Hicks, Tribes, and Dirty Realists

Hicks, Tribes, & Dirty Realists

American Fiction after Postmodernism

Robert Rebein

THE UNIVERSITY PRESS OF KENTUCKY

Publication of this volume was made possible in part
by a grant from the National Endowment for the Humanities.

Editorial and Sales Offices: The University Press of Kentucky
663 South Limestone Street, Lexington, Kentucky 40508–4008

05 04 03 02 01   5 4 3 2 1

Library of Congress Cataloging-in-Publication Data
Rebein, Robert, 1964–
    Hicks, tribes, and dirty realists : American fiction after postmod-
    ernism / Robert Rebein
        p.   cm.
    Includes bibliographical references and index.
    ISBN 0-8131-2176-0 (cloth : alk. paper)
        1. American fiction—20th century—History and criticism.
    2. Experimental fiction, American—History and criticism.
    3. Postmodern (Literature)—United States. 4. Realism in literature.
    I. Title.
    PS374.E95 R43 2001
    813'.540911—dc21   00-047306

for A.C.

Contents

Contents
Contents

Acknowledgments

Acknowledgments
Acknowledgments

In writing this modest book I have incurred the debt of many people I am happy to acknowledge here. Among those who educated and encouraged me, offered advice, discussed ideas, assigned books for review, or read and commented on parts of the manuscript, I would like to thank in particular Leslie Fiedler, Bruce Jackson, Mark Shechner, Marcus Klein, Jack Cohn, Peter Casagrande, Cheryl Lester, Charles Masinton, Clark Coker, Peter Hulme, Michael Wood, Charles Newman, Wayne Fields, Jonathan Eller, Nick Gillespie, Katharine M. Gillespie, Mary Obropta, Charles Jones, Benjamin Clay Jones, Joe Croker, Elaine Pfefferblit, Heidi Burns, Eddie Silva, Jack Goldman, Millie Clark, Leif Peterson, Neal Durando, Andy Mozina, Paul Rebein, and Alyssa Chase. Any mistakes or wrong moves remaining here are my own affair.

1 / After Postmodernism

1 / After Postmodernism

Studies of twentieth-century American fiction published before 1985—and even some published after that date—share a certain beautiful symmetry, a sort of pristine academic logic that is as pleasing to the eye as it is compelling to the intellect. In the early decades of the century, so the story goes, fiction writing in America came roaring out of the backwaters of nineteenth-century naturalism and into a revolutionary period of modernism and experimentation that was symbolized, in painting, by the New York Armory show of 1919. In the years immediately following World War I, American modernism flowered in the works of Ernest Hemingway, Gertrude Stein, and F. Scott Fitzgerald, expatriate Americans well versed in European forms. In the 1930s, admittedly a period dominated by works of social realism, the modernist banner was nevertheless carried forward by the "Camera's Eye" section of John Dos Passos's *U.S.A.* trilogy, the isolated formal experiments of southern writers such as William Faulkner and Thomas Wolfe, and the surrealism of Henry Miller, Djuna Barnes, and others. The 1940s and 1950s saw the rise of an existential movement dominated by Jewish writers who, more than anyone else in America except blacks and a few unreconstructed southerners, understood the alienation that more and more characterized life in the United States. The two great writers of this period were Saul Bellow, whose 1944 novel *Dangling Man* brought postwar angst to the literary mainstream, and Ralph Ellison, whose 1952 novel *Invisible Man* made use of a mixture of naturalism, expressionism, and surrealism to powerfully depict the plight of the black man in America. From here, it was but a hop and skip to the next "evolutionary" stage, which was marked by a progression from the tentative modernism of the first five decades of the century to the "postmodern" masterpieces of the 1960s and 1970s, those self-reflexive, end-of-the-line works of fantasy and fabulation most powerfully represented in the "fictions" of John Barth, Donald Barthelme, Robert Coover, William H. Gass, and Thomas Pynchon. These were the Last Writers. Anything after or beyond postmodernism was by definition impossible—as difficult to imagine as an end to the cold war.

This, at any rate, is the story I was told in English departments in both the United States and England throughout the 1980s and even into the early 1990s. Whatever else may have been going on in publishing, in the rapidly expanding creative writing programs, in the literary magazines, or in the review pages of newspapers and magazines, in academe postmodernism still held sway—this despite the fact that by the late seventies even Robert Scholes, author of the largely celebratory *Fabulation and Metafiction* (1979), considered "self-reflection in fiction" to be "essentially a short-term trend . . . nearing its end."[1]

Stranger still was the fact that so many critics and scholars who publicly supported literary postmodernism would readily confess, when asked in private, to little or no joy in reading the books themselves. As Charles Newman observed in *The Post-Modern Aura* (1985), books such as Pynchon's *Gravity's Rainbow* (1973) or Coover's *Public Burning* (1977) were capable of creating a power feeling of ambivalence in readers, an ambivalence Newman described well when he wrote, "As the plot progresses, we come to notice that *it's as good as it's going to get;* and so for the first time in the history of literature we respond with a version of: 'It's terrific. But I wish it were over.'"[2]

Tremors of dissatisfaction with literary postmodernism could be felt in even the most thoroughgoing apologies for the new fiction. For example, Frederick Karl's monumental *American Fictions, 1940–1980: A Comprehensive History and Critical Evaluation* (1983), which pushes the postmodernism-as-destiny story line harder (and at greater length) than perhaps any other literary history of the period, contains strained and awkward confessions such as the following: "Literature in the modern or postmodern period is often inaccessible or even disagreeable—as were Joyce's *Ulysses* and Eliot's 'Waste Land' in 1922—but it has a shaping vision that goes beyond the novel of the 'now.' We must once more make that leap, as though it had not been made before."[3]

For Karl, although many works of literary postmodernism are "disagreeable" (and many more are not "experimental" at all but in fact repetitions of once-startling maneuvers reduced now to tired mannerism), the responsible critic must still praise these works because of their "shaping vision." Exactly what this "vision," so dearly bought, might be is notoriously difficult to define, but that it is of little immediate consequence becomes clear once we see the diminished role Karl assigns writers ("fiction-makers") in the fallen, postmodern world. For Karl, the postmodern writer is neither a prophet, a voice for the multitude, nor even much of an artist. Instead, the writer is a "trickster," a "coyote" whose ultimate goal is to survive in a world that has superseded him. "The novelist survives, of course," Karl writes,

> but like the coyote, he must work along the contours of different frontiers; he must approach borders differently, and he must be prepared to accept his lesser role in white man's America. The magic has gone out, not only from his world but from the world; and it has passed elsewhere or been extinguished. What the novelist needs, now, is not only a vision but strategies for holding on; for he/she still embodies the crises, conflicts, and tensions which we associate with a culture—although precisely what the culture embodies has become a part of America's fictions. (xiv)

No longer does the novelist hold center stage in the culture (if, indeed, he ever did). Literature itself is threatened with extinction, its meaning having fled or been sucked into the great void of the media age. In this fallen world, the writer is a kind of glorious victim, Christ minus the miracle of resurrection, a cosmic joker in the land of nada. The writer does not interpret, does not represent, does not dramatize nor even reveal the crises and conflicts in American culture—for these are all *active* constructions. Instead, the writer "embodies" these crises and conflicts and tensions, much as Bartelby in the Melville story embodies the tensions in his culture (that is to say, *passively*). Karl means to invoke here both Jung's "Trickster Figure" and a similar presence in Native American myth, showing thereby how the death of modernism after World War II left a world that can only be haunted, not saved. Hence his conclusion: "To negotiate as ghosts in the shadow—not as saviors—is the function of the novelist, the one-time shaman now turned trickster" (xiv). And yet, there remains the central irony of Karl's argument, which is that this Last Writer, so impotent and passive, is at once the culmination and the antithesis of an entire tradition. Hubris and abjection are so mixed here as to become finally inseparable. As Charles Newman observed in *The Post-Modern Aura*, "It is typical of Post-Modernism to inflate the riskiness of the literary impulse in exact proportion to literature's diminishing influence" (82).

By the early 1980s, when Frederick Karl wrote the above sentiments, one had become accustomed to such melodramatic descriptions of the author's reduced state. Indeed, one often heard them from the mouths of writers themselves. There was Philip Roth's famous midcentury complaint, in the essay "Writing American Fiction" (1961), that American reality as represented in the media had become so bizarre, so protean and huge as to constitute "a kind of embarrassment" to the writer's, by comparison, "meager" imaginative gifts. "The actuality," Roth wrote, "is continually outdoing our talents, and the culture tosses up figures almost daily that are the envy of any novelist."[4] More famous still was John Barth's lament in "The Literature of Exhaustion" (1967) that the techniques and forms used by fiction writers are somehow subject to becoming "used-up." At a certain point in the development of any art form, Barth implied, it becomes depressingly clear to the artist, at least with respect to technique, that *it has all been done before.* "Our century is more than two-thirds done," Barth wrote, striking the typical desperate note of this period; "it is dismaying to see so many of our writers following Dostoevsky or Tolstoy or Balzac, when the question seems to me to be how to succeed not even Joyce and Kafka, but those who *succeeded* Joyce and Kafka and are now in the evenings of their own careers."[5]

Taken at face value, Roth's despair about content and Barth's about form would seem to justify all that Frederick Karl has to say about the American writer's loss of faith and cultural authority in the late twentieth century. Against such statements, however, we must pause to add a few observations from our own time. In fact, far from having become paralyzed by the situation he described in 1961, Roth has gone on to write novel after novel—not least 1997's *American Pastoral,* a book that treats the 1960s in the context of all that has happened since. In recent years John Barth has also adjusted his tune, distancing himself from his former statements. Collecting "The Literature of Exhaustion" in *The Friday Book* (1984), Barth paused long enough to add this "Author's Note" to the above statement about Kafka and Joyce: "Did I really say this remarkably silly thing back in '67? Yup, and I believed it, too" (67). According to Barth, such "silliness" was attributable to a certain "Make-It-New" spirit that operated as the bright side of the "American High Sixties"— about which, more later—the dark side being summed up by what Barth called, ominously, "traces of tear gas" (63–64).

To be sure, there is something of a Sputnik-era, arms-race lunacy about both Roth's and Barth's statements. In retrospect, they say a lot more about the cultural and political climate of the American 1960s than they do about either the nature of "American reality" or the "usability" of inherited forms.

And it is in the above context of doubt and upheaval that Frederick Karl's assessments in *American Fictions, 1940–1980* make the most sense. When we read, for example, that in Karl's view "the postwar novel has striven for precisely this achievement: to defamiliarize the familiar, to make the reader reinvent the world, and while moving human experience to the margins, to move the margins to the center" (xi), we glimpse some of the diversity of experience represented in today's American novel while at the same time recognizing that the tendency to understand literary achievement so strictly in terms of *form* (at the ultimate expense of content) is not nearly so urgent today as it was even ten years ago. Indeed, how strange today to read the following, from Susan Sontag's 1964 essay "Against Interpretation": "Whatever it may have been in the past, the idea of content is today mainly a hindrance, a nuisance, a subtle or not so subtle philistinism."[6]

We may also recognize a practice many of us indulge in when thinking about our literary history—our tendency to read backward from the present, starting with whatever is lately in ascendancy and interpreting all that came before it as a movement toward that ascendancy. If, to take an example, Henry James's brand of psychological realism is currently important, then earlier writers in the tradition such as Hawthorne and Charles Brockden Brown increase in importance, too. If Ernest Hemingway sits atop the throne of American literature, however, we had better look to frontier writers like Mark Twain or pared-down stylists like Kate Chopin. In the case of Faulkner, Poe. In the case of Toni Morrison and Cormac McCarthy, Faulkner . . .

But I have jumped ahead of myself here. If the present moment is *1980,* as is the case in Frederick Karl's assessment, and literary postmodernism is— if no longer new or even very interesting, at least a sort of reigning lame duck—then our tendency will be to read all that came before postmodernism in light of its peculiar strategies and concerns. The progression we come up with, not surprisingly, is Karl's beautifully symmetrical realism ' modernism ' postmodernism. The problem, of course, is that by the early 1980s such a model no longer described what was actually happening in contemporary American fiction (if, indeed, it ever did).

Perhaps no critic in America understood this better than Larry McCaffery, author of *The Metafictional Muse* (1982), a work that celebrates the "self-reflexive," "metafictional" narrative strategies of Robert Coover, Donald Barthelme, and William H. Gass. From 1978 to 1980, when he was working on *The Metafictional Muse,* McCaffery was also traveling around the United States conducting formal interviews and "late-night discussions" with writers of the day. It isn't hard to imagine what McCaffery, long known for his vocal support of experimental fiction, hoped to hear in these interviews. What he actually heard was another matter altogether. "The most important conclusion I've reached," McCaffery would write of those interviews, "is that experimentation per se—especially experimentalism in the direction of reflexive, nonreferential works—is not nearly as important to writers today [i.e., in 1980] as it was a decade ago." The reasons for this shift, as McCaffery points out, are not difficult to understand:

> [S]o-called artistic revolutions have a natural life span, and they are inevitably succeeded by a new artistic climate generated by practitioners who do not share the enthusiasms of a previous group and who are anxious to define themselves as artists in new ways. Then, too, the energy and hard work of any significant creative movement will eventually produce, in the course of its development, works of surpassing and even intimidating success. Finally, a sense develops among the artists who have defined themselves as part of a movement that most of its possibilities have been explored.[7]

We should add to these reasons a few others. The fact is, literary post-modernism, especially of the sort practiced by the subjects of McCaffery's book, appealed to far fewer writers, readers, and critics than what one would guess from reading Robert Scholes or Larry McCaffery. From the beginning, its primary home was the university, a status that explains not only why metafiction in particular was often said to be fiction "of the academy, by the academy, and for the academy" but also why so many academics who clearly found it "disagreeable" felt called upon to support and defend it (there were other reasons, of course, as I will make clear in a moment). Outside the English departments—and, indeed, even in "antithetical cells" within them, such as the creative writing programs—literary postmodernism was often seen as either ridiculous in its assumptions (all magic has fled from the world, it's all been done before, etc.) or simply too limiting in its strictures. Women writers, especially, seemed far less drawn to it than men, and a similar observation (with appropriate footnotes) would have to be made about minority writers, who simply could not say, along with the mostly white, eastern males of postmodernism, that their world had been represented to death. On the contrary, it had been represented hardly at all.

And yet, for all that, the narrative of realism giving way to modernism giving way to postmodernism continues to provide the primary lens through which contemporary American fiction is viewed in the university, this even as

the works of those writers most identified with literary postmodernism—
Barth, Barthelme, Coover, Gass, and Pynchon—find fewer and fewer readers.
The only real change has been a broadening of the notion of what constitutes
literary postmodernism. As the editors of a recent anthology, *Postmodern
American Fiction* (1998), put the matter, "The history of postmodern American
fiction belongs to those authors who, in any idiom and for any audience, for
brief passages or for entire careers, shared a new cultural sensibility as a response
to an altered world."[8] As becomes evident when one flips through the book's
table of contents, such a broad definition allows the anthology's editors to
include a host of writers we would not normally associate with literary
postmodernism—Truman Capote, Bobbie Ann Mason, Toni Morrison, E.L.
Doctorow, to name a few—while at the same time ensuring that pride of place
is reserved for the usual suspects (Gass, Pynchon, et al.).

What could possibly account for such a bizarre state of affairs—one in
which the books one constantly hears praised go largely unread because of
their apparent barrenness and willful difficulty, while the books that might be
said to come *after postmodernism,* many of them masterpieces, go largely
unrecognized because of their relative accessibility and ties to a native tradition that predates postmodernism? The answer to this question turns out to be
relatively simple, if somewhat difficult to explain, and it has to do with several
likely responses to the seeming paradox I have just put in italics—*after
postmodernism.*

For what could possibly come "after" postmodernism? Does not postmodernism itself connote a kind of finality, "the end of things"—not least of
which would be the end of innocence with regard to language and mimesis?
Does not the term refer to a period of time we are still, demonstrably, in? And
anyway, doesn't a denial of the dominion of postmodernism amount to a de
facto admission of artistic and cultural conservatism? Are we not speaking here
of a kind of *regression,* aesthetically speaking?

As I have intimated, the climate that gives rise to these questions is one of
much fear and confusion and not a little willful blindness as regards what has
actually been taking place in American fiction writing in the last two decades
of the millennium. In the pages that immediately follow, I want to take up
these questions more or less one by one (albeit in no particular order), and by
doing so clear the air for a discussion of what I take to be the most significant
developments in late-twentieth-century American literature—namely, the
revitalization of realism, the renewed importance of the concept of place, and
the expansion of our traditional ideas of authorship to include those who in

the past would have appeared in our literature only as characters, and stereotypes at that.

But first, a brief archaeology of the term "postmodern."[9]

In the introduction to *Postmodern American Fiction*, anthology editors Paula Geyh, Fred G. Leebron, and Andrew Levy make an important distinction between use of the term postmodern as a period concept and use of the term as a marker for a particular aesthetic around which to gather writers, architects, musicians, and so forth. "For many observers," they write,

> the term "postmodern" refers to "postmodernity," a historical period stretching from the 1960s to the present, marked by such phenomena as upheavals in the international economic system, the Cold War and its decline, the increasing ethnic heterogeneity of the American population, the growth of the suburbs as a cultural force, the predominance of television as a cultural medium, and the rise of the computer. For others, however, the term "postmodern" connotes "postmodernism," a tentative grouping of ideas, stylistic traits, and thematic preoccupations that set the last four decades apart from earlier eras. In the arts, postmodern traits include pastiche, the incorporation of different textual genres and contradictory "voices" within a single work; fragmented or "open" forms that give the audience the power to assemble the work and determine its meaning; and the adoption of a playful irony as a stance that seems to prove itself endlessly useful. (x)

There can be no real argument about the existence and continued importance of what the authors here call "postmodernity" (although in the inevitable battle of nomenclature it appears likely this term will lose out to others with more descriptive power, for example the "postindustrial era," the "computer age," the "media society," the "information economy," etc.).

According to this usage, pretty much everything written during the postmodern period should be thought of, in some sense, as postmodern literature. A story such as Raymond Carver's "Cathedral," for example, with its reference to an America uprooted by divorce and relentless in its mobility, a world in which cathedrals have been reduced to "something to look at on late-night TV," would qualify as postmodern by virtue of its content alone, as would David Foster Wallace's novel *Infinite Jest* (1996), with its reference to such local contemporary phenomena as junior tennis and Boston, Massachusetts, Alcoholics Anonymous. There is something both convenient and liberating in thinking about our recent literature in this way. The *period* becomes the unifying factor, and, as people living in the period, we are bound to find it interesting. And yet, what two works of recent fiction could be more different than "Cathedral," with its low-rent, minimalist style, its depressed, earnest tone and barely contained sentimentality and understated, "epiphanic" ending, and *Infinite Jest,* with its maximalist spill (1,079 pages), its futurism and footnotes and willfully stupid jokes and pointed lack of an ending? Clearly any term that can so easily encompass both of these narratives does not mean all it could.

About the existence and/or importance of something called *postmodernism,* however, there has been no end of debate. But here we encounter the opposite problem: where *postmodernity* as an organizing principle is too broad, threatening to eliminate all distinctions, sweeping everything into its purview, *postmodernism* is too narrow, tending always to fragment and self-divide. Once formal difference becomes the criteria by which we catalogue different groups or schools of writers, who is to say where we quit remarking differences and similarities? The tendency has been to exclude rather than include. Thus, for example, in a book such as Jerome Klinkowitz's *Literary Disruptions: The Making of a Post-Contemporary American Fiction* (1975), John Barth and Thomas Pynchon are treated as "regressive parodists" while Donald Barthelme, Jerzy Kosinski, and Kurt Vonnegut Jr. are said to be "fictionists" of a "new disruptivist school" whose definitive arrival on the literary scene is pinpointed quite precisely to "the publishing season of 1967–1968." Yet the list of attributes by which Klinkowitz identifies the work of the disruptivists— "formal experimentation, a thematic interest in the imaginative transformation of reality, and a sometimes painful but often hilarious self-conscious artistry"—applies to most writing we would ordinarily describe as postmodern, including the works of Barth and Pynchon, writers Klinkowitz blames for, among other crimes, "confus[ing] the course of American fiction" and holding back "the critical (although not the popular) appreciation" of the writers he admires.[10] Twenty years later, in the introduction to Larry McCaffery's *After Yesterday's Crash: The Avant-Pop Anthology* (1995), we are told that Pynchon's *Gravity's Rainbow* and Vonnegut's *Slaughterhouse Five* (1969) are both seminal works of "Avant-Pop," a movement which, according to McCaffery's definition, "combines Pop Art's focus on consumer goods and mass media with the avant-garde's spirit of subversion and emphasis on radical formal innovation."[11] The separate efforts of Klinkowitz and McCaffery on behalf of writers they obviously admire are fine as far as they go. But in the end, who beyond the obsessed fan visiting various Pynchon web sites would want to argue whether the writer is a parodist, a disruptivist, a maker of avant-pop, or just a plain old postmodernist?

Despite the tendency toward narrowness in definition, which may or may not be inherent in the whole idea of postmodernism, the past thirty years have provided any number of mostly useful and interesting attempts to enumerate the strategies and explain the impulses behind the movement—books such as Ihab Hassan's *Dismemberment of Orpheus* (1971), Alan Wilde's *Horizons of Assent* (1981), Brian McHale's *Postmodernist Fiction* (1987), and Fredric Jameson's *Postmodernism, or, The Cultural Logic of Late Capitalism* (1991). Each of these works has its own distinctive thesis, its own canon of definitive texts, and yet each may be said to hover about a single cultural moment—what Leslie Fiedler, in his essay "Cross the Border—Close the Gap" (1970), called "the death throes of Modernism and the birth pangs of Post-Modernism."[12] The problem with these works, at least in the present context, occurs when we turn to them for answers about what is happening in fiction writing *today*. It is here that the whole concept of postmodernism begins to lose its currency. For not one of these books can speak to us about the strange similarities and even stranger differences between "Cathedral" and *Infinite Jest*, why each of these works is in some sense "postmodern" while each may also be said to have arrived "after" postmodernism. And that is because the authors of these studies, caught up in a cultural moment in which formal experimentation still held sway, have tended, whether consciously or unconsciously, to treat the surface effects of literary postmodernism as *absolute symptoms* of the condition of postmodernity. The tendency has been to treat the works of formally experimental writers like Barth and Pynchon as *the real postmodern literature*, while all work deemed not experimental enough has been thought to be behind the times—holdovers from or throwbacks to another era. So pervasive has this tendency been that even a critical work ostensibly written as an attempted *way out* of the binary opposition represented by realism vs. experimental—Wilde's *Middle Grounds* (1987)—still somehow manages to place the work of Pynchon and Barthelme in this privileged middle space.[13]

And yet when American literary critics first began to speak of a "postmodern" American fiction, in the late 1950s and early 1960s, they were not using the term as a synonym for the experimental, nor were they necessarily dishing out compliments. Rather, as I have suggested, they were announcing—often with disappointment, sometimes with actual trepidation—what they took to be a significant break with the high religion of modernism. The titans who had dominated the first half of the century—

Faulkner, Hemingway, Fitzgerald, and Stein—were either dead or past their prime, and no figure of equal stature had arrived on the scene. Beyond this, the very air of postwar America seemed filled with anxiety and alienation. There had been the Holocaust, then the bomb, then the onset of the cold war. Who imagined anymore that the world's problems could be solved with mere words?

In "Mass Society and Post-Modern Culture" (1959), for example, Irving Howe complained of what he termed "a certain obliqueness of approach" in the work of postwar writers like Saul Bellow, Bernard Malamud, Wright Morris, and J.D. Salinger—an obliqueness Howe traced to the rise of a mass society characterized by its passivity, alienation, atomization, and rampant consumerism. "They do not represent directly the postwar American experience," Howe wrote of these writers, "yet [they] refer to it constantly": "They tell us rather little about the surface tone, the manners, the social patterns of recent American life, yet are constantly projecting moral criticisms of its essential quality. They approach that experience on the sly, yet are colored and shaped by it throughout. And they gain from it their true subject: the recurrent search—in America, almost a national obsession—for personal identity and freedom."[14]

According to Howe, it all came down to a curiously long view, a strange "distance" in the new fiction. "In their distance from fixed social categories and their concern with the metaphysical implications of that distance," he concluded, "these novels constitute what I would call 'post-modern' fiction." For Howe, then, postmodern fiction was defined by what he took to be its essential passivity—its impotence in the act of representation, its failure to engage social conditions, its escape into the metaphysical. In Howe's depiction, postmodern fiction resembled, in its overall weariness, nothing so much as a burned-out soldier returned home from a far-off war, a mere shell of his former self. In a 1960 essay entitled "What Was Modernism?" Harry Levin exhibited less contempt for the present than Howe, but more nostalgia for the past. In Levin's hands, postmodernism is primarily a period concept referring to a conservative age of consolidation and assimilation following the radical experiments of modernism. "Looking back toward the Moderns," Levin wrote, "we may feel as Dryden did when he looked back from the Restoration on the Elizabethans, contrasting their strength with later refinement." In Levin's conception, "revolutionary" periods in the arts are regularly followed by "reactionary" periods, "tougher" minds" by "tender minds"—the whole process taking place at "roughly 30 year intervals."[15]

Both of these critics, each in his own way, viewed the onset of postmodernism (as they defined and understood it) as an alarming decline in the importance and quality of American fiction. For Howe, the change was permanent and irreversible (or at least as permanent and irreversible as mass society itself), while for Levin the change was both temporary and relatively long-term, the whole business of "strength" vs. "refinement" in the arts being rather like the cycles of bull and bear markets on Wall Street—observable but sadly out of our hands.

For Fiedler, who entered the conversation in the more turbulent and exuberant days of the mid- to late-1960s, the arrival of the postmodern age in literature was still something to be announced with some gravity, but it also promised to bring with it a few welcome changes, most notably a turning away from modernist "seriousness" and authority, as well as what Fiedler liked to call a "closing of the gap" between any number of previously separated entities, including artist and audience, critic and audience, amateur and professional. As a matter of course there would come a new and slightly terrifying freedom, a new pluralism of forms, and a breaking of the barrier between "high" and "low" culture.[16]

There is a tone and attitude in Fiedler's work from this period, a change in diction and sometimes in long-held positions—it is almost as though you can see the man's hair growing. The fifties have given way to the sixties, the Korean conflict to the Vietnam War, Eisenhower to Kennedy to Johnson. It is in this turbulent era that the concept of literary postmodernism will be remade in the minds of critics, transformed from the disappointing fall from greatness Howe and Levin observed and lamented in the fifties into the radical, "Make It New" experimentalism that Barth and others explored and affirmed in the sixties and seventies. The aesthetic ambitions and biases of literary postmodernism, that is to say, are more or less *inseparable* from their time and place. They simply do not make sense outside the context of what Barth, in his 1984 preface to "The Literature of Exhaustion," called "the American High Sixties":

> Those years—1965–1973—were the American High Sixties. The Vietnam War was in overdrive through most of the period; the U.S. economy was fat and bloody.... Eighty percent of the populous English department I joined had been hired within the preceding two years, as additions to the original staff; so numerous were our illustrious immigrants from raided faculties, troubled marriages, and more straitlaced lifestyles, we came to call ourselves proudly the Ellis Island of Academia. . . .

The politically active among our faculty and students had their own ambitions for the place: the Berkeley of the East. . . . They struck and trashed; then the police and National Guard struck and trashed *them*. Mace and peppergas wafted through the academic groves; the red flag of communism and the black flag of anarchism were literally waved at English Department faculty-student meetings, which—a sight as astonishing to me as those flags—were attended by *hundreds*, like an Allen Ginsberg poetry reading with harmonium and Tibetan finger-cymbals.

Altogether a stimulating place to work in those troubled years. . . .

In that time and place, *experimental* was not yet an adjective of dismissal. On the contrary: As in the European Nineteen Teens, artistic experiment was in the Buffalo air.[17]

Those of us who were educated in whole or part by refugees from this era will recognize both the overwhelming *nostalgia* of Barth's reminiscence and its latent thesis—that *one had to be there* to understand. This is no doubt true. But to move beyond this point, note how thoroughly Barth has situated the impulses behind literary postmodernism not only within the specific *time-frame* of the "American High Sixties" but also within the *place-frame* of academia. It is a time of political unrest but also of economic boom; the country's university system is expanding rapidly to meet the needs of the baby boom generation; both students and faculty are politically active and understand themselves to be playing the role of "revolutionaries"; their relationship to art is conditioned by an ongoing comparison between themselves and the denizens of the European avant-garde circa the First World War. . . . All of which is easy enough to mock from a millennial perspective, but that is not my intention. Rather, I would simply like to point out that much of what we experience today as a continuing in-words-if-not-in-deeds support of the whole project of literary postmodernism is actually a continuing nostalgia for the time and place in which this project made the most sense.

Most commentators on the phenomenon of American literary postmodernism have taken note of the two positions I've outlined above—the first of which views postmodernism as a definitive break with modernism and laments this fact, the second of which admits the same break with modernism but tends to treat it as a positive development. But there is also a third position, one whose arguments I find instructive though not fully convincing, and that is the view that *no definitive break with modernism has occurred*, whether fortunately or unfortunately, and therefore most of what has been said in the above debate about postmodernism is either premature or hopelessly flawed.

In a 1988 essay entitled "The Problem of the Postmodern," C. Barry Chabot surveys the theoretical statements of four of American postmodernism's most tireless and prolific commentators—Hassan, Klinkowitz, Wilde, and Jameson—and reaches the following somewhat surprising conclusions: "(1) that no satisfactory and widely accepted account of postmodernism now exists; (2) that much of what is called postmodern in fact derives directly from modernism; and (3) that most arguments for its existence achieve their initial plausibility largely through impoverished characterizations of modernism, especially characterizations that neglect its nature as a second-order concept."[18]

Of course, a certain amount of doubt about postmodernism's usefulness as a concept has always been a part of this debate. Even Ihab Hassan liked to point out that modernism did not completely die out when postmodernism came along, that in fact at certain points the two could be said to coexist. In *The Post-Modern Aura,* Charles Newman wrote that in his view "the Modern and the Post-Modern share an unbroken (and largely unexamined) aesthetic tradition" (10). But neither of these writers take the matter as far as Chabot, for whom postmodernism becomes finally "an empty marker" that exists only to "hold a place in our language for a concept that might one day prove necessary."

These are strong sentiments, but they are hardly new. A decade before Chabot's essay, Gerald Graff reached the same conclusion in *Literature Against Itself* (1979), arguing that "postmodernism should not be seen as a break with romantic and modernist assumptions but rather as a logical culmination of the premises of these earlier movements, premises not always clearly defined in discussion of these issues." "To characterize postmodernism as a 'breakthrough'—a cant term of our day—" Graff wrote, "is to place a greater distance between current writers and their predecessors than is, I think, justified." To pretend otherwise was to fall into what Graff called the "Myth of the Postmodern Breakthrough."[19]

For Graff, there was little in postmodernism that could not be fitted into the ongoing project of modernism. Even postmodernism's vaunted lack of seriousness, its playful calling into question of literature's traditional claims to truth, was anticipated not only by modernism in the twentieth century but also by romanticism in the nineteenth—postmodernism simply accentuated and extended these ideas. "The postmodern temper has carried the skepticism and anti-realism of modern literary culture to an extreme beyond which it would be difficult to go," Graff concluded. "Though it looks back mockingly on the modernist tradition and professes to have got beyond it, postmodern literature remains tied to that tradition and unable to break with it. The very concepts through which modernism is demystified derive from modernism itself. The loss of significant external reality, its displacement by myth-making, the domestication and normalization of alienation—these conditions constitute a common point of departure for the writing of our period" (62).

As I have said, I find Graff's notion that postmodernism can be so neatly folded into the overall project of modernism more than a little problematic, if only because, for me, it is finally too difficult to reconcile modernism's heroic stance, its faith in the imagination's ability to create order out of chaos, with postmodernism's essentially antiheroic stance, its loss of such faith and lapse into irony and language games. Where I do find both Graff and Chabot useful is in their unwillingness to allow postmodernity to stand as a ready justification for the set of specific literary strategies that have come to be identified as postmodernism.

For postmodernity—or the information age, or the media society, call it what you will—is the one great reality of our times. The end of the cold war and the spread of information technology, especially the development of the Internet and the World Wide Web, have made this abundantly clear, if it was not clear before. At the same time—perhaps paradoxically, perhaps not— postmodernism as a literary strategy no longer pertains in the way it once did, its peak having come probably as early as 1974, the year Pynchon's *Gravity's Rainbow* won the National Book Award. As literary postmodernism has waned in influence, new definitions of postmodern fiction have begun to emerge, definitions that remain true to postmodernity but offer a different set of features than what we have come to think of as postmodernism.

"As American culture has become more fragmented," write the editors of the anthology *Postmodern American Fiction,* "its literature has also become more pluralistic" (xiii). Demographic changes in the American population, together with the rise of identity politics, have led to an increase in the kinds of voices—Native American, Asian American, Caribbean, Hispanic, gay and lesbian, and so on—that now present themselves as some version of American in our literature. It is entirely possible, as the editors of this anthology imply, that *these changes* in our literature and not the formal experiments of the 1960s and 1970s constitute the real break with modernism. For not only do many of these new writers consciously or unconsciously reject the cultural legacy of modernism, perhaps even much of what we think of as the Western tradition, they also reject experimentation for its own sake. "For this most recent generation of writers," the editors note, "postmodernism does not foreground formal difficulty, but combines formal innovation with shifts in context, tone, and audience to create forms of fiction that sometimes feel old but read new" (xix).

All of which is well and good. But the question remains: Is this postmodernism?

Let us return to some of the questions I posed earlier, all of which had to do with a certain understandable difficulty we might have accepting the idea that our most recent writers have somehow moved beyond postmodernism, or have successfully ignored it, or are now writing "after" it.

I hesitate to use the word "beyond" here, if only because it implies acceptance of an idea I take to be at the heart of the problem—namely, the notion that the history of art is to be understood as a series of "progressions" or "breakthroughs" or "innovations" in technique or form. As Newman and others have noted, there are really two metaphors at work here, neither of them very plausible or useful. The first, drawn from science, sees the history of literary art in essentially evolutionary terms, as a progression of forms, each better or more advanced than those that came before—an idea best illustrated by those drawings in grammar school science books showing the gradual development of club-wielding Cave Man into briefcase-bearing Business Man. This is an idea, we may pause to remark, that could only be taken seriously in a country like America with a relatively brief and not particularly impressive literary past, where the whole point of the college literature survey is to show how sophisticated Gertrude Stein is when compared to Anne Bradstreet. Can anyone imagine such a program in England or Italy or Greece? Among other things, I want to suggest here that a large part of the cosmic despair commonly associated with literary postmodernism is actually a drawn-out mourning for the loss of this rather adolescent idea. The second metaphor, drawn from politics, suggests that there is something "revolutionary" or "subversive" about formal innovation in the arts. Certainly this is the tenor of McCaffery's avant-pop anthology, the back cover of which promises an introduction to "a new, subversive aesthetic sensibility" that McCaffery, echoing Fredric Jameson, refers to as "the Cultural Logic of Hyperconsumer Capitalism" (xvii). And yet the persistence of this idea is nothing short of amazing given the lessons provided by modernism, in which many of the most "radical" formal innovators—Pound and Eliot, for example—turned out to be politically the most reactionary. As was the case with the evolution metaphor, this revolution metaphor relies on an American innocence with regard to social and political change, for as Newman pointed out in *The Post-Modern Aura*, "the Avant-Garde was for Europe a profoundly cultural and political revolution, while for America, from the first, it was essentially an *aesthetic* movement" (46).

That the appeal of literary postmodernism was at its most powerful, especially for academics, in the years 1967–74, the heart of Barth's American High Sixties, tends to prove rather than disprove this point, for who would attempt to connect any of the canonical works of postmodernism with progress in civil rights or the end of the Vietnam War? Even Barth, waxing nostalgic about the Buffalo sixties in *The Friday Book*, attempts no such connection—political protest and avant-gardism exist, at best, side by side, both breathing the same air but at work at essentially different tasks. But this is hardly surprising given the fact that from the proletarian novel of the thirties to the most angry novel of our own times, the exact opposite axiom has held true—the greater the social content and protest in a work of fiction, the less likely it is that the work will also be experimental or innovative in terms of form.

However, the question remains: Insofar as metafiction was a response to a supposedly naïve view of language and reality, isn't the abandonment of self-conscious narration in our time a doomed and renegade attempt to return to the days of unproblematic mimesis? To put the matter another way, isn't the writer of such neorealist fare pretending, in essence, that poststructuralist theory never happened?

We should first of all be clear about the fact that some sort of revitalization of realism has taken place. Writers themselves have declared it. Against the separate pronouncements of Philip Roth and John Barth in the sixties, we must now balance more recent statements by the likes of Tom Wolfe and Robert Stone. "One of the axioms of literary theory in the Seventies," Wolfe wrote in his essay "Stalking the Billion-Footed Beast" (1989), "was that realism was 'just another formal device, not a permanent method for dealing with experience'":

> I was convinced then—and I am even more convinced now—that precisely the opposite is true. The introduction of realism into literature in the eighteenth century by Richardson, Fielding, and Smollett was like the introduction of electricity into engineering. It was not just another device. . . . For writers to give up this power in the quest for a more up-to-date kind of fiction—it is as if an

engineer were to set out to develop a more sophisticated machine technology by first of all discarding the principle of electricity, on the grounds that it had been used ad nauseam for a hundred years.[20]

What America needed in the late twentieth century, Wolfe argued, was a legion of "big novels" that took the "billion-footed city" or "any other big, rich slices of contemporary life" as their subject matter. In writing *The Bonfire of the Vanities* (1987), apparently just such a novel, Wolfe had tried to fulfill a prediction he had made almost fifteen years earlier in his introduction to *The New Journalism,* "namely, that the future of the fictional novel would be a highly detailed realism based on reporting, a realism more thorough than any currently being attempted, a realism that would portray the individual in intimate and inextricable relation to the society around him" ("Billion-Footed Beast," 50).

Three years later, in his introduction to *The Best American Short Stories 1992,* a volume that included stories by, among other writers, Alice Munro, Rick Bass, Robert Olen Butler, Denis Johnson, Thom Jones, Lorrie Moore, David Foster Wallace, Joyce Carol Oates, and Tobias Wolff, guest editor Robert Stone made the following unequivocal statement: "In their variety, these stories reflect what is probably the most significant development in late-twentieth-century American fiction, the renewal and revitalization of the realist mode, which has been taken up by a new generation of writers. This represents less a 'triumph' of realism than the obviation of old arguments about the relationship between life and language. As of 1992, American writers seem ready to accept traditional forms without self-consciousness in dealing with the complexity of the world around them."[21]

Stone's choice of words here is canny and interesting. To obviate means to anticipate or forestall, to clear away or effectively dispose of, as when an orator anticipates arguments and disables them. But obviate also means to render unnecessary. One of the word's roots is the Latin *obvius,* which translates roughly as both "in the way" and "obvious"—which in turn suggests that something is evident without need of further reasoning or investigation. I want to suggest that this has been precisely the contemporary writer's response to the questions about language and mimesis raised by poststructuralists in the seventies. As Brian McHale observed in the conclusion to *Postmodernist Fiction,* "Everyone knows that the conventions of nineteenth-century realism were just that, conventions, and not a transparent window on reality."[22] The question, however, becomes what we do with this knowledge.

Do we back ourselves into a corner and insist, as so many of the postmodernists have, on a completely different set of conventions with their own peculiar limitations? Or do we simply accept the mimetic limitations of realism, as Robert Stone suggests today's writers have, *as obvious* and move on from there to build what Tom Wolfe insists will be a bigger, better realism? Recent history provides the answer. Taken together, then, these separate statements by Wolfe and Stone declare not the return of realism but rather its continuing relevance.

But then there have always been those willing to make the case. In *Literature Against Itself,* Gerald Graff admitted as valid Philip Roth's insight that there was something decidedly *unreal* about modern technological reality, but he stopped far short of the conclusion that "literature must for this reason abandon its pretensions to represent external reality and become either a self-contained reality unto itself or a disintegrated, dispersed process."[23] And in an essay entitled "The Nine Lives of Literary Realism" (1987), Keith Opdahl argued that "the realistic novel has remained our single major literary mode for over 125 years, habitually springing back to outlast those movements that have ostensibly buried it." According to Opdahl, realism has lasted "because it is adaptable, borrowing all kinds of techniques from the movements that would supplant it," including, of course, postmodernism itself. But above all, Opdahl insisted, realism offered readers something they could not get from any other kind of fiction, "recognition of their own experience, particularly when that experience is private, subjective or intangible." Though he was concerned in his argument with realists of the immediate postwar period—Bellow, Mailer, Roth, Updike, and so on— Opdahl's description of what made the work of these writers appealing fifty years ago still holds true for today's so-called neorealists: "Like Robert Penn Warren, whose *All the King's Men* (1946) set the tone, these writers used their heightened prose to examine social issues through the prism of personal experience. Never before, it seemed, had such a large number of writers rendered with such exact insight the daily experience of ordinary citizens."[24]

The great Jewish writers of the 1940s, 1950s, and 1960s—Bellow, Mailer, Malamud, and Roth—provided us with an elaborated and precise (not to say objective) view of an intensely urban, ethnic experience that would be difficult to imagine without recourse to the lessons and techniques of realism. In our own time, this project has been carried forward by a new breed of ethnic writer—Native American, Chinese American, Latino/a, and so on. Books like Sherman Alexie's *Reservation Blues* (1995) or Amy Tan's *Joy Luck*

Club (1989) or Sandra Cisneros's *House on Mango Street* (1984) are designed to provide, among other things, a window on a world that is both alien and recognizably our own.

In some ways, then, Tom Wolfe's prediction that the immediate future of the American novel would be in the realist mode has largely come to pass. But that is not to say that postmodernism somehow never happened, that contemporary writers have simply gone back to realism. Indeed, with the obvious exceptions of Faulkner and Hemingway, few writers have exerted as great an influence on the contemporary American novel as Vladimir Nabokov and Gabriel García-Márquez. Of course, it could be argued that neither of these writers was, in his bones, a postmodernist—that despite their obvious interests in word games, literary allusions, and indeed the whole impulse toward reflexivity in fiction, both writers maintained an equal if not greater interest in linear narrative, vivid characters, and what Nabokov called, in his 1956 afterward to *Lolita,* "a certain exhilarating milieu." It could even be argued that Nabokov's most lasting contribution to American fiction came not as a result of any impulse toward language consciousness or reflexivity but from the pair of sharp, outsider's eyes he brought to bear on the world of American strip malls and motels.[25] But beyond such arguments, what stands out finally is that contemporary realist writers have *absorbed* postmodernism's most lasting contributions and gone on to forge a new realism that is more or less traditional in its handling of character, reportorial in its depiction of milieu and time, but is at the same time self-conscious about language and the limits of mimesis.

"I like the feeling of unexpectedness and verbal decoration that is part of the experimental," the novelist Nicholson Baker has said, "but I like to be as close to the truth as I can be. So I do tracery work on the hinges of the cabinet, but want to be building a functional object, as opposed to a piece of nonsense sculpture." Thomas Mallon, author of, among others, the novel *Aurora 7* (1991), an account of Scott Carpenter's 1962 space flight, concurs. Although he doesn't necessarily agree with the tenets behind much experimental writing, Mallon acknowledges that many of his novel's more startling and successful narrative devices, for example its periodic revelations of its characters' futures, could not have been pulled off without his exposure to the example of postmodernism.[26]

At first glance, these statements may appear to ignore postmodernism's larger aims, but upon further reflection it becomes clear that both Baker and Mallon are treating the experiments of postmodernism as just that—

experiments. It is not the job of later writers to simply *repeat* these experiments but rather to take what has been proven useful and put it to work where and how they may. That today's writers have done this within the overall context of a continuing tradition of realism should not really surprise us since, as both Wolfe and Opdahl suggest, realism has proven itself far more adaptable and, paradoxically, more open to new techniques and influences than has literary postmodernism.

2 / Minimalism and Its Di

2 / Minimalism and Its Discontents

Although it would be difficult to pinpoint the exact moment when the first cracks began to appear in the edifice of literary postmodernism, a good guess might be December 1966, when a gaunt, low-rent tale called "Will You Please Be Quiet, Please?" was chosen for the *Best American Short Stories* anthology of 1967. It would be a full fourteen years, many hardships and much rejection, before Raymond Carver and his particular brand of realist short story came to dominate the American literary scene, but the signs of this coming, we can see now, were already in the air.

Contrary to what many people believe about him, Raymond Carver was not a latter-day Sherwood Anderson, a late-bloomer who had already lived several lives before he discovered his gift and became a writer. Although his breakthrough collection of stories, *Will You Please Be Quiet, Please?* did not appear until 1976, when he was thirty-eight years old, Carver had been writing seriously since the late 1950s. His first short story, "Pastoral," was published in 1963, and most of the stories that appeared in his first collection had been written by 1971. If recognition for Raymond Carver was a long time coming, that had more to do with the literary climate of the sixties and seventies—that is to say, the reign of literary postmodernism—than any lack of effort on Carver's part to either write or attempt to publish what he had written. Right up to 1976, when *Will You Please Be Quiet, Please?* was nominated for a National Book Award, and even beyond that time, Carver had trouble placing his stories in literary magazines because, as Tobias Wolff has recalled, "they were considered rather odd and old-fashioned . . . because they weren't in the experimental mode" favored by the journals of that era.[1]

Aesthetic prejudice aside, Carver was also held back by the simple facts of book publishing in his time. By the early 1990s, it was no longer unusual for promising writers to publish a collection of short stories as their first book. Even a short list of story writers who began their careers in this way would include Ann Beattie, Amy Hempel, Jayne Anne Phillips, Bobbie Ann Mason, Thom Jones, Chris Offutt, Pam Houston, and Sherman Alexie, not to speak of writers we otherwise think of as novelists, for example, Barbara Kingsolver, Dorothy Allison, E. Annie Proulx, and others. When Raymond Carver began publishing, by contrast, story collections were often viewed as vanity publications, favors done for successful writers who had already proven their worth as novelists. Carver himself was instrumental in changing all that. Yet as amazing as it may seem today, even after his first collection had been nominated for a National Book Award, Carver's second collection, *Furious Seasons* (1977), could find no other home than the tiny Capra Press. Thus it was that by 1981, when he finally began to receive national recognition as a major writer and the principal force behind the renaissance of the American short story, Raymond Carver had already been writing his own distinctive brand of fiction for more than twenty years.

To write about Raymond Carver today is to first of all confront the myriad myths and legends that surrounded the man even before his death in 1988 at the age of fifty. The most persistent of these myths would have us understand Carver as a hero of the masses, an uneducated man made good, the son of a sawmill worker and part-time waitress who first learned to write by enrolling in the Palmer Institute of Authorship, a correspondence course he failed to complete. This is the Carver who is remembered as the Last of the Nonliterary Literary Men, heir to a heroic tradition that includes Melville, Twain, Hemingway, and above all Jack London, whose No Mentor But Myself philosophy defines the myth almost as much as the requisite lack of college credits. Visit any of the unlikely places where the dream of becoming a writer still somehow manages to take root in this country, from rural truck stops to urban unemployment offices, and you will hear of this Carver: how he persevered and by dint of hard work turned all of his most glaring weaknesses into strengths, how he survived to beat the odds. This is the view of Carver from below, as it were.

The view of Carver from above sees him as a kind of idiot savant, a naïve artisan whose largely autobiographical tales of life in the American underclass succeed because of their blunt and shocking "inarticulateness." This is the Carver who was married at age eighteen, the father of two children by age twenty, twice bankrupt by age forty, and by age fifty was dead of lung cancer. It is this Carver who lived for years performing a series of demeaning "crap" jobs, including janitor, stock boy, motel clerk, and so on. Above all, this is the Carver who by all reports nearly drank himself to death between the ages of thirty-five and forty, and whose later life of sobriety with the poet Tess Gallagher is to be viewed as an inexplicable species of cosmic good luck—which is, of course, exactly as Carver himself regarded it.

The truth is a bit more complex and makes far less interesting copy. For although Raymond Carver indeed hailed from humble origins and experienced more than his share of hardship—much of it self-inflicted—he is also perhaps the first major American writer whose entire career was informed and shaped by the world of the university. As Carver's friend Richard Ford recalled in an essay published on the tenth anniversary of Carver's death, "Ray and I were so typical of Americans who decide to try being writers, and were products of the environment that included college, writing workshops, sending stories to quarterlies, attending graduate school, having teachers who were writers . . . all of us seeking improvement in the standard postwar American way: through some sort of pedagogy."[2] Indeed, it would be difficult to posit a career more thoroughly conditioned by this university world of writing (unless that career is John Barth's). And if earlier writers like Flannery O'Connor and Tennessee Williams were among the first who, as Ford has it, "entered the writing world by institutional means," then it must be said that Carver helped to establish the later pattern of full "institutionalization."[3]

These are the relevant facts of the Carver resume: in 1959, at the age of twenty, he was already enrolled in an undergraduate workshop run by a pioneering teacher of creative writing, the novelist John Gardner. (Carver's tribute to these years, "John Gardner: The Writer as Teacher," first published as the forward to Gardner's *On Becoming a Novelist* (1983) and reprinted many times since, stands as a classic in the emerging genre of pedagogical reminiscence.) By the time Carver graduated from Humboldt State in 1963, he had taken more fiction workshops from the writer Dick Day, had edited several issues of the campus literary magazine, and had begun submitting his own work nationally. It was on the strength of the stories he wrote in undergraduate workshops, as well as the recommendations written by Gardner and Day (both graduates of Iowa), that Carver was admitted to the prestigious Iowa Writer's Workshop later in 1963. By 1967, as I've noted, his work had appeared in the *Best American Short Stories* anthology—a coup that must have made further success seem tantalizingly near. In 1968 or 1969, while working as a textbook editor in California, Carver met the other major influence on his writing, the writer and editor Gordon Lish, who would later ascend to the position of fiction editor at *Esquire* magazine and from that post help launch Carver's larger career. In 1972, Carver held a Wallace Stegner Fellowship at Stanford, managing to teach at the same time at the University of California at Berkeley. The next year, Carver returned to the Iowa Writer's Workshop, this time as a teacher. In later years, even as he struggled mightily with alcoholism, Carver taught creative writing at a number of institutions, including the University of California at Santa Barbara, Goddard College in Vermont, the University of Texas at El Paso, and eventually at Syracuse University, where he was appointed professor of English.[4]

Knowing all of this about Carver does tend to dilute some of the legends surrounding him, but it in no way diminishes his achievement. Rather, it forces us to grant him awareness of pretty much all that was going on around him in the literary culture of his time, and this insight is crucial if we are to position his work accurately viz-à-viz what I have called the reign of literary postmodernism. For example, there can be no doubt that Carver knew very early on about the experimental bent of much American writing of the 1960s. In his essay on Gardner, Carver recounts how the older writer tried to introduce him to William Gass's experimental novella *The Pederson Kid* even before it appeared in the first issue of Gardner's literary journal *MSS.*[5] In time, Carver would articulate his own individualized response to the experiments of literary postmodernism, a response grounded in the ideas about craft he absorbed from Gardner and his own ideas about what constituted responsibility to the reader. For example, in the essay "On Writing," which first appeared in the 15 February 1981 *New York Times Book Review* as a belated response to John Barth's lament, in the same publication, that student fiction writing in the eighties was less formally innovative than student writing of the sixties and seventies, Carver offered the following complaint about "formal innovation" in fiction: "Too often 'experimentation' is a license to be careless, silly or imitative in the writing. Even worse, a license to try to brutalize or alienate the reader. Too often such writing give us no news of the world, or else describes a desert landscape and that's all—a few dunes and lizards here and there, but no people; a place uninhabited by anything recognizably human, a place of interest only to a few scientific specialists."[6]

Carver went on to note that what he considered "real experiment in fiction" was "original, hard-earned and cause for rejoicing." Unlike traditional techniques, however, real experiment could not be learned through imitation. The "real experimenters," of whom Carver mentions only Donald Barthelme, had to "find things out for themselves," and the best of these writers continued to "want to stay in touch with us . . . to carry news from their world to ours."

Elsewhere, in a 1986 interview with William L. Stull, Carver reiterates a key idea, drawing a distinction between *communication,* which continually takes audience into account, and *expression,* which is more private and often operates outside concerns of audience. "In trying out different ways of expressing themselves," Carver argues, "the experimental writers failed to communicate in the most fundamental and essential way. They got farther and farther away from their audience. But maybe that is what they wanted." He finishes his response by speculating that later literary scholars will look back on literary postmodernism and see it "as an odd time in the literary history of the country, an interruption, somehow." Asked by Stull if what he means by this is an interruption "in the course of realism," Carver answers, "I don't really think in those terms, but now that you ask me, yes."[7]

In the essays and interviews of the mid- to late 1980s, we encounter a confident Carver who elaborated freely on an aesthetic that grew out his apprenticeship under John Gardner, the early examples of Chekhov and Hemingway, his relationship with Gordon Lish, and his own natural tendencies as a fiction writer and poet (to say nothing of his precarious mode of living during most of the years when his best work was produced—which Carver always counted, along with the fact of early fatherhood, as the most important influence on his work).[8]

Recently there has been much speculation about Lish's exact role in all this—specifically, the aggressive and at times "overweening" (Richard Ford's phrase) approach Lish took in editing the stories that appeared in *Will You Please Be Quiet, Please?* and *What We Talk About When We Talk About Love.*[9] Indeed, it appears Lish played a major role, cutting some of the stories by more than half, changing titles and endings at will, at times even making additions of his own to the text of the stories. These are serious revelations Carver scholars will debate for years. For now, however, it must be said that it is only in the context of Carver's other influences and his origins in the workshop method that Lish's contribution makes sense. Seen in this light, Lish simply pushed Carver further in the direction he had already chosen for himself—which is, among other reasons, why Carver not only stood for Lish's treatment of his work but also welcomed it and remained more or less grateful for it even to the end.

We have already seen, in his comments on experimental writing, how important Carver thought it was to write about *people* and to allow emotion into his stories. For Carver, stories were meant to deliver what he liked to call *news* and to do so with both beauty and economy. Indeed, concision was a lesson learned early on from Gardner, of whom Carver, in his essay "Fires," wrote, "He helped me to see how important it was to say exactly what I wanted to say and nothing else" and "He helped show me how to say what I wanted to say and to use the minimum number of words to do so" (38). In the Stull interview, Carver credits Lish as well, remarking that whereas Gardner had said, "[D]on't use twenty-five words to say what you can say in fifteen," Lish "believed that if you could say it in five words instead of fifteen, use five words."[10]

Beyond these two powerful mentors, all of Carver's primary *literary* influences—Chekhov, the early Hemingway, the Joyce of *Dubliners,* Flaubert—were believers in a necessary unity of part and whole in the short story, which is why the first three of these four, together with Edgar Allan Poe, are regularly cited as having more or less *invented* the modern short story with its emphasis on a single effect (Poe), an economy of words (Hemingway), and an epiphany that registers as much with the reader as with the central character (Joyce). These writers were also, as was Flaubert, great believers in the art of revision—about which Carver heard quite a lot from Gardner. "It was a basic tenet of his," Carver wrote in his tribute to Gardner, "that a writer found out what he wanted to say in the ongoing process of *seeing* what he'd said. And this seeing, or seeing more clearly, came about through revision. He *believed* in revision, endless revision" (43).

That Carver fully absorbed Gardner's sermons about "endless revision" there can be little doubt. It is a topic in every major essay Carver wrote and nearly every interview he ever gave. But by revision Carver meant not only cutting (although he would eventually become most famous for this, his name a sort of ready-made metaphor for the practice) but also adding, moving, changing around. Indeed, in his short career Carver became famous for two distinctive kinds of revision—revision by way of cutting, associated with his early work, especially the Lish-edited stories in *Will You Please Be Quiet, Please?* and *What We Talk About When We Talk About Love,* and revision by expansion or amplification, associated with his late work, especially the alternate versions of some of the stories from the early collections that made second appearances in *Cathedral* and *Where I'm Calling From.* It should be noted that each of these distinctive Carver modes has found its champions, as have the different published versions of particular stories, with the end result being that no real consensus has emerged about which Carver, early or late, is the "real" or the "best" Carver.

Take, for example, the story known variously as "The Bath" and "A Small, Good Thing." In its Lish-edited, minimal incarnation ("The Bath"), the story won *Columbia* magazine's Carlos Fuentes Award and helped launch the movement or school later either celebrated or derided as minimalism. Two years later, in its expanded or "restored" version ("A Small, Good Thing"), the story appeared in the Pushcart Prize annual and won an O. Henry Award. Still later, the two versions were published side by side in a chapter on revision in multiple editions of Janet Burroway's *Writing Fiction,* the leading textbook used in college fiction writing workshops. That Burroway meant the "expanded" version, "A Small, Good Thing," to be taken as the superior work of art is clear by the way she introduces the two stories, with "A Small, Good Thing" referred to as "the new version," said to have undergone "major expansion in the revision process," and "The Bath" said (by Carver himself, no less) to have been "messed around with, condensed and compressed," so that the story itself "hadn't been told" in that version. Despite Burroway's obvious prompts, however, routinely half the writers in my workshops still say they prefer "The Bath" to "A Small, Good Thing."[11]

No doubt readers will continue to disagree about this and other Carver stories, the whole issue of where particular readers come down always tending to say more about who is doing the choosing than about Carver or his work. The differences are, after all, fairly substantial. The Lish-edited versions from the seventies tend to foreground despair and crop sentiment (often at the expense of significant detail), offering readers a hard, highly stylized surface, while the "restored" versions of the eighties tend to reintroduce hope (also sentimentality) into the stories, offering readers a more complete and expansive view of the characters and their situations. It is my position, however, that as great as this difference can be, it is negligible when compared to the persistent overall *effect* Carver's stories tend to have on readers, which remains remarkably consistent from version to version and even from early career to late.

In his tribute to Carver, Richard Ford has created a kind of composite picture of that effect. It is the fall of 1977, and both Ford and Carver are at a writer's conference at Southern Methodist University in Dallas, where Carver, just off booze and trying desperately to put his life back together, gives a public reading of the story later known as "Are These Actual Miles?"

> Ray read the story in near-dark conditions, hugely hunched over a glaring little podium lamp, constantly fiddling with his big glasses, clearing his throat, sipping water, beetling down at the pages of his book as if he'd never really thought of reading this story out loud and wasn't finding it easy. His voice was typically hushed, seemingly unpracticed, halting almost to the point of being

annoying. But the effect of voice and story upon the listener was of actual life being unscrolled in a form so distilled, so intense, so *chosen,* so affecting in its urgencies as to leave you breathless and limp when he was finished. It was a startling experience—wondrous in all ways. And one learned, from the story, many things: Life was this way—yes, we already knew that. But *this* life, *these* otherwise unnoticeable people's suitability for literary expression seemed new. One also felt that a consequence of the story was seemingly to intensify life, even dignify it, and to locate in it shadowed corners and niches that needed revealing so that we readers could practice life better ourselves. And yet the story itself, in its spare, self-conscious intensity, was such a *made* thing, not *like* life at all; it was a piece of nearly abstract artistic construction calculated to produce almost giddy pleasure. That night in Dallas, Ray put on a blatant display of what a story could do in terms of artifice, concision, strong feeling, shapeliness, high and surprising dramatics. The story was definitely *about* something, and you could follow it easily—it was about what two people did in adversity which changed their lives. But here was no ponderous naturalism. Nothing extra. There were barely the rudiments of realism. This was highly stylized, artistic writing with life, not art, as its subject. And to be exposed to it was to be bowled over. (72)

I have quoted Ford at length here because what he says in this remarkable paragraph foregrounds not only what I take to be the overall effect of Carver's work on readers generally, but also its specific effect on writers, particularly young writers, circa 1977. The general effect, as Ford notes, is that of the "actual life" of imperfect characters being put before the reader in ways that are at once disturbing and aesthetically pleasing. Readers fresh from an encounter with Carver often speak of the "dread" or "menace" they felt reading a particular story, following this by remarking on how "beautiful" or "perfect" they felt the work to be. Writers can be expected to experience much the same thing, of course, but they will also tend to remark on any issues of technique a story raises and what possibilities it seems to open. Ford isolates several here, including Carver's depiction of working-class characters, his willingness to display raw emotion, his choice of moving or changing action over irony, and his refining or "distilling" of all this by way of a conscious economy of means. As Ford ticks off these elements, each of them coming with the force of revelation, one can feel him building to a kind of joyous climax: Carver has shown him, and everyone else present that night, how to be a serious artist without taking art as his subject matter, how to be the most literary of writers without becoming thereby a literary postmodernist. And it is this, as I have suggested above, that constitutes Carver's true and lasting legacy.

"What We Talk About When We Talk About Love," the title story of Carver's 1981 collection, provides a good example of what can be achieved through close cutting and the marshaling of a limited repertoire of techniques in service of a single effect.[12] Like Hemingway's classic story "Hills Like White Elephants," "What We Talk About When We Talk About Love" is composed almost entirely of dialogue—very sharp dialogue, dialogue that not only propels the story's minimal plot but also acts as an ongoing characterization of the people speaking. There is no action, no summary exposition, no outside commentary or interpretation. Even so, the story is rich in nuance and complexity—more so, perhaps, than "Hills Like White Elephants."

Whereas Hemingway's story features two characters, a man and a woman, who reveal themselves and the state of their relationship through small actions and the loaded things they say, Carver's story features four characters, two married couples, each of whom has been married before. "Hills Like White Elephants" is written in the third person, a strategy that puts the reader in the position of eavesdropper on a tortured, private conversation. "What We Talk About When We Talk About Love," by contrast, is narrated by one of the story's speakers, Nick, a thirty-eight-year-old man eighteen months into his second marriage.

The story's title describes the subject of the couples' conversation, while the narrator's background gives some indication of his investment in it. Background, mostly via dialogue, is also given for the other important characters. Mel, a cardiologist and the main speaker in the story, has been married to his present wife, Terri, for four years. Before this he was married to a woman he now hates because she's "bankrupting" him with alimony payments while living with another man she refuses to marry. In the face of this, Mel fantasizes about killing his ex-wife, who is allergic to bees, by going over to her place "dressed like a beekeeper," with "that hat that's like a helmet with the plate that comes down over your face," and setting "loose a hive of bees in the house" (184–85). Terri's previous relationship was with Ed, a violent, unstable man who used to beat her and who killed himself after she left him. These separate pasts weigh heavily on Mel and Terri, providing both a catalyst for the conversation depicted in the story and a key to its meaning.

Mel and Terri and Nick and his wife Laura are sitting in Mel's kitchen in Albuquerque, New Mexico, drinking gin and working up an appetite for dinner at a new restaurant they've heard about. "The gin and tonic water kept going around," Nick says, "and we somehow got on the subject of love" (170). They discuss love's passion and mystery, its transience, the way it can turn so quickly into hate. Hovering over all this talk is the characters' histories of failed relationships and the possibility—on the face of it, a very real one for Mel and Terri—that even their current marriages won't last. Initially at issue is Terri's former relationship with Ed, which she sees as having been "abnormal in most people's eyes" but filled with love nonetheless, especially since Ed "was willing to die for it . . . did die for it" (174). But for Mel, who professes a more "spiritual" view of the subject, Terri's relationship with Ed was merely "dangerous," and her insistence that "there was love there" only indicates that she has bought into the "kick-me-so-I'll-know-you-love-me school" (171). Nick and Laura, meanwhile, obviously uncomfortable with the conversation, hold that no one "can judge anyone else's situation," especially since they never knew "anything about Ed" (172). As the couples finish one bottle of gin and start on a second, Mel attempts to prove his point by telling a story that shows what "real love is" (176).

An elderly couple whose camper has been "plowed" down on the interstate by a drunken teenager is brought into the hospital where Mel works. They are both badly injured, and Mel and a team of doctors work though the night to keep them alive. Though initially given little chance to live, somehow they pull through and eventually are given a room off the ICU, where Mel visits them while making his rounds. "I dropped in to see each of them every day," Mel tells the others, "sometimes twice a day if I was up doing other calls anyway."

> Casts and bandages, head to foot, the both of them. You know, you've seen it in the movies. Little eye-holes and nose-holes and mouth-holes. And she had to have her legs slung up on top of it. Well, the husband was very depressed. Not about the accident, though. I mean, the accident was one thing, but it wasn't everything. I'd get up to his mouth-hole, you know, and he'd say no, it wasn't the accident exactly but it was because he couldn't see her through his eye-holes. He said that was what was making him feel so bad. Can you imagine? I'm telling you, the man's heart was breaking because he couldn't turn his goddamn head and *see* his goddamn wife. . . . I mean, it was killing the old fart just because he couldn't *look* at the fucking woman. (183)

In the aftermath of his speech, the others "all looked at Mel." "Do you see what I'm saying?" he asks them. They all just sit there, drunk and unable to focus. "The light was draining out of the room," Nick observes, "it was hard keeping things in focus," yet no one makes a move "to get up from the table to turn on the overhead light" (183). The story ends with Mel announcing that the gin is gone. "Now what?" Terri asks ominously. "I could hear my heart beating,"

Nick observes in the story's last paragraph. "I could hear everybody's heart. I could hear the human noise we sat there making, not one of us moving, not even when the room went dark" (185).

As most critics have noted, the characters in this story are "unconscious." Even Nick, the narrator, makes no attempt to interpret what's been said or how it affects his life. The true epiphany in the story happens to the reader, who is outside the relationships described in it and so can see the special problems each character is up against: for example, Mel's fear of injury by love, which leads him to wish he'd been born in another time, a knight protected and "safe wearing all that armor" (or, in his beekeeper fantasy, wearing "that hat that's like a helmet" and "the plate that comes down over your face"); Terri's desperate need to believe that Ed killed himself because of her, even though, as Mel points out, one rarely knows why another person commits suicide; and lastly, Nick and Laura's requirement that none of these stories touch them, that regardless of what has happened in Mel and Terri's previous marriages (or their own, for that matter), they still "know what love is" (175).

Each of these problems is a problem of vision, an inability to see things clearly, to "keep things in focus." As is often the case in Carver's work, the reader is confronted with a similar problem, but it is only by attending closely to Carver's often mundane language that we begin to see how tightly the story has been constructed.

For example, in the passage from Mel's speech I've quoted above, the words "look" and "see" are repeated over and over, each time with a slightly different meaning: to visit ("I dropped in to see them"), to be ("That's just the way they looked"), to love ("The man's heart was breaking because he couldn't *see* his goddamn wife"), to know ("Do you see what I'm saying?"), to not know ("We all looked at Mel"). Each of these meanings is a variation on a theme that becomes finally the larger theme of the story itself: to "talk about love" is ultimately to talk about a persistent failure to clearly see or communicate to others all that is closest to the human heart.

Seen in this light, "What We Talk About When We Talk About Love" stands out as a small masterpiece of understated realism and an excellent example of the Carver idiom. Written in the simplest of styles and making use of a bare minimum of literary devices, it nevertheless exerts a mesmerizing power and speculates on important aspects of the human condition.

Working independently of Carver, several other writers, most notably Grace Paley and Ann Beattie, had been for years perfecting a similarly abbreviated style that in the 1980s took the American literary scene by storm. It wasn't long before book reviewers and literary critics, borrowing a term from the art criticism of Richard Wollheim and others, began to speak of the new writing as "minimalism."

Writing in *Arts Magazine* in January 1965, Wollheim, a professor of logic at the University of London, had observed that a lot of postwar painting and sculpture shared "in looks, in intention, in moral impact" a certain similarity that could best be described by saying that these works displayed a "minimal art-content." "Either they are to an extreme degree undifferentiated in themselves," Wollheim wrote, "and therefore possess a very low content of any kind," or else "the differentiation that they do exhibit, which may in some cases be very considerable, comes not from the artist but from a nonartistic source, like nature or the factory."[13] Reading this description, it is easy to see why literary critics were drawn to Wollheim's term. Much literary minimalism was remarkably similar in its lack of "differentiation"—so much so, in fact, that many readers complained of an inability to tell one minimalist's work from another's. Beyond this, there was the feeling that what the old-fashioned realists had called "milieu" had been replaced by brand names and other "surface details" that clearly came not from the individual artist but from a "nonartistic source"—the world of the television sitcom and the shopping mall, for example.

At about the same time as literary critics began to take notice of minimalism, publishers discovered that story collections that were "high concept," unified by a single theme, and, above all, easily digested in the time it took to ride the subway to work, were suddenly good risks for an industry that was having a hard time competing with other mass media. As writer and teacher Eve Shelnutt ran it down, "With what is called the 'renaissance' of American fiction post-1970, the publishing industry began to see, with minimalism in particular, a way to package American fiction almost the way New Journalism was being packaged: writing that talks about the way we live now, writing that appeals to a reader who spends a lot of time in front of the television."[14]

Midway into the 1980s, several writers attempted to step back and define the movement, often by way of attacking its techniques and the philosophical positions underpinning them. John Barth, writing in the *New York Times* in December 1986, offered this definition:

Minimalism (of one sort or another) is the principle (one of the principles, anyhow) underlying (what I and many another interested observer consider to be perhaps) the most impressive phenomenon on the current (North American, especially the United States) literary scene (the gringo equivalent to el boom in the Latin American novel): I mean the new flowering of the (North) American short story (in particular the kind of terse, oblique, realistic or hyperrealistic, slightly plotted, extrospective, cool-surfaced fiction associated in the last 5 to 10 years with such excellent writers as Frederick Barthelme, Ann Beattie, Raymond Carver, Bobbie Ann Mason, James Robinson, Mary Robinson and Tobias Wolff, and both praised and damned under such labels as "K-Mart realism," "hick chic," "Diet-Pepsi minimalism" and "Post-Vietnam, post-literary, postmodernist blue-collar neo-early-Hemingwayism").[15]

Minimalism, which for Barth exists outside the parentheses of his own definition, is lean, declarative, and punctuated by a colon, but it can't begin to tell the whole story, which is parenthetical, listlike, ugly by comparison. Barth's string of descriptive adjectives ("terse," "oblique," "extrospective," "cool-surfaced") quietly calls into question the fiction's commitment and passion, while what qualitative assessment he offers ("most impressive," "excellent") sounds like the sort of faint praise with which a bored professor might damn a "B" paper. And no wonder: Barth, an avowed "maximalist" himself, taught any number of budding minimalists at Johns Hopkins in the seventies, the most notable being Frederick Barthelme and Mary and James Robinson.

Madison Smartt Bell, writing in *Harper's* in April 1986, was at once less kind and more thorough than Barth. Bell's essay took the form of a review of recent story collections by Carver, Beattie, Barthelme, David Leavit, Amy Hempel, and Bobbie Ann Mason. Some who read the piece, however, knew it for what it was: a full-scale assault on "the minimalist school." Minimalism, Bell wrote, "may fairly be described as a school because its representative work contains, as if by prescription, a number of specific elements": "a trim, 'minimal' style, an obsessive concern for surface detail, a tendency to ignore or eliminate distinctions among the people it renders, and a studiedly deterministic, at times nihilistic, vision of the world."[16] For Bell, minimalism's accomplishments were purely technical; beneath its cool surfaces and lean prose style lurked a subtle and terrible estimation of human possibility. "The characters come to resemble rats negotiating a maze that the reader can see and they cannot" (67), he wrote of Carver's story "The Bridle." He was similarly dismissive of the work of the other minimalists, especially with regard to their handling of character, summing up his view of the movement as a whole by remarking, apropos one of Hempel's "spare, elliptical" works, "It is an admirably well-made story, as tidily constructed a bit of nastiness as anyone could wish for" (64).

As Bell points out, the problem with minimalism as it came to be practiced by writers such as Amy Hempel, Frederick Barthelme, and others was that, unlike Hemingway and Carver, these later writers did not seem to be meticulously cutting fat from stories that said too much; rather, they seemed to be cynically knocking out stories that deliberately said too little. This is a damning assessment, to be sure—if you agree with Bell's basic assumptions about plot, character, dialogue, and motivation. In his response to the "charges" leveled against "so-called 'minimalist' fiction," Frederick Barthelme, whose *Moon Deluxe* (1983) collection Bell had called "the literary apotheosis of the condominium and the mall" (68), argued that the new writing did not come out of the theories or practices of Hemingway, Carver, or even Samuel Beckett, but instead was an attempt on the part of members of his generation to separate themselves from both the postmodernism of an older generation (including Barthelme's older brother Donald) and the traditional realism these older writers had themselves rebelled against.[17] For writers coming of age in the mid-1970s, Barthelme wrote, "neither realism nor the adventure of post-modernism was going to get it":

> What you wanted to do was draw a distinction between realism, standing for a whole system of literary artifice, and representation, standing for only one part of that system. What you figured was that you could try some of this representation stuff, and do your dog and cat too, and see what happened. So suddenly you had characters that looked as if you just slowed for them in the parking lot of the K & B drugstore, but instead of waiting patiently and driving off, as you would in life, now you were talking to them, and they were talking back—not in conventional "realist" fashion or as people might in life, but like some characters in trees, or somebody discovering ice, or some other artificial beings in some other artificial text—very careful, very clear, achingly pristine and precise. But because you'd put them right down on an ordinary planet that looked strikingly like ours, the readers were reading right along as if what you'd written was some kind of one-for-one depiction of the real world. And, you know, you couldn't say for sure that it wasn't; maybe it was sort of a well-edited, delicately vetted, meticulously rendered, persnickety version thereof, even if it also was as wholly constructed, as made up as any post-modernist's, made somehow remarkably real because the context and components were not obviously fantasies, abstractions, assertions about the language, arguments dressed up as fictions, but ordinary things, ordinary places, just the stuff literary people were trying to flick off the shoulders of their jackets 20 years ago.

Like minimalism itself, Barthelme's description of the practice behind it is more focused on style than substance. There's a roguish humor about it that pokes fun at the seriousness of minimalism's detractors and promotes a view of the artist as a happy-go-lucky creator, one who is simply out to "do his dog and cat," seriousness be damned. Apart from the hipness of its style, however, Barthelme's "confession" is about as breathtaking an admission of artistic bankruptcy as anything Madison Smartt Bell could have devised for him to say. The kind of hybrid story he is describing purports to take the best from both worlds, representation from realism and invention from postmodernism, throwing out along the way all that was "conventional" in the one and "obvious" or "dressed up" in the other; but what is actually created in such a process is hardly clear, even to Barthelme himself. Minimalism, according to his description, can finally claim to be neither honestly representational nor honestly abstract, but instead turns out to be little more than a deliberate failure of context, an elaborate joke on readers whose punch line is informed by a sort of gleeful nihilism.

As tongue-in-cheek as it may seem, Barthelme's description of minimalist practice paints all too accurate a picture of what one finds in much of the fiction itself. The typical minimalist story, post-Carver, is set in a narrow domestic space, usually the living room or kitchen of a one-bedroom apartment, and features at most three characters (though two is the norm). As a rule, these stories begin in medias res and make use of first-person, present-tense narration (though second person is also popular), a tactic designed to bring a sense of immediacy to common events and circumstances. The language is flat, unadorned, highly stylized. The theme is invariably captivity, which is to say, the characters are "trapped" where they are, bored beyond words, and only vaguely conscious of how they got there in the first place. Perhaps they are husband and wife, but more often they are merely roommates or hospital patients on the same ward, people with no real connection to each other besides the "situation" they share. The action in these stories, such as it is, usually entails a domestic chore such as washing the dishes or a passive activity such as watching television. This allows the minimalist writer to concentrate on small things, little disturbances in language and gesture, and to bring dialogue to the fore. The space between action and dialogue, where we would normally expect to find narration, is reserved for the sort of clipped one-liners that in television sitcoms are traditionally followed by canned laughter. Terse, often witty, and ominous in the extreme, these one-liners serve to move the story toward its inevitable conclusion, which is rarely the culmination of any significant action, or even the end of a particular conversation, but rather a deadly pause that leaves the future open at the same time as it assures us that what follows will be undoubtedly more of the same. The overall effect such a story attempts to create is a thoroughgoing sense of irony.

A good example of the kind of story I'm talking about—and there are literally thousands to choose from—appears in Amy Hempel's 1985 collection *Reasons to Live*. The story, entitled "Tonight Is a Favor to Holly," concerns two women who are living in an apartment by the ocean while their usual dwelling, damaged in a mud slide, is undergoing repairs. The story begins in the classic first-person, present-tense manner:

> A blind date is coming to pick me up, and unless my hair grows an inch by seven o'clock, I am not going to answer the door. The problem is the front. I cut the bangs myself; now I look like Mamie Eisenhower.
>
> Holly says no, I look like Claudette Colbert. But I know why she says that is so I will meet this guy. Tonight is a favor to Holly.[18]

The language here is spare in the extreme. Hempel's narrator, like those in a lot of minimalist stories, is neither insightful nor even reasonably articulate. Where narration is concerned, indirection and evasion will be the rule. Since we have already been told, by way of the title and the second paragraph, that the blind date is a "favor to Holly," we expect that the rest of the story will develop this idea (we are wrong). As for the references to Mamie Eisenhower and Claudette Colbert, these are throwaway lines, the sort of surface details minimalist writers build up layer upon layer in place of milieu. The blind date, needless to say, will not be treated in the story; and not because of the "hair problem," either, but because the story itself will come to its quiet, ironic close long before seven o'clock rolls around.

What follows Hempel's flat, declarative opening is a series of equally detached examples of where these women are, both physically and emotionally. Physically, of course, they are at the beach: "Out the front door is sand. There's the ocean, and we see it every day of the year" (7). What do they do at the beach? Well, what they "usually do": "mix our rum and Cokes, and drink them on the sand while the sun goes down" (7). Also, they do "research," which is to say, they look at men on the beach and talk about them: "It's the other thing we do together on my days off" (10). Small details accumulate. Holly, a backup singer who "sometimes records" (8), is divorced. However, she still sees her ex-husband; they "sit around and depress each other" (11). The narrator, for her part, is a travel agent (no real details are given), but she hopes only to hold this job "until my parents die" (8). The men in the story—the "beach guys," Holly's ex-husband, the blind date who is about to arrive—hover over these tiny details in an ominous way, and yet it is difficult to pinpoint the reason for this. The most we get are cryptic comments such as "These men, it's not like we don't see them coming. Our intuition is good; the problem is we ignore it" (11). Along the same lines, the narrator mentions two other characters, Hard and Suzy, who live in an aluminum shack at the end of the block. Suzy "has massive sunburned arms and wide hips that jerk unevenly when she walks" (9). Hard is "tall and thin" (9). Characteristically, the relationship is filled with violence. Standing before the kitchen window the night before, the narrator had seen Suzy attacking Hard in the alley. The origins of this violence, however, remain a mystery, and there is no real sign that the narrator has been affected by it. She merely "views" it as one would watch a movie on television, later imagining herself as "Claudette or Mamie," her blind date as "Hard's brother . . . so dumb there aren't any examples" (12).

Apart from the dialogue ("You wash, I'll dry," says Holly), the rest of the story consists of one elliptical comment after another, most of which serve, as far as we can tell, to reinforce the story's mood. Such as: "My job fits right in. I *do* nothing, it *pays* nothing, but—you guessed it—it's *better* than nothing" (8). Or: "What you forget, living here, is that just because you have stopped sinking doesn't mean you're not still underwater" (10). Or: "There are two kinds [of people] to choose from: those who are going under and those who aren't moving ahead" (11). Or: "The truth is, the beach is like excess weight. If we lost it, what would the excuse be then?" (13).

The story ends when the narrator mentions that she once moved east, "a mistake." Moving back, the truck carrying her things crashes and spills her "whole life down a muddy ravine" (13). This reminds her of the place on Highway 1 where people sometimes "fall over these cliffs, craning to see the bottom of them" (13). The message of all this is, the narrator admits, "heavyhanded," however—and here the story closes—"I say an omen that big can be ignored" (13).

What we are to make of all this is hard to say. Considerable energy has gone into creating a mood of impending doom, but other than the rather obvious idea that these women are waiting around for men and hate themselves for it, nothing much seems to be behind this mood. We know as little about the narrator at the story's end as we did at the beginning. No explanation is offered for why these women live the way they do, why it's so important for Holly that the narrator go on the blind date, what in their previous relationships has gone so wrong, or what, if anything, they intend to do about it. To be sure, we are given plenty of Hemingway's tip of the iceberg, but by the time we finish the story we are far from believing that anything substantial remains below the surface.

One of the more depressing things about the story is its lack of concrete and believable detail. The divorced Holly is said to be a "backup singer who sometimes records," which sounds like nothing so much as a twenty year old's vague notion of what someone might do after graduation. The same must be said of the narrator's occupation, which she only plans to pursue "until my parents die." The domestic situation in the story is equally unbelievable. The reader is never able to accept the idea that these two women, who barely know each other, own a house together, and the idea that Holly and her ex-husband still "sit around and depress each other" would appear to describe a failed dormitory romance much more accurately than it does an actual divorce. In fiction, as John Gardner liked to point out, the vast majority of an author's authority resides in his or her ability to serve up and control convincing detail, and in this regard, as in so many others in this particular story, Amy Hempel comes up spectacularly short.

However, if a story like "Tonight Is a Favor to Holly" lacks what I have called concrete and believable detail, we may at least be thankful it is not filled with what passes for such detail in Frederick Barthelme's 1983 collection *Moon Deluxe*. Consider, for example, the openings to the following stories.

"You watch the pretty salesgirl slide a box of Halston soap onto a low shelf, watch her braid slip off her shoulder, watch like an adolescent as the vent at the neck of her blouse opens slightly—" ("Shopgirls").

"Kathleen Sullivan is back on CNN, a guest on the call-in interview show. She's supposed to be talking about the boom in news, but the callers, who are all men, only want to talk about her bangs, and the new drab-look clothes she wears on ABC" ("Violet").

"You're stuck in traffic on the way home from work, counting blue cars, and when a blue-metallic Jetta pulls alongside, you count it—twenty-eight" ("Moon Deluxe").

"Harry Lang's company Chevrolet breaks down on the highway fifteen miles outside of Dallas. He gets the car to a small old town called Cummings, leaves it at the gas station, and calls Fay, a woman he met at a corporate sensitivity workshop in San Antonio and the reason for this trip" ("Trip").

"First you see the woman's beautiful hair, steel gray and cut to brush the shoulders of her vanilla silk blouse. She is thin and too elegantly dressed for the supermarket" ("Safeway").[19]

Of these five stories (there are seventeen in the collection), two take place in stores, three make use of the once-rare second-person mode of narration, and all are in present tense. Clothing gets a lot of play here, as does hairstyle and the names of specific companies or products—Halston, CNN, ABC, Jetta, Chevrolet, Safeway. None of this is done in the name of specificity or depth, but on the contrary to underscore the commonness of the situations and the superficiality of the narrative consciousness. Who hasn't been stuck in traffic, had a car break down, or stood in line at the supermarket? When are we not surrounded by trademarks? And yet, as the above examples perhaps begin to show, there is something deadening and depressing about seeing such trivia take the place of significant action and detail in fiction. At best, the practice strikes the reader as a failed shortcut and a cheapening of literary art. At worst, it seems neurotic and obsessive and—when matched with the ubiquitous second person—vaguely insulting.

In the end, the example of both Raymond Carver and minimalism more generally must be seen as an ambiguous inheritance for today's writer. On one hand, Carver and the minimalists provided a much-needed alternate route to that traveled by the postmodernists in the sixties and seventies, their best work tending to revitalize both realism and a once-proud American tradition in the short story. On the other hand, by limiting themselves to such a meager repertoire of techniques, and by repeating these techniques ad nauseam, the minimalists who followed Carver and in some cases imitated him too often appear to lack both a coherent and compelling view of the world (never true of Carver) and the skill and ambition necessary to embody that view with any kind of lasting power. Read today, the work often seems shallow and dated, the insights predictable and slight—a mere step toward better work to come.

3 / Dirty Realism

3 / Dirty Realism

Minimalism goes by another name in England, where it has been widely discussed as a result of two issues of the literary journal *Granta* conceived and put together in the mid-1980s by the expatriate American editor Bill Buford, who a decade later would become the literary editor of *New Yorker* magazine: *Granta 8: Dirty Realism* (1983) and *Granta 19: More Dirt* (1986).

In his introduction to *Granta 8,* which included stories by Raymond Carver, Richard Ford, Jayne Anne Phillips, and others, Buford described the new American writing as "a curious, dirty realism about the belly-side of contemporary life."[1] Dirty realism differed from both the traditional realistic writing of John Updike or William Styron, which was "ornate, even baroque in comparison," and the "consciously experimental" writing of the postmodernists—Barth, Pynchon, and others—which "seemed pretentious in comparison." The new writing was a fiction of "a different scope" altogether than either these or the "inflated," "epic ambitions" of Saul Bellow and Norman Mailer. Dirty realism focused on the small instead of the large, and the stories it told were so spare that it took some time before the reader realized how completely "a whole culture and a whole moral condition" were being represented. "These are strange stories," Buford wrote,

> unadorned, unfurnished, low-rent tragedies about people who watch day-time television, read cheap romances or listen to country and western music. They are waitresses in roadside cafes, cashiers in supermarkets, construction workers, secretaries and unemployed cowboys. They play bingo, eat cheeseburgers, hunt deer and stay in cheap hotels. They drink a lot and are often in trouble: for stealing a car, breaking a window, pickpocketing a wallet. They are from Kentucky or Alabama or Oregon but, mainly, they could just about be from

anywhere: drifters in a world cluttered with junk food and the oppressive details of modern consumerism. (4)

On a purely technical level, the new fiction was indeed minimalist ("unadorned," "unfurnished"), but it was also realist insofar as it dealt with a specific class of people (the working class) living in specific places (Kentucky, Alabama, Oregon) holding down specific jobs (construction, ranch work, waitressing). Its dominant themes—dislocation, drifting, malaise—presented an image of America as at once free and *pursued:* wealthy beyond words and yet crime-ridden, arrogantly confident and yet horribly dissatisfied. For the British, in short, dirty realism was a kind of truncated documentary naturalism that told the "truth" about America in the 1980s, even as imported television shows such as *Dallas* and *Dynasty* traded in "lies."

Of course, foreigners have long been fascinated with American violence, consumerism, and pop culture iconography, and Bill Buford's designation of the new American writing as dirty realism was in part an inspired marketing strategy to sell the new fiction to a well-read English audience that could not be expected to take much interest in something as innocuous as minimalism. Whereas Americans tend to look to Europe for examples of "high" culture (so goes conventional marketing wisdom), Europeans tend to look to America for examples or treatments of "low" or popular culture.

But in coining the term dirty realism, Buford was on to far more than a marketing strategy. There is indeed a movement of this sort in American fiction, but the authors who come to mind in relation to it have, for the most part, gained prominence in the 1990s and share little in terms of artistic practice or subject matter with the minimalists. I have in mind writers such as Thom Jones and Denis Johnson and William T. Vollmann, all of whom are more indebted to the intense, post-Vietnam realism of Robert Stone than they are to the pared-down style of Carver or the Richard Ford of *Rock Springs*. In Vollmann's work in particular, especially *The Rainbow Stories* (1989) and *The Atlas* (1996), the contemporary fascination with street life and marginalized people is taken to an extreme beyond which it would be almost impossible to go.

In his introduction to *Best American Short Stories 1992*, which included Johnson's "Emergency" and Jones's "The Pugilist at Rest," Robert Stone, as noted earlier, made a special point of linking the writers in his anthology to a "renewal and revitalization of the realist mode" that he regarded as "probably the most significant development in late-twentieth-century American fiction" (xviii). "As of 1992," Stone wrote, "American writers seem ready to accept traditional forms without self-consciousness in dealing with the complexity of the world around them" (xviii). Stone's assessment was echoed in early reviews of both Johnson's collection *Jesus' Son: Stories* (1992) and Jones's *The Pugilist at Rest* (1993). Madison Smartt Bell wrote of *Jesus' Son*'s "grinding realism," Gail Caldwell of its "tough-guy realism." British reviewers, meanwhile, thought Johnson's stories took "the American 'Dirty Realism' of Raymond Carver and Richard Ford into new depths" and called *The Pugilist at Rest* "Dirty Realism welded to pessimistic philosophy."[2]

Dirty realism, as I would like to employ the term, refers to an effect in both subject matter and technique that is somewhere between the hard-boiled and the darkly comic. It refers to the impulse in writers to explore dark truths, to descend, as it were, into the darkest holes of society and what used to be called "the soul of man." Not the trailer parks and fern bars of minimalism, though Conrad's heart of darkness might lurk in these places, too, but rather the more intense worlds of war, drug addiction, serious crime, prostitution, prison. In terms of technique: not the detached, "unconscious" narrations of minimalism, but rather the probing, superconscious narrations of a Henry Miller or Hubert Selby Jr. I'm thinking of a kind of fiction that goes beyond what has been called, at one time or another, "tough-guy realism," "under-world realism," "hard-boiled fiction," "southern Gothic," and so on, a fiction that incorporates all this but also includes what Harry Levin used to call, following Melville's view of Hawthorne, "the power of blackness."[3]

Melville is in fact instructive here. "For spite of all the Indian-summer sunlight on the hither side of Hawthorne's soul," he wrote in a famous passage,

> the other side—like the dark half of the physical sphere—is shrouded in blackness, ten times black. . . . Whether Hawthorne has simply availed himself of this mystical blackness as a means to the wondrous effects he makes it to produce in his lights and shades; or whether there really lurks in him, perhaps unknown to himself, a touch of Puritanic gloom,—this, I cannot tell. Certain it is, however, that this great power of blackness in him derives its force from its appeals to that Calvinistic sense of Innate Depravity and Original Sin, from whose visitations, in some shape or other, no deeply thinking mind is always and wholly free.[4]

What Melville is describing here is not merely an aspect of the Hawthorne psyche as he sees it. He's describing a kind of transaction between Hawthorne and his nineteenth-century readers, a place where Hawthorne's "Puritanic gloom" met their "sense of Innate Depravity and Original Sin," creating in the process a "power of blackness" in the work itself.

Despite the distance between Melville's time and our own, we can still recognize what he is talking about in writers like Jones and Johnson and Vollmann, the power of whose work, it seems to me, derives from their handling of certain subjects and themes that are for the twentieth-century American conscience what "Innate Depravity" and "Original Sin" might have been for Hawthorne's nineteenth-century audience. A short list of these subjects would include the lingering anger and guilt surrounding America's involvement in the Vietnam War, the legacy of crime and violence to which America's drug trade gives rise, the stark worlds of street life and the prison, and the cauldron of disappointment, bitterness, and fear characterizing race relations in the post–civil rights era.

Although it has been roughly a quarter century since the last U.S. helicopter lifted off from the last embattled U.S. embassy building in Southeast Asia, the memory of Vietnam still haunts American culture and literature in ways we are only beginning to understand. In *Re-Writing America: Vietnam Authors in Their Generation* (1991), the second book he has written on the subject since 1982, Philip Beidler argues that the war and its aftermath have irrevocably changed the American literary landscape. Far from having been forgotten, Vietnam is one of the most important cultural referents in our writing. The Vietnam veteran, for years a sort of Bartleby the Scrivener roaming our collective conscience, has since become a persistent protagonist in our literature and frequently the author of some of our most compelling and important books. The works of Robert Stone, Michael Herr, Philip Caputo, Tim O'Brien, and Ron Kovic come immediately to mind. But beyond these nearly household names, there are the subsequent careers of writers as varied as Larry Heinemann, Robert Olen Butler, Tobias Wolff, and Bobbie Ann Mason to consider. Taken together, Beidler insists, the work of Vietnam-era writers constitutes "nothing less than a whole vast heterotopia," a major reorientation of "the very myth of national culture itself."[5]

It is just this subject that Thom Jones, not a Vietnam veteran himself, takes on in *The Pugilist at Rest*. A finalist for the 1993 National Book Award, Jones's collection came into print with back-cover praise from Vietnam heavyweights like Herr and Stone. Herr speaks of Jones's Hemingwayesque subject matter, "the codes and rituals of what we call American manhood"; Stone speaks of his style, which mixes "knowledge and skill" with "terror and release."[6] Neither writer mentions the war; but *there it is,* as they used to say in Vietnam, hanging about their very names like napalm above a burned-out forest.

Jones, a former marine and a boxer with more than 150 fights to his credit, has remarked how intimidated he felt by the prospect of writing about the war: "There has been such superlative work written about Vietnam that I never considered writing about that war until the Persian Gulf War of recent times coincided with the birthday of a Marine buddy who died in Vietnam."[7] At that point, says Jones, he sat down and wrote his most famous short story, "The Pugilist at Rest," essentially in one sitting. Such a statement speaks volumes about the continuing power of Vietnam as a subject. The Gulf War, as immediate and unreal as it was, is by comparison relegated to the status of mere *reminder,* a kind of Proustian tea biscuit to a larger experience that is past but far from forgotten.

The first three stories in Jones's collection, "The Pugilist at Rest," "Break on Through," and "The Black Lights," deal directly with the experience of the gung-ho "recon" foot soldier "dealing death in the 'Nam." These stories are both brutal and brutally moving. In the title story, which was originally published in the *New Yorker* and later won an O. Henry Award, the narrator survives three tours in Vietnam, exorcising along the way all the "malice, poison, and vicious sadism" in his soul, only to get his brains hopelessly scrambled in a boxing match upon his return to Camp Pendleton (20). His health gone, suffering from recurrent bouts of left-temporal-lobe epilepsy, he becomes introspective and timid. He reads Schopenhauer, learns to love the pair of Staffordshire terriers that keep him from swallowing his own tongue, and comes finally, like the "epileptic saint" Dostoyevsky, to see through the "veil of illusion which is spread over all things":

> You lose your health and you start thinking this way. . . . The world is replete with badness. I'm not talking about that old routine where you drag out the Spanish Inquisition, the Holocaust, Joseph Stalin, the Khmer Rouge, etc. It happens in our own backyard. Twentieth-century America is one of the most materially prosperous nations in history. But take a walk through an American prison, a nursing home, the slums where the homeless live in cardboard boxes, a cancer ward. Go to a Vietnam vets' meeting, or an A.A. meeting, or an Overeaters Anonymous meeting. *How shallow and unreal a thing is life, how deceitful are its pleasures, what horrible aspects it possesses.* (22)

This bald statement of shock and horror might be taken as the thesis statement of Jones's entire book. The world is a bleak, brutal place; people are both sadistic and superficial; unspeakable crimes are awarded with medals, while to seek the truth is to risk madness or lobotomy. Man, in the present configuration of his world, is utterly without hope.

Jones's handling of his Vietnam material in these stories differs considerably from the way the same material is handled in the work of, say, Tim O'Brien, whose 1990 collection, *The Things They Carried,* won the *Chicago Tribune*'s Heartland Award for fiction that year. *The Things They Carried,* like O'Brien's National Book Award–winning novel *Going After Cacciato* (1979), is essentially an autobiographical work. The book's narrator is a forty-three-year-old writer named Tim O'Brien whose take on the war is that of the soldier-turned-protester. The war was wrong. O'Brien knew it but went anyway, because he was afraid of what people would say, afraid of "embarrassment." Twenty yards from the Canadian border in the summer of 1968, O'Brien turns back. "I passed through towns with familiar names," he writes at the end of "On the Rainy River," "through the pine forests and down to the prairie, and then to Vietnam, where I was a soldier, and then home again. I survived, but it's not a happy ending. I was a coward. I went to the war."[8]

For Jones, by contrast, Vietnam is not about the personal demons O'Brien's narrator grapples with here and throughout *The Things They Carried.* Instead, it is a metaphor. Like more than a few American authors before him—Crane, Hemingway, Mailer, Stone—Jones believes that, at bottom, life is war. This is made perhaps most clear by the boxing motif that counterbalances the Vietnam sections in "The Pugilist at Rest," a motif that is carried forward in the story by the narrator's experiences in the ring and his comments on Theogenes and the Roman statue from which the story's title has been taken. For the narrator of this story, boxing is an art, a beautiful and sweet science, but like war, and indeed like life itself, it also has its dark side, which operates as an outlet for the "hatred, anger, envy, rancour and malice" that is in "every human breast" (227). Theogenes, we are told, "was the greatest of the gladiators" (17): "He was a boxer who served under the patronage of a cruel nobleman, a prince who took great delight in bloody spectacles. Although this was several hundred years before the times of those most enlightened of men Socrates, Plato, and Aristotle, and well after the Minoans of Crete, it still remains a highpoint in the history of Western Civilization and culture. It was the approximate time of Homer, the greatest poet who ever lived. Then, as now, violence, suffering, and the cheapness of life were the rule" (17). As in the previous quotation, where "one of the most materially prosperous nations in history" is found to be "replete with badness," here a "highpoint in the history of Western Civilization" is found to be replete with "violence, suffering, and the cheapness of life." In such a world, the question is not Mailer's "Why Are We in Vietnam?" or even O'Brien's "Why Did I Go?" but rather, "What Devil of Violence, Greed, and Hot Desire" (to paraphrase Conrad) "Lurks in the Heart of Man?" In short, politics can never be the salvation of man; only philosophy can.

Apart from the three stories set in Vietnam and its aftermath, Jones takes his reader into the hostile, dark territory of the cancer ward, the boxing ring, the broken American family. These settings are rendered in the darkest of tones. Even so, the world Jones depicts allows for the possibility of an existential sort of grace. This, more than anything else, is what separates Jones from the polite nihilism of the minimalists. Jay McInerney, Raymond Carver's most celebrated disciple, once remarked that the major contribution of Carver's brand of minimalism was that it "completely dispensed with the romantic egotism that made the Hemingway idiom such an awkward model for other writers in the late 20th century."[9] Thom Jones, for his part, seems hardly to have heard the news. His characters, though downtrodden, remain heroic; though in a bad place existentially, they continue to bark their defiance. Facing desperate, last-ditch brain surgery to cure him of his recurrent seizures, the narrator of "The Pugilist at Rest" retains the humor and the bravado to say, "If they fuck up the operation, I hope I get to keep my dogs somehow—maybe stay at my sister's place. If they send me to the nuthouse I lose the dogs for sure" (27).

"Unchain My Heart," a story that appears toward the middle of the book, displays both Jones's verbal virtuosity and his uncanny ability, when dealing with the right material, to let a story unfold on the razor's edge of his reader's credulity. In the first paragraph we are introduced to Bocassio, a three-hundred-dollar-an-hour deep-sea diver with a powerful build and a thick, black beard. He has just come up from a dive, five hours on the bottom of the ocean. He's got a "cigarette jones moderate to medium-heavy" and is bitching that the crane operator, the stupid "motherfucker," nearly killed him when he moved a length of pipe too quickly. "If you ever fuck up like that again, you're through," Bocassio says (114). It is only in the second paragraph that we learn that this picture of absolute machismo is actually being narrated by a woman, Bocassio's lover, who is herself defiantly AWOL from her editorial job in New York. What follows is an account of one woman's addiction to a vaguely caricatured, hard-core masculinity—her love for the tattooed, pockmarked

Bocassio. At the story's end, another twist. When Bocassio dies in a deep-sea accident, the narrator aborts his baby, "unchains" her heart, and moves on to a Marine Corps fighter pilot. "I've learned deep," she says in the story's last sentence, "now I want to learn fast" (128). There is something very hard, almost cutthroat, about this woman's ability to move on so soon after her lover's death. Yet while we might want to condemn her callousness, we are also compelled to admire her tenacity, the hard-won ability to survive in an essentially hostile world.

The violence Jones depicts in *The Pugilist at Rest* is even more apparent in Denis Johnson's recent collection of stories, *Jesus' Son*. Writing in the *Atlantic Monthly* in June 1993, Jack Miles declared that Johnson, who started his career as a poet, had "found a new, poetically charged way to turn American violence into prose."[10] Johnson's work, which took as its subject "the menacing, menaced side of American life," had little in common with conventional crime fiction, Miles argued, and even less with the sentimentalized depictions of drugged-out "bad boys" offered up by William Burroughs or Jean Genet. Whereas "Burroughs moons over the badness of bad boys," Johnson does not. Whereas Jean Genet makes criminals into "brave boys coerced by force majeure into taking up arms," Johnson "makes no more of his characters' violence than he does of their ineptitude," wherein lies "the deeper realism of his imagination of them" (121).

Denis Johnson was born in Munich in 1949. His father worked for the U.S. Information Agency, and throughout Johnson's childhood the family bounced around from one foreign post to another, with regular stints back in Washington D.C. and Alexandria, Virginia, in between. Ages seven to twelve were spent in Tokyo, twelve to sixteen in Manila. By the time Johnson made it back to Virginia, as a teenager, the American sixties were in full swing. The young Johnson abused both drugs and booze with abandon. Somehow he also managed to graduate college, attend the Iowa Writer's Workshop, and publish two books of poetry. But heroin was his life's main activity. By 1978, however, the jig was up. Johnson quit writing, went through withdrawal and detox, then made a second career as a fiction writer in the early 1980s. A novel, *Angels*, appeared in 1983, followed quickly by three more: *Fiskadoro* (1985), *The Stars at Noon* (1986), and *Resuscitation of a Hanged Man* (1991). A fifth novel, *Already Dead*, appeared in 1998.[11]

Jesus' Son is a collection of eleven interrelated short stories narrated by a young, introspective, drug-addicted drifter known simply as "Fuckhead." From the stark and disturbing "Car Crash While Hitchhiking" to the final story in the collection, "Beverly Home," we follow this drifter from state to state, bar to bar, drug deal to drug deal, until he finally lands in rehab in Phoenix, Arizona. He's married at one point, then divorced, then holed up in the Holiday Inn with a beautiful, heroin-shooting girlfriend, still later in the "Rebel Motel" with yet another girlfriend who survives an abortion only to die of an overdose in another man's bed. Written in a spare, poetic language, Johnson's stories continually juxtapose straightforward descriptions of death and violence with strange, drug-induced moments of lucidity and alarming addresses made directly to the reader. Take, for example, the following paragraphs that close the story called "Dundun":

> Dundun tortured Jack Hotel at the lake outside of Denver. He did this to get information about a stolen item, a stereo belonging to Dundun's girlfriend, or perhaps his sister. Later, Dundun beat a man almost to death with a tire iron right on the street in Austin, Texas, for which he'll also someday have to answer, but now he is, I think, in the state prison in Colorado.
>
> Will you believe me when I tell you there was kindness in his heart? His left hand didn't know what his right hand was doing. It was only that certain important connections had been burned through. If I opened up your head and ran a hot soldering iron around in your brain, I might turn you into something like that.[12]

The quiet, straightforward narration of the first paragraph is in stark contrast to its violent subject matter, yet the effect of this narration is to make the acts depicted all the more alarming and believable. The second paragraph goes even further in this direction, pleading, in an understated manner, for Dundun's basic humanity, his capacity for kindness. But all is changed by the narrator's last, terrifying observation, which leaves all question of Dundun far behind, suggesting instead what the narrator himself might be capable of: "If I opened up your head, and ran a hot soldering iron around in your brain . . ."

The story called "Work," originally published in the *New Yorker*, further illustrates some of the different moves Johnson is capable of making in his short fiction, the way he weaves in and out of graphic description, spare metaphor, drug-induced hallucination, and sudden shifts in address or point of view. The story begins with the sort of sharp rendering of circumstance that leads readers to believe that the very essence of all that is to follow has been summed up in a single sentence: "I'd been staying at the Holiday Inn with my girlfriend, honestly the most beautiful woman I'd ever known, for three days under a phony name, shooting heroin" (55). The first two clauses of the sentence, with their mention of the hotel and the beautiful girlfriend, set the reader up for its startling end, "under a phony name, shooting heroin." The rest of the paragraph expands this contrasting of dark and light elements, telling how the two of them "made love in the bed, ate steaks at the restaurant, shot up in the john, puked, cried, accused one another, begged of one another, forgave, promised, and carried one another to heaven" (55). The graphic details, "puked, cried, accused one another," are oddly balanced by the narrator's memory of the experience as two people carrying "one another to heaven."

In almost any other writer's work, the richness of this dichotomy could be counted on to become the subject matter of all that follows. In "Work," by contrast, all is changed in the very next paragraph, which begins, "But there was a fight" (55). Just like that, just two short paragraphs in, the story completely shifts its focus, and the narrator finds himself at 9:00 A.M. in a bar called the Vine, talking to his friend Wayne "about making some money" (56). Piling into the narrator's "sixty dollar Chevrolet," the two men drive off to a small housing development built along a river bank. There has been a flood here, and all the houses are abandoned. "Are we doing a burglary?" the narrator asks. But the house, it turns out, used to belong to Wayne, who lived there with his wife in better times. "Fuckhead" and Wayne are only there now to rip out its copper wiring, which Wayne intends to sell for scrap.

The work is hard, and the narrator complains that it is "fucking with my high," but after a while they have all the wire out and piled in the front yard. Looking up from the last of their work, they see a boat coming up the river pulling a "tremendous triangular kite on a rope," behind which flies a suspended woman, naked except for her beautiful red hair. "Now, that is a beautiful sight," says Wayne. On the way back to town, they stop at a farmhouse, where Wayne has a conversation with his wife, who is also red-headed, though older and more haggard looking than the woman from the river. Nevertheless, there is "no doubt" in the narrator's mind. "As nearly as I could tell," he observes, "I'd wandered into some sort of dream that Wayne was having about his wife, and his house. But I didn't say anything more about it. Because, after all, it was turning out to be one of the best days of my life, whether it was somebody else's dream or not" (62). Heaven has turned into hell, then, via hallucination, back into heaven again.

Having sold the wire, the two men head back to the Vine, where Wayne picks a fight with a huge man during a card game. Suddenly it looks as though things will turn ugly, but then, just as quickly, the moment passes and they all go back to their drinks—which on that day are being poured by their favorite bartender (indeed, their "very favorite person"), a young woman who "doubles their money" by filling their glasses without bothering to measure the shots. For the narrator, the whole afternoon has turned into "one of those moments," so rare in his life, when his high is a good one and disaster has been averted and he feels lucky just to be alive. "We had money," he says in the story's penultimate paragraph. "We were grimy and tired. Usually we felt guilty and frightened, because there was something wrong with us, and we didn't know what it was; but today we had the feeling of men who had worked" (66).

Were the story to end here, it would simply underline the theme alluded to in its title, a regular theme in all of these stories: the good feeling that comes over these outcasts when they participate, however marginally, in the normal workings of the world. In the story's final paragraph, however, the narrator turns his attention back to the bartender, and Johnson achieves yet another of his "moments": an image of extreme violence that is followed by a sympathetic comment meant to include this violence in all that is most human:

> "Nurse," I sobbed. She poured doubles like an angel, right up to the lip of a cocktail glass, no measuring. "You have a lovely pitching arm." You had to go down to them like a hummingbird over a blossom. I saw her much later, not too many years ago, and when I smiled she seemed to believe I was making advances. But it was only that I remembered. I'll never forget you. Your husband will beat you with an extension cord and the bus will pull away leaving you standing there in tears, but you were my mother. (66)

How strange and shocking that last sentence is. And how far this slim story, barely twenty-five hundred words, has come from its first sentence about the Holiday Inn, the beautiful girlfriend, and heroin. Perfectly unpredictable as it goes along, the story ends making perfect sense, from its theme of the lost home (the Holiday Inn, Wayne's flood-damaged house, the Vine bar itself) to its theme of the lost woman (the girlfriend, Wayne's dream of his wife, the bartender who is finally the narrator's surrogate mother) and lastly to its theme of all those "lost days" in the life of the narrator, who can only recount them now, this side of detox, with a nostalgia typical of the recovering alcoholic or drug addict. "That world!" he says at the end of another story, "Emergency." "These days it's all been erased and they've rolled it up like a scroll and put it away somewhere" (88). Or again, in the story called "Out on Bail": "Sometimes what I wouldn't give to have us sitting in a bar again at 9:00 a.m. telling lies to one another, far from God" (40).

This last comment underlines what is a persistent theme in both Thom Jones's and Denis Johnson's work: the search for meaning in a fallen world through some hard-pressed form of religious belief. The narrator of "The Pugilist at Rest," suffering from epilepsy, comes close in his recurrent fits to experiencing Dostoyevsky's "aura" of "the Supreme." Dostoyevsky "said that he wouldn't trade ten years of his life for this feeling," he observes, "and I, who have had it, too, would have to agree. I can't explain it, I don't understand it—it becomes slippery and elusive when it gets any distance on you—but I have felt this down to the core of my being. Yes, God exists! But then it slides away and I lose it. I become a doubter" (23–24).

Jack Miles has called this, with regard to Johnson's work, a "pre- rather than post-religious" feeling, a nostalgia for "and despairing of the human as the post-religious are nostalgic for and despairing of the divine." For men who have seen and done what Johnson's characters have seen and done, "it is easier to believe in God than to believe any longer in man" (121). This search for meaning, most often a failed one, is what finally separates these writers' characters from the mouthpieces for bored nihilism we find in minimalism. For Jones's characters, as for Johnson's, life is a dangerous, harrowing, desperate thing. It must be made sense of at all costs. That's why the stories these characters tell are so intense, and ultimately, so true. Annie Dillard once remarked that writers should write as if both they and their readers were dying, since that is literally the case. Thom Jones and Denis Johnson write in just this way.[13]

But it is in the work of William T. Vollmann, particularly *The Atlas* (1996), that this direction in recent American writing has reached its most profound completion. Once virtually unknown to mainstream readers, although long the subject of a cult following, Vollmann has recently attracted a level of critical praise few authors allow themselves to hope for, being pronounced everything from "the reigning kid genius of American fiction" to "the most prodigiously talented and historically important American novelist under 35" and, most recently, "among the eight or 10 greatest novelists America has produced."[14] Not since Pynchon has an American author received such praise so early in his career, and not since Cormac McCarthy has one been, at the same time, so little known by the public at large. This is all the more interesting given the fact that Vollmann, unlike Pynchon and McCarthy, is far from being reclusive or shy of the media. In fact, as a sometime special assignment reporter for magazines like *Esquire* and *Spin,* Vollmann is himself a part of the media. In this regard, as well as in his penchant for autobiography and his love of being photographed, Vollmann more closely resembles writers like Hemingway and Norman Mailer, who deliberately courted celebrity, than he does those American writers, Faulkner among them, who have famously shunned not only celebrity but also any autobiographical impulse in their work.

The facts about Vollmann's life are well known and bear directly on the work and in some cases are inseparable from it. He was born in Los Angeles in 1959, the son of an itinerant college professor; the family moved often. Tragedy struck early and with great force. When Vollmann was nine years old, a younger sister, Julie, three years his junior, drowned in a shallow pond in New Hampshire while he was apparently in charge of watching her but instead was absorbed in reading a book. After a subsequent childhood filled with nightmares and an awkward adolescence, Vollmann won a scholarship to Deep Springs College, an alternative, all-male academy in the desert mountains of eastern California that admits only twenty-five students and mixes a demanding academic program with mandatory ranch work and participation in all matters pertaining to the college's governance. According to his mentors at Deep Springs, the young Vollmann "lived inside his mind a lot" during these years and was already driven to write. "He had such unusual things on his mind," remembers one professor, "that his writing wasn't like anyone else's. It was often sadistic, strange animals being dismembered. . . . We tried to make his writing more normal." From Deep Springs, Vollmann went on to Cornell University, where he studied comparative literature and wrote an eclectic thesis treating, among other subjects, Dante, deconstruction, and a group of antinuclear protestors whose exploits he observed and reported. "It was three times the required length," recalls a member of Vollmann's thesis committee. "Not polished, but original, special. It was clear he wanted to be a writer and a witness."[15]

In 1982, Vollmann left Cornell and traveled to Afghanistan in an attempt to help the Mujahedin in their war against the Soviet Union—a mad, yearlong trip, ultimately a failure, born equally (one supposes) of a hands-on, activist impulse the writer acquired at Deep Springs College as well as of a ubiquitous and overarching death wish. Not incidentally, the trip also supplied the material for Vollmann's first-written book, *An Afghanistan Picture Show; or, How I Saved the World,* which would not be published until 1992. Back from Afghanistan, Vollmann at first enrolled in graduate work at Berkeley, but he soon dropped out and took a job as a computer programmer in Silicon Valley.

It was here, sleeping in his work station between shifts, that Vollmann wrote his first novel, *You Bright and Risen Angels* (1987), a playful work of metafiction that inspired comparisons to Pynchon and William Burroughs but that the author himself would later repudiate as "a kid's book" because, as he came to believe, "it was too easy to go on and on and have a good time making things up."[16]

The real breakthrough, at least as regards what we now think of as the signature Vollmann stance and method, came in 1989 with *The Rainbow Stories,* a book that mixed reportorial and fictional techniques to powerfully evoke the lives of prostitutes and skinheads on the streets of San Francisco's Tenderloin district. It was with *The Rainbow Stories* that Vollmann first began to fulfill the specific promise he had shown at Cornell, a promise that figured him as both writer and witness (or, as Vollmann himself would put it in the book's preface, a "recording angel").

In the half decade after *The Rainbow Stories,* Vollmann earned a dual reputation as a kamikaze travel writer bent on visiting the world's most exotic and dangerous places (an impulse carried over from his trip to Afghanistan and repeated in Bosnia, Somalia, the Magnetic North Pole, etc.) and as the most prolific author of his generation, publishing nine books in just under six years and developing, in the course of marathon sessions at the computer, a bad case of carpal tunnel syndrome. During this period Vollmann also embarked on what may be the most ambitious and important fictional project of our era, the monumental and as yet unfinished *Seven Dreams: A Book of North American Landscapes,* a multivolume work that promises to chronicle nothing less than the entire history of European involvement with Native Americans and the New World, from the arrival of the Norse in Greenland in the tenth century right up to our own century's part in what the author has called, in the preface to volume 1, a progressive "undermining of trees and tribes." Three volumes in the series, totaling more than eighteen hundred pages, have been published so far: *The Ice-Shirt* (1990), *Fathers and Crows* (1992), and *The Rifles* (1994), with more apparently on the way. Should Vollmann live long enough to finish the project—and it is by no means certain that he will—*Seven Dreams* could go down as the most significant contribution to our literature since Faulkner's Yoknapatawpha County series. So far, however, the *Seven Dreams* books have been more or less respectfully ignored, and this is perhaps as it should be, given their length, difficulty, and the overall project's radical state of incompletion.

Of Vollmann's work in what I have called the dirty realist vein—*The*

Rainbow Stories (1989), *Whores for Gloria* (1991), *Thirteen Stories and Thirteen Epitaphs* (1991), *Butterfly Stories* (1993), and *The Atlas* (1996)—*The Atlas* is without question the masterpiece. Not only is it the most finely observed and written, it also collects and distills what was distinctive and original about its predecessors; it is the most *mature* and fully realized of Vollmann's works to date; and finally, it exists as a kind of key to the entire oeuvre (and may eventually provide a needed bridge between the dirty realism books and the volumes in the *Seven Dreams* series).

According to Vollmann's cryptic and dryly humorous "Compiler's Note," which begins the book, *The Atlas* was inspired by the Japanese writer Yasunari Kawabata's "palm-of-the-hand" stories. Kawabata, who won the Nobel Prize in 1968 and committed suicide in 1972, had experimented since the early 1920s with a form of miniature story or vignette that was at once autobiographical and fantastical, reduced plot to a minimum, and achieved most of its effects through a sustained lyricism that explored themes of loneliness, sorrow, love, and death. It is not difficult to understand why Vollmann would be drawn to this form (or these themes), especially when one considers that the vignette has served as the basic unit or building block of nearly all of this writer's books. *The Atlas* is, in part at least, a compilation of discreet material Vollmann published between 1990 and 1994 in magazines like *Esquire* and literary journals like *Conjunctions* and *Grand Street;* in his compiler's note, Vollmann invites us to dip into the work "in no particular order," as one would a collection of poems or a book of maps or a "pillow-book" kept by one's bed and perused "in the five minutes between lying down and turning out the light." However, this is not all. A certain transforming ingenuity has guided the book's construction. "For those who require games and calculations in order to drowse," Vollmann writes in his compiler's note, "I should state that this collection is arranged palindromically: the motif in the first story is taken up again in the last; the second story finds its echo in the second to last, and so on."[17]

A palindrome, in its dictionary sense, is a word or phrase that reads the same backward or forward, for example, "Madam, I'm Adam," or "A man, a plan, a canal, Panama!" The Greek root of the word suggests another meaning—running back again, recurring. Thus *The Atlas'* table of contents lists a front section of stories or vignettes numbered 1 through 26, then an unnumbered novella, "The Atlas," and finally a back section numbered 26 through 1. As one would expect, there are indeed correspondences or "echoes" between the front and back of the book, so that for example both stories listed as number 14 are from Vollmann's "Butterfly Stories" series and are set in Cambodia in 1993 and 1994. But it is to Vollmann's and the book's credit that this structural conceit is never allowed to become too predictable or an end in itself. In fact, as we shall see, its main purpose is to frame and accentuate the book's centerpiece and title story, a job it does very well indeed.

Dipping into the book, as its author suggests, we find ourselves in the usual Vollmann territory: the dangerous, gonna-die-young worlds of the war zone, the barroom and brothel, the boxing ring, the late-night bus station and volatile international airport, the prisons of three continents, wherein we encounter all the usual toxins, bullets and booze and drugs and disease, as well as the usual bodies absorbing them, prostitutes and pimps, drug addicts, petty criminals, soldiers and other aficionados of violence. Also all the usual Vollmann places, given to us in their usual specificity: Canada, Thailand, Cambodia, Bosnia, Madagascar, California, Montreal, Bangkok, Phnom Penh, Sarajevo, San Francisco. We are even given, in the form of a gazetteer, each place's exact address on the face of the earth, for example, Eureka, Ellesmere Island, Northwest Territories, Canada, 80.00 N, 85.40 W; or Roberts Camp, Wyman Creek, Deep Springs Valley, California, U.S.A., 37.21 N, 117.59 W. "What you hold, then," Vollmann declares in the compiler's note, "is but a piecemeal atlas of the world I think in" (xv).

In one sense, *The Atlas* appears to be just that—a partial list of its author's obsessions, the places and the people and the situations Vollmann finds interesting. "The truth is," he has said in an interview, "I get kind of bored with a lot of ordinary people. It's not that I think I'm better than they are (if anything, I think they're probably better than I am, because it's easier for them to be happy and just live their lives, whereas for some reason I don't seem to be happy just living my life; it always feels like I'm looking for something new, not ordinary). Given that predisposition, I try to find people who don't feel familiar."[18] But in another, equally important sense, the meaning of the individual vignettes is startlingly up in the air. Vollmann has merely presented us with the raw materials, choosing to draw no conclusions himself, a strategy for which, on occasion, he has been roundly criticized, as when one of this author's most perceptive readers, Tom LeClair, complained in the *Nation*, "In *The Atlas*, Vollmann seems not to care about the causes and contexts of worldwide degradation. He's too guilty. . . . All that train travel and auto-revelation are just jerking off unless Vollmann gives us some understanding of a world we couldn't imagine without him."[19] In large part, how we make sense of this seeming paradox at the heart of Vollmann's work—Is the author there or isn't he? Is this autobiography or passive documentary?—will ultimately determine how we make sense of the work as a whole.

So far, Vollmann has been read as either a New Journalist or as part of a second wave of "metafictional" writers, a direct descendent of the literary postmodernists. But as Madison Smartt Bell among others has argued, neither of these descriptive tags does the work itself justice.[20] The case against Vollmann as a New Journalist is clear once one encounters the work itself, for while Vollmann does indeed insert himself into his reports from far-flung corners of the globe, he also (particularly in the books) juxtaposes the journalism and travel writing with work that is immediately recognizable as fiction. Typically the more journalistic vignettes are written in first person and submerge the narrator's involvement in the action being portrayed, while the more fictional episodes are written in third person and feature one of Vollmann's regular protagonists—the "man in the camouflage coat," the reporter or war correspondent, the "angel" who visits people in prison, the traveler, and so on—figures whose actions, many of them questionable, are dramatized much more fully than those of the first-person narrators.

For example, in *The Atlas,* Vollmann juxtaposes the vignette "No Reason to Cry," which recounts a first-person narrator's attempt to rescue a child prostitute in Thailand, with a second vignette, titled simply "Blood," which shows the "man in the camouflage coat" murdering a Thai prostitute by injecting her with his own HIV-infected blood. The tone and stance of the two vignettes are strikingly different, as can be seen in their respective endings. Here is the last paragraph of "No Reason to Cry": "At the end, the nurse told her what AIDS was. I gave her a handful of condoms. . . . (She understand now AID, the nurse later told me, with weary satisfaction.) She was going back to work. A case can be made that if a girl is going to get AIDS there is no reason to cry while she is getting it" (33). The stance taken here is controlled and detached, almost Hemingwayesque in its brevity and lack of affect. The writer-witness has done what he can; perhaps he has done too much, more than a reporter ought to do. But in no way are we meant to judge *his* actions; ultimately, the vignette is not about him, but about some nameless cruelty in the cosmos that allows such situations to exist. Compare this with the last few paragraphs of "Blood":

> Close your eyes, bitch, he said to the slender girl. I don't want you looking into my eyes while I do this. Don't worry. I'll pay you one thousand baht. Make a fist. Make a fist, I said. Yeah, that's a good vein. You've got such pretty little veins.

Thank you, sir.

Okay, it's going in. Don't move. Don't move. There it goes.

Thank you very much, sir.

What the fuck are you thanking me for? I just murdered you.

Excuse me sir me no no understand you speak.

I apologize, he said. It's just that I've been feeling pretty down lately. (393)

Here the opposite situation prevails; the subject of the vignette is neither the prostitute nor her world but the third-person protagonist and his capacity to commit evil. We are even given his motivation: someone has given him the AIDS virus, therefore he will pass it on. His actions are central; it is the protagonist, not the cosmos, we judge.

The first vignette, "No Reason to Cry," reads very much like a species of New Journalism, and, in fact, a similar story was financed by and published in *Spin* magazine in 1993. But that is only when it is read alone. Read alongside "Blood," the vignette is transformed by the part it plays in a larger whole; which is to say, Vollmann has succeeded here in turning *both* vignettes into fiction. And yet, the complexity of Vollmann's strategy of juxtaposition, the extent to which he has effectively mixed genres, does not stop here, for even in the highly fictionalized horror show that is "Blood," the author apparently cannot keep himself from adding the following footnote to his use of the word "baht": "About U.S. $40 in 1993. About what an all-night girl might expect to receive" (393).

The case against Vollmann as a metafictionalist is even more clear, and can be made without resort to further examples. As Madison Smartt Bell has observed, "Most typically, a metafictionalist enters the text in order to reveal that its artifices are only that, to collapse whatever mimetic illusion may obtain, to reveal (from the detractor's point of view) that the whole work is predicated on bad faith." Vollmann, however, "has turned his presence within his work into a declaration of engagement. Instead of entering the work to declare that it is a trick, he stands inside it as a witness—vouching for its authenticity" (44). Clearly this is just what Vollmann is up to in the above footnote explaining the value of one thousand baht in 1993—he is using a nonfictional technique to authenticate a detail in an elaborately created fictional world. That he is doing so apparently without irony, in a manner unimaginable in the work of, say, Borges or David Foster Wallace, stands as a further illustration of the ways in which Vollmann has, according to Madison Smartt Bell, "broken out of metafiction's self-reflexive squirrel cage" and "shown a way for an author to be present in the work and to manipulate it without undercutting its credibility" (44).

As I have said, that credibility is arrived at in Vollmann's work in two powerfully different ways that at first glance appear to be mutually exclusive but later come to make perfect sense. On one hand, there is the sense in which Vollmann remains passive in his work, a spectator and "recording angel," refusing to judge the people and situations he depicts. On the other, there is the growing sense that everything Vollmann depicts in his work is *chosen,* and that its ultimate *significance* is highly autobiographical in nature.

Take, for example, the following scene from the vignette titled "The Best Way to Shoot H," which takes place in a residence hotel in San Francisco's Tenderloin, where Vollmann's ubiquitous "john" character is living amid a gaggle of prostitutes and street folk, silently observing their comings and goings, all the while holding out some vague hope that one of them will "smash through his soul-eye's smooth flat window to kill him or make him free" (275):

> There was a knock.
> Who is it? she cried ferociously.
> It's me, said a sad shy voice.
> Grunting, the old lady popped her hernia back in and opened the door. It was the whore who'd been raped with a vacuum cleaner. (Two days afterward, her stomach had suddenly swelled up, and she fainted from the pain.)
> You get it? said the old lady.
> Got it right here, the girl whispered.
> They heated the bottlecap with the old lady's lighter, untwisted the paper, added water from the brandy bottle (the white stuff in the cap was already fizzing), stirred it lovingly with the needle end.
> Just draw it up, the old lady snarled.
> I'm tryin' to. . . .
> They were almost ready now to bare their arms to the needle, like children who didn't have a ticket to a carnival, stretching their hands out from so far behind the fence.
> Well, that came out right, said the old lady with satisfaction.
> I'll come back. Where's the restroom? I gotta stick myself in a personal place.
> The old lady shot her a glare. — You'd better come back, or I'll hunt you down and kill you.
> The girl cringed in terror. — I'm sorry, I'm sorry, she said almost inaudibly. I'll do it here.
> Go to the restroom if you want. You heard what I said.

I'll do it here.

Well, stop whining and do it here, then. You need me to hit you? Which personal place is it today?

My pussy.

That's where the happy veins are, the old lady laughed, the needle already in her wrist, the smelly pantyhose knotted around her upper arm. (277)

As is often the case in Vollmann's work, we are not told what to think, nor do we know what the narrator thinks. We sense empathy in the image of the children holding out their arms for carnival tickets, some slight disgust in the adjective "smelly." But beyond this, we are on our own. The *effect* of this distance between narrator and event, however, is to create a sense of immediacy and closeness between reader and event. We, too, are witnesses, eavesdroppers. The older prostitute's hernia, the younger prostitute's swelled stomach and weak plea for privacy in a world where there is none, the bare ferocity of both characters' terrible need—these details are offered up to convince us of the scene's *authenticity,* not to influence our judgment of its *meaning.*

And yet, there is always *more* meaning in Vollmann's work than can be gotten from an individual vignette. His fiction, like that of Faulkner and Louise Erdrich, gains its power exponentially, over time and across sections. It also does so within a specific context that is autobiographical in origin, which is to say that Vollmann's fiction is in a profound sense *inseparable* from his life. Near the center of all his work is a single, real-life event: the death by drowning of his younger sister in that shallow pond in New Hampshire in 1968.

Indeed, it would be difficult to overestimate the importance of this event as a kind of primal scene for the work as a whole. Its explanatory power is enormous, its associations rich and various, its potential exploitation as a metaphor almost unlimited. Indeed, one might speak here of a central Vollmann myth, the details of which are as compelling as those surrounding the famous "Hemingway code." As a boy, the writer witnesses his own sister's death. It is, at least in part, his fault, which is why it is registered as a double wound, both a loss and a source of guilt. In later years, the writer travels to all of the world's most dangerous places in an effort to get himself killed, but alas, he appears to be bullet-proof and invincible. He befriends prostitutes and other lost women, falling in love repeatedly and with abandon. Yes, he is attempting to "rescue" these women, but even more he is inviting them to hurt and perhaps even kill him. Along the way, the writer rids himself of illusions and money but not of guilt. For him writing is not some cold career choice or even an art he masters through patience and cunning; it is an addiction, a burning, driving need, a form of penance, and, finally, a bit of black magic with which he conjures his dead sister's spirit and ensures her immortality.

Book reviewers, as might be expected, are well aware of this myth and evoke it regularly. In his review in the *Nation,* titled "His Sister's Ghost in Bosnia," Tom LeClair brilliantly links *The Atlas* to Hemingway's *In Our Time* and Thoreau's *Walden* because, as he observes, "[a]t the center of Hemingway's alternating stories and sketches is 'Soldier's Home,' in which a battle-shocked and prostitute-experienced veteran fails his little sister," while "the middle chapter and symbolic center of Walden is 'The Ponds,' where Thoreau lies on the ice, peers into the world's axis and discovers how to complete his sojourn, book, and life" (72). In fact, the power of LeClair's observation cannot quite survive our revisiting either "Soldier's Home" or "The Ponds," but his point nevertheless underscores how thoroughly our experience of Vollmann's work is conditioned by its *allusiveness,* its continual (and largely uncomplicated) *reference* to a real world of action and event outside its pages.

With *The Atlas,* Vollmann for the first time brings his sister's death *fully into* his fictional project, rather than allowing it to exist according to an "exclusionary conceit" whereby it is nowhere mentioned but everywhere felt (103). Before *The Atlas,* Vollmann had mentioned his sister's death only once in writing, in a one-sentence reference in *An Afghanistan Picture Show,* where he wrote, "When I was growing up, my little sister drowned because I hadn't paid attention."[21] Along with the other vignettes in this book's front section, however, is one called "Under the Grass," set in Hanover, New Hampshire, 1968, in which Vollmann's narrator addresses his sister directly and steps forward to acknowledge his debt to her. "Until now I've scrubbed at the stain of your face on my brain's floor, your sky, your headstone—I never wanted you to come back!" he writes (102). Now however things are different. "Your death was a great gift you gave me," he continues (103), and by now we must understand what he means. "Suppose I'd never done what they never said I did, my executioneering I mean, would I still have been brazed to ferocity year by year by the memory of your blue face?" (104).

It is a good question, perhaps *the question* as regards Vollmann's work, and of course it is unanswerable, just as the deed or event of the sister's death is irrevocable. Given a choice, the narrator would take it all back, trade it all in, but of course there is no choice, but only a wish that will never come true. "My blood-writing has quarried you," he writes in the section's final sentence, "but I wish that you were still my sister, dancing above grass" (104).

One of the more beautiful and satisfying things about *The Atlas* is the fact that we do not encounter this sentence either at the beginning or the end of the book, but rather in the run-up to its middle, the sixty-page title story that must surely stand as Vollmann's most accomplished piece of writing to date. The frame for "The Atlas" is a train trip taken from Montreal to Canada's far Northwest Territories in 1993, a trip that will recall for Vollmann's traveler a great many other trips, other places, and other women. It is a trip taken after all the others have failed. "He had used up every place now," we are told. "Everywhere he went, he'd say to himself: There's nothing for me here anymore. No more nowhere nobody" (202). A trip, that is to say, taken in full knowledge of the ultimate futility of travel as a cure for inner wounds. For traveling, the traveler explains, "is equivalent to dying, swimming through a night of sleep-choked houses, carrying one's baggage the last few steps to the place where it must be surrendered, entering the irrevocable security zone, then waiting in monotonous chambers to be taken away" (202). In a sense, of course, the narrator's whole life is waiting—waiting for death, so he can join his sister. But then "living, too, is a likeness of dying. Living means leaving, going on trying not to hear the screams" (202).

Within the frame provided by the train trip, the narrator revisits, in memory, many iconic Vollmann places, including Bangkok, Cairo, Madagascar, Sarajevo, Budapest, and, above all, Canada, which for the traveler is "an infallible country," a flawless landscape "full of nature and loneliness," the "world's edge" (207). Each of these places is an occasion for remembering a particular woman or revisiting a particular reverie. For example, the thought of Australia recalls a vision of "ants crawling by the hundreds across his hands in the Blue Mountains of New South Wales," which in turn recalls "ants in Mae Hong Song," which recalls Bangkok and "the grand oval windows of the massage parlor, ladies with numbers, ladies as numerous as ants," which recalls Mogadishu and "Somali women in flower-robes . . . who sold mangoes inside the corrugated metal boxes under pale yellow-leaved toothbrush trees" (205). The thought of Yugoslavia calls forth "Beograd, where he knew that he would be the enemy," which calls forth Lenin on "infantile romanticism," which calls forth the question of why he traveled to that country in the first place, which calls forth, seemingly out of nowhere, the following explanation: "By his own standards, he was simply looking for something. He wanted to see the world, that was all. He wanted to know and love the entire atlas" (224).

That last line is rather splendid. One is tempted to take it as the crux of the matter. Our man the traveler is motivated by a desire the attainment of which is impossible, hence its appeal. He is the white man set loose upon the globe to encounter and perhaps marry the other. "It's a comfort to picture him," Tom LeClair observed in his *Nation* review, "the Great White Male Scapegoat, roaming the planet, risking his life and degrading himself for my sins" (75). He is Melville's Ahab and Ishmael rolled into one, Kurtz in *Heart of Darkness*. He is the Frederick Henry of *A Farewell to Arms* who leaves the Italian front to visit prostitutes in Milan and Rome. He is Rimbaud in North Africa, D.H. Lawrence in Mexico. He is the narrator of Tennyson's "Locksley Hall," who brags, "I will take some savage woman, she shall rear my dusky race." Above all, perhaps, he is Gauguin in Tahiti, whose ghost the traveler encounters in a museum in Paris:

> When he met the surviving wooden panels of Gauguin's House of Joy from that dreamworld we call Oceania—*les îles Marquises,* to be precise (1901)—he remembered how priests had burned the rest as soon as the artist died, leaving orphaned his bas-relief girls with negroid shell-faces, idol-faces, who dwelled within the world he'd once called *"Soyez mystérieuses."* A little yellowish-green pigment remained on their faces; their hair was painted red or bluish-green; one tawny-buttocked nymph grappled at a greenish darkness, gazing at another woman's face which shone in isolation like the moon; as it seemed, the nymph supplicated and the moon gazed back at her and the traveller, tight-lipped. On the far left another woman sadly drowsed, faded like so many of Gauguin's dreams—sentimental, pornographic dreams, yet not without merit; the man wanted to be loved, let's say; he was a traveller; he wanted to possess the alien; his flaw was that he was unwilling to be possessed by it. (233–34)

Like Gauguin, Vollmann's traveler knows what it is to live in the House of Joy. He has visited the brothels and massage parlors of the world, slept with Inuit women in Canada, Asian women in Thailand and Cambodia, African women in Somalia, Arab women in Cairo. He gives them his money, he refers to them all as his "wives," he loves them all indiscriminately. Could there be any, he asks at one point, "whose recollection he'd ever fail to praise?" (245–46). The answer, it goes without saying, is no. "Their tears and reproaches, silences, farewells, laughter and whispered words were marked on the atlas pages like nations" (246). The title of another Gauguin painting promises, "SOYEZ AMOUREUSES—VOUS SEREZ HEREUSES" (Be loving; you will be happy), and indeed this would appear to be the hopeful formula Vollmann's traveler professes himself willing to be possessed by, even as he knows it is hopeless. His desire to know and love the entire atlas is an impossible desire, but his attempt to do so in the face of certain defeat makes of him a hero in the tragic sense of that word.

At the center of the novella "The Atlas"—which, as we have seen, is itself at the center of *The Atlas*—is the traveler's recollection of a "strange concession" in San Francisco, a camera obscura that he paid a dollar to enter and in which he saw—what else?

> A little girl. . . . The girl was lost. The traveller was lost. Lives sped like arrows, and the world turned upside down again with the turning of the great lens. The world was so blue and so excellent, and even though it was just outside this dark room, he could never get there. If he were to climb over the railing and lie down in that pale bowl upon which the lens projected its findings, then he could not get there, either, even though the image of that world might be tattooed upon him. The world was lost, and the more precious for being so. Was that so strange? Was it the secret at the center of the world, that the rest is lost? (254)

The world was lost, and the more precious for being so. This, then, is the "great gift" his sister's death has given the traveler. This is why he is capable of searching for belief in a world in which belief is impossible. And why he travels from that pond in "Under the Grass" to the frozen cap of North America in the last few pages of "The Atlas." But this is not all. In the same paragraph we are told that the world, which looks round, is in fact "only an asymmetric rotational spheroid—that is, a pear," and so it is that "the center"—of the world, or Vollmann's book—"is not quite where intuition might lead us to expect" (253). In the end, we are each a center, or sun; we "make our own planets wherever we go, with . . . our own idées fixes or lunar satellites to accompany us in orbits of measurable eccentricity" (253). In his search for the "other," the guilt-ridden white man has discovered that there is no center, only centers.

Is Vollmann's use of submerged autobiography to create the ultimate *context* for his fiction the great and surprising strength or the great weakness of that work? I myself am undecided on this point; perhaps it is enough, for now, that the work resonates so powerfully and strangely, something new and surprising on the landscape. I do know that, in *The Atlas*, at least, Vollmann has succeeded in creating a completely self-contained work of surpassing beauty and power, a work that may one day take its place alongside some of the flawed masterpieces of American literature, not only *Walden* and *In Our Time*, but also *Leaves of Grass* and *Moby-Dick*, with which it shares a certain inclusiveness with regard to place and character type; *The Sound and the Fury,* with which it shares an obsession with sisters and with history; and *The Waste Land,* with which it shares a mood or atmosphere as well as a broad range of allusion.

At the end of his journey, Vollmann's traveler arrives on Ellesmere Island in Canada's Northwest Territories, a country of snow and ice that "was for Kawabata's protagonist the end of this world and the beginning of another, . . . the zone of that uncanny whiteness hymned by Poe and Melville, the pole of transcendence" (251). Here the traveler leaves the train and walks out on the ice and in his final reverie lies down on the ice and hears the legendary Native American Willow Lady speaking to him. The wind is her voice and breath and she has "a face like a sly brown mask" and "Inuk eyes" (261). She tells him to go, hit the road, just as she always has, and he still does not know where; he tells her about all of his "wives," the women who populate his life and book. One by one he recalls them, including the woman he held at the hospital while she underwent an operation that would render her sterile, a woman whose screams recalled to him those other screams he has spent his life trying not to hear. It is in this moment that he understands what any fool ought to know: "The screams were so horrible because life was so beautiful" (259).

Composing his "Traveller's Epitaph," Vollmann's hero at first writes, "I'm not well or wise; I fear death; but I've never failed any woman I've loved" (259). But he knows this does not "ring true": "He hadn't loved enough (how can one love enough?); and how could he dare to say he hadn't failed anybody? Whom hadn't he failed? He could only say that he loved life. He closed his eyes, and a screaming grey face exploded into crimson goblets" (259). This, then, is the ultimate message of *The Atlas,* and perhaps of dirty realism as I have defined it: that one cannot truly claim to love life until one has witnessed it in all of its cruelty and stupidity and poverty and abjection and *still* loved it, despite the screaming that will never fully go away.

4 / Hick Chic, or,
the "White Trash Aesthetic"

4 / Hick Chic, or,
the "White Trash Aesthetic'
4 / Hick Chic, or, White Trash Aes

Bill Buford's introduction of dirty realism to Britain led to two important studies of the new fiction written by British authors. The first of these, Duncan Webster's *Looka Yonder!: The Imaginary America of Populist Culture* (1988), looked at the new fiction (as well as American movies, plays, and popular music) in relation to populist ideas both past and present. Webster's analysis is important because it locates the new fiction not only in relation to a revival of the American short story but also to a "return to regional voices," a movement in subject matter "away from the cities and campuses and suburbs to uncover forgotten regions and characters."[1] For Webster, "[t]here is an ambivalent sense of place" to the new writing, a "transformed regionalism testifying to the relationship between the local and the national popular culture": a regionalism, in other words, that has to admit to the presence of McDonalds and cable TV, for as Webster points out, "a South watching MTV is a long way from the world of Faulkner" (4). A follow-up book-length study is Nick Hornby's *Contemporary American Fiction* (1992), which has chapters on the *New Yorker* short story, Raymond Carver, Anne Tyler, Bobbie Ann Mason, Richard Ford, Jayne Anne Phillips and Joy Williams, and Andre Dubus. Like Buford and Webster, Hornby is more interested in content than form, finding, for example, that nearly all of the writers he discusses "have made attempts to come to terms with the demands of topography which inevitably accompany realist fiction."[2]

Return to regional voices. Ambivalent sense of place. Transformed regionalism. It is interesting to hear the British using these terms so unselfconsciously. American literary critics, by contrast, tend to look on the whole concept of regionalism with fear and suspicion. Our writers avoid such a designation like some dread disease because they know that "locale" is often read to mean "local," and "local" to mean "marginal" or "unimportant." Thus the regional is taken to be the opposite of national, and regionalism is taken as minor league at best.

However, what happens when the margins become the center, as has been taking place in American writing for going on two decades now?

In March 1985, Jonathan Yardley, the *Washington Post*'s Pulitzer Prize–winning book critic, published a column in which he scanned the horizon of contemporary American fiction and found it dominated, much to his chagrin, by something he called "Hick Chic." "Here's a tip for trendies," Yardley wrote: "Keep an eye out for Hick Chic. The first to spot it was my friend the ferociously opinionated novelist, who recently sent along this order: 'Here is your assignment. Would you please write an essay explaining why in a nation full of yuppies, conservatives and materialists, with college campuses full of business students and future lawyers, rural poverty is all the rage, as in *Love Medicine* and *The Beans of Egypt Maine?*'"[3] Yardley's answer was to proclaim the new rural writing a fad, the literary equivalent of disco or the Hoola Hoop. (Hence the term "chic," which implies a certain mindless conformity to the current fashion.) As long as fickle, middle-class readers in the cities retained a taste for it, hick chic would enjoy its brief moment in the sun; afterward, it would be consigned, as all fads eventually are, to the back closet of yesterday's fashion. After all, Yardley wrote, "[t]he urban faddists haven't fastened on Hick Chic out of any inherent merit or interest that they discern in it, but because they see it as yet another product with which to bedeck their lives." What urban readers were after (and for Yardley, all readers are "urban") was not "the real life of the countryside" but "the *idea* of country" and the various consumer products that went along with it—Jeep Cherokees, renovated barns, Ralph Lauren apparel, and, yes, a few trendy rural novels to throw on their faux-antique coffee tables. Far from signaling any real return to the land, hick chic was just a slick repackaging of a worn pastoral myth.

In coining the term hick chic, Yardley lumped together a vast array of eighties cultural phenomena—everything from serious literary novels to Hollywood films to country-and-western line dancing—without ever distinguishing between their different origins and effects. Nevertheless, a broad cultural note had been struck, and several more sophisticated critics responded with analyses of their own.

The first was Ann Hulbert, whose review article "Rural Chic" appeared later that year in the *New Republic*. Hulbert began by distinguishing between Hollywood's take on the rural—movies such as *Country, Places in the Heart,*

The River, Witness, and so on—and the more serious literary efforts of writers such as Louise Erdrich, Bobbie Ann Mason, Larry McMurtry, and Douglas Unger. "'Hick chic,' a craving among the quiche crowd for pure country vistas and prettified country values, helps account for the screen fad," Hulbert wrote. "But what might be called 'hick shock,' the fall-out from recent decades of change in rural America, lies behind the more serious literary rural renaissance."[4] For Hulbert, the deeper inspiration for hick chic was not materialism but "populist romanticism, what [Richard] Hofstadter called the 'soft' side of America's agrarian ethos" (25). This "soft" version of the agrarian myth, which typically features a rugged, embattled individual (or family) standing up to a corrupt, eastern power (the banks, say, or the government), has always existed alongside a less popular, "harder" version, which doesn't "invoke a golden agrarian age destroyed by a capitalist conspiracy" but instead emphasizes "a sense of isolation, interrupted by crises that promote a tenuous, not triumphant, solidarity" (29). What Yardley had been calling "hick chic" was about romanticism, pure and simple; whereas "hick shock"—its dark, literary other—was more about realism, the grim realism of the countryside, "where discontent and disorientation have long been as common as dirt" (29).

Diane Johnson added her voice a few weeks later in a November 1985 *New York Times* review of Mason's *In Country* and Anne Tyler's *The Accidental Tourist.* Johnson, like Hulbert, distinguished between the two dominant takes on the rural, the one tending toward romanticism, the other toward a grim, Tobacco Road–style realism. But for Johnson, what was at issue in the new fiction was not just the question of content and its interpretation. There were formal questions to be raised as well. Novels like Mason's and Tyler's shared a "meticulous, literal description, the faintest hint of caricature, and a long narrative distance in which the author is very detached, a viewer rather than an interpreter."[5] Gone from the American literary landscape were the subjective, writer-as-hero novels of the 1970s "in which the character is identified with the real life of the author." In place of this "fiction of the self," Johnson wrote, the new fiction had constructed a "fiction of the 'other,'" in which the authors, very detached, describe mostly what can be seen, and the clarity of the visual detail strangely objectifies the characters." Of course, it was not as if such a technical shift could be achieved without serious consequences for both content and interpretation. Books like *In Country* or *The Accidental Tourist,* with their long authorial distance and brand-name realism, were effectively empty of any real substance, Johnson implied. They were "Reaganesque dream novels," Norman Rockwell–like takes on the country life that lacked "confrontation" with "the real world" and offered, in the end, only a sort of "folksy escapism." Nevertheless, as such they were "books of our times," dull reflections of the "national mood," which was also, in the mid-1980s, lacking in "confrontation."

Writing in the *Nation* in May 1986, Jack Killey found fault with the new fiction for exactly the opposite reason. For Killey, a self-proclaimed "rube" from Hiram, Ohio, the "perpetrators of hick chic"—Carolyn Chute, Bobbie Ann Mason, Anne Tyler, and others—had "loosed upon the serious reading public a menagerie of troubled, gloomy hayseeds and ruminative rustics" who had nothing in common with their real-life counterparts in places like Hiram, who were for the most part stable and satisfied, having not "read enough modern fiction to know that they should be unhappy."[6] "These are the sins of the country," Killey concluded: "smooth diurnal rhythms; relatively stable social institutions; a propensity to cure rather than court ornamental disease; indifference to self-flagellation and neurotic self-examination; above all, flat rejection of oppression as the universal human condition. For these sins, the country is being ravaged by writers whose pleasant and rather tame surroundings cannot provide the emotional pain and the Dostoyevskian troika traces that their craft and their readers demand." The "wimps, losers, sociopaths, psychopaths, drunkards, malcontents and sleazebags" of contemporary rural fiction were simply not drawn from real life, Killey argued, but were the self-conscious creations of the "jangled minds of attitudinizing, cosmopolitan authors who have run out of asphalt and crabgrass on which to park their garish sound trucks."

These separate meditations on the meaning of hick chic foreground some of the problems readers in the mid-1980s had when encountering the new fiction. For despite their differences, which are really more political than aesthetic anyway, all three reviewers were pointing to essentially the same problem: a certain discrepancy between the avowed *content* of the new fiction, which was regional in orientation, and the *form* it tended to take, which, while realist at its core, was also disturbingly minimalist in its assumptions about narration ("long narrative distance") and character ("the faintest hint of caricature"). It is not surprising that a literary development that followed so closely upon the heels of minimalism (and for some critics was indistinguishable from it) would display a certain residue of minimalist technique. Writers like Bobbie Ann Mason, Jayne Anne Phillips, and Richard Ford are in some respects strayed minimalists for whom place, region, and landscape became far more important than it ever was for Raymond Carver or Ann

Beattie. However, their subject, especially in the case of Mason, is not popular culture per se, but how pop culture intersects with, and sometimes overwhelms, regional cultures once thought to be isolated and unique.

In Country (1985), Mason's first novel, is a case in point. It would be difficult to think of another novel as thoroughly concerned with the world of popular culture as this one is. Samantha Hughes, the novel's seventeen-year-old protagonist, is characterized far more by what television shows she watches (*M*A*S*H*) and what popular music she is obsessed with (Michael Jackson, Bruce Springsteen) than by the fact that she lives in Kentucky or has a grandmother she calls "Mamaw." Yet *In Country* is a long way from being a typical minimalist story in which brand names and other references to popular culture are carted out as mere surface details.

Mason has worked hard (too hard, probably) to document not just a particular era or year, but a particular summer. The songs her characters hear on the radio, the movies they see, the episodes they watch on television (including the reruns), the events they hear about on the nightly news—all of these are as faithfully reported as the details in a work of nineteenth-century naturalism. But more than this, Mason has also endowed these details with a certain metaphorical power. The novel is above all about Samantha Hughes's attempts to come to terms with the death of her father, who was killed in Vietnam, and the deteriorating condition of her uncle Emmett, who has begun to show signs of exposure to Agent Orange. The *M*A*S*H* episodes Samantha and Emmett watch throughout the novel work as constant reminders of the lingering effects of the Vietnam experience (*M*A*S*H*, as pop culture critics have long noted, was always more about Vietnam than Korea), as do the Michael Jackson *Victory* tour and the Bruce Springsteen *Born in the U.S.A.* tour.

Ultimately, there is even a kind of historical resonance in the fact that this novel is set in the South, for as Fred Hobson points out in *The Southern Writer in the Postmodern World* (1991), "*In Country* is a novel very much concerned with history, and Sam a character nearly as single-minded as Quentin Compson and Jack Burden in her attempts to unlock the secrets of the past."[7] Hobson goes to great lengths to show how similar in spirit were the South after Appomattox and America after Vietnam, but what concerns us here is just his underlying point: that minimalist fiction of the sort represented by *In Country* "requires a nonminimalist reader" (19). That is to say, if we are to get beyond the problems experienced by readers like Diane Johnson and Ann Hulbert in the eighties, we must bring to our reading an understanding of how the minimalist idiom is forever limiting, sometimes interestingly, sometimes not, the content it would nevertheless have us explore in depth.

Larry Brown's *Father and Son* (1996), to take a more recent example by an otherwise excellent writer, notably fails in this regard. Set in 1968, the novel traces the doings of "bad seed" Glen Davis in the five days following his release from Mississippi's Parchman Prison. Glen drinks, he rants, he rapes and murders. When not raping or murdering, Glen drives around in his beat-up car, visits family in the backwoods, goes fishing, drinks some more. In pursuit for most of the novel (although not when it counts), is right-minded sheriff Bobby Blanchard, Glen's half-brother. Bobby is light to Glen's dark, a good man disgusted by evil. He's also, quite naturally, in love with Glen's girl, Jewel.

Depending on how you look at it, Brown has either created a hopelessly clichéd plot or made a heroic attempt to take on big themes and trade in powerful archetypes. The situations depicted in the novel, and the aura pervading its every word, remind one of Faulkner's *Sanctuary* (1929) and Cormac McCarthy's *Child of God* (1973), which is another way of saying that *Father and Son* aims for inclusion in a very exclusive tradition of southern Gothic. But in the end, *Father and Son* feels like a decidedly small creation. Its frame has been built to bear the weight of epic tragedy, but the characters at its center have been lightly, even shallowly conceived. Unlike Faulkner's great villains, Popeye and Joe Christmas, there is nothing about Glen Davis to make the reader think, "There go we all, but for the grace of (God/education/upbringing/economic advantage, etc)." Nor is there anything about the town—Faulkner's old stomping ground, after all—to make us think this is our town, all towns. Instead, we are made to respond as we do to the pointless violence of so much recent cinema; we are merely appalled.

The problem, as I've hinted above, is the small arsenal of technique with which Brown goes after his subject. The action is divided into short sections, each either objectively reported or seen from the point of view of a particular character. Thoughts are rarely reported, and background information is fed to us primarily as images, never in full-blown flashback—a technique that keeps the book moving, to be sure, but finally leaves the reader disappointed in the terrain that's been covered. The prose is spare and unadorned, reading very much like the descriptive passages in a screenplay. The whole book, in fact, has a decidedly cinematic feel; what's been lost is a certain richness in the depiction of inner and outer motivation we expect when reading a novel. Glen's actions are indeed horrible, and Brown does not flinch in delivering them to us, but in the few times when the narrator does attempt to account for them, either by letting us catch glimpses of Glen's past or by recording the jumble of his thoughts, the effect is to create more distance between reader and characters, not less.

Take, for example, the method by which we are given to understand that Glen accidentally killed his own brother in childhood. The information comes to us not through Glen himself, but through his father, Virgil. Even when ideas do come to us through Glen, as when he thinks of his dead mother in the moment before he commits his second rape, the effect is almost cartoonish in its spareness and the depth of feeling it insists upon: "She was almost as beautiful as his mother, and he began to undress slowly, quietly, taking great pleasure in it, thinking of how it was going to be, how fine to finally join with that flesh."[8] Moments like these seem contrived, insisted upon, precisely because the technique used to register them is at odds with the gravity of what's being registered. Throughout *Father and Son,* it is as if Brown has gone hunting big game with the smallest caliber of rifles; again and again, he strikes out at his subject, but in the end it merely limps off, wounded but never fully laid to rest.

In truth, hick chic caused more problems for book reviewers than just its mixing of minimalist techniques with regional subject matter. Another problem reviewers like Yardley had in assessing the new fiction—one that they rarely confessed to in their reviews but that became obvious once they began to grapple with content—was that, by the mid-1980s, American literature was being authored increasingly by just the sorts of people who once only appeared as characters. I refer, of course, to the "great unwashed": the legions of southern "white trash," Appalachian poor, reservation Indians, and barrio Hispanics who, through government loans and the presence of the writing programs, had gained for the first time in American history not only literacy in the sense of being able to read the newspaper but also the expertise and knowledge to write books about who they were and where they came from. (African Americans, with their long history of authorship in this country, are clearly a separate category altogether.) Larry Brown is a case in point. The son of a sharecropper and poorly educated, Brown became a writer largely through a tremendous act of will.

Consider also the case of Dorothy Allison, author of the short story collection *Trash* (1988) and the amazing first novel *Bastard Out of Carolina* (1992). There was a time, not so long ago, when it would have been unthinkable for someone of Allison's background—grinding, "white trash" poverty, by her own description—to have read much in the way of American literature, let alone to have written it. In cases where it did happen, the odds were high that the writer in question would attempt to write about the class into which she had just risen, not the one from which she had just escaped. Today, just the opposite is true. Writers are, if anything, downwardly mobile when it comes to the kinds of characters they choose to populate their fiction.

As are, apparently, Americans in general when it comes to the style they have come to emulate in the 1990s. In a 1994 article in *New York Magazine* that in many ways echoed Jonathan Yardley's "Hick Chic" essay, authors Tad Friend and Anya Sacharow argued that all eras in American history have been dominated by "charismatic stock figures" such as the cowboy, the robber baron, the flapper, and so on, figures that "bestride the popular imagination by sheer bravado" and become, "for a time, the lodestars by which the rest of the country defines itself."[9] Our own era is no exception. According to Friend and Sacharow, we are now (and have been since the mid-eighties) in "the age of white trash." Citing television shows such as "Cops" and "Hard Copy," movies such as *Natural Born Killers, True Romance,* and *A Perfect World,* "media celebrities" such as Tonya Harding and John Wayne Bobbitt, and advertising campaigns such as those for Guess jeans, Friend and Sacharow argue that America has become obsessed with what they call "the white trash aesthetic":

> The Guess? jeans ads have been only the most visible manifestation of a whole white-trash fashion movement: candy-apple lipstick, chipped cherry-red nail polish, fishnet stockings, rhinestone earrings and dime-store barrettes, Candie's mules, tattoos—of which Drew Barrymore alone has five.
> Courtney Love's dark roots and dirty baby-doll dresses are as sophisticated an appropriation of the childlike white-trash aesthetic as was the Rolling Stones' homage to black urban style; Love's delight in looking like "a 14–year-old battered rape victim," a "kinderwhore," is a nutshell of white-trash chic.... The slumming well-to-do believe that by affecting trash poses they are tapping into authentic despair and alienation, just as certainly as if they had styled a beret and black turtleneck in the fifties. (22)

"The form of trash is attractive," Dorothy Allison herself is quoted as saying, "but the content is not. Americans are into form without content" (22).

Whatever the truth of such observations, the revolution in the class origins of so many of our writers has led to a fundamental change in the way different regions are represented. As Fred Hobson has noted, authors like

Bobbie Ann Mason, Jayne Anne Phillips, and Richard Ford "write about rural and urban working-class people unselfconsciously and, more to the point, approvingly" (21). Not only do writers like Ford approve of their characters, in a very real sense they identify with them, a change that naturally begets other changes. While it is true, for example, that the new southern writers are less likely to celebrate the same qualities the Agrarians did, such as an awareness of history, a regard for tradition and hierarchy, a reverential sense of place, and so on, that is only because southern fiction as we have it today "is written by *different* Southerners, not only black Southerners (who *do,* curiously, often embrace these qualities) but white Southerners whose families had little past to hold on to, little history in which ancestors had played important parts, little reason to live dramatically, little high culture to protect" (22).

Allison's novel *Bastard Out of Carolina,* a finalist for the 1992 National Book Award, is a perfect example of Hobson's point. The book is narrated by Ruth Anne "Bone" Boatwright, the bastard of Allison's title, and features a cast of characters that includes a snuff-taking Grandma, a mother who has her first child at fifteen and is on her second marriage by twenty-two, and a virtual horde of aunts, uncles, and cousins, all poor, who are either unemployed or, more often, working the sort of backbreaking, low-paying jobs that are killing them just as surly as the whiskey they drink, the cigarettes they smoke by the carton, and the beatings they take from one another and the law. Yet each of these characters, though derived from a stereotype, comes vividly to life in Allison's plot, which turns on the abuse and then molestation Bone receives at the hands of her stepfather, "Daddy Glen."

As George Garrett noted in his review of Allison's novel, material such as this is explosive and dangerous, "strewn with booby traps where the least false step could lead to disaster."[10] To begin with, there is the danger of turning poor characters into "case studies" and thus leaving readers "relieved by that abstraction from the pain of felt experience." A second danger, just as serious, is that of dealing in sentimentality, which plays too much on readers' emotions and in the end creates a similar distance.

In *Bastard Out of Carolina,* Dorothy Allison falters in neither of these directions. Her depiction of the extended Boatwright clan is precise and "typical," in the old Balzacian sense, without ever becoming stereotypical. Take, for example, her extended description of the dynamic at work between the men and women in the Boatwright clan. "I worshipped my uncles," Bone says:

They were all big men with wide shoulders, broken teeth, and sunken features. They kept dogs trained for hunting and drove old trucks with metal toolboxes bolted to the reinforced wood sides. They worked in the mills or at the furnace repair business, or sometimes did roofing or construction work depending on how the industry was going. They tinkered with cars together on the weekends, standing around in the yard sipping whiskey and talking dirty, kicking at the greasy remains of engines they never finished rebuilding. Their eyes were narrow under sun-bleached eyebrows, and their hands were forever working a blade or piece of wood, or oiling some little machine part or other.

"You hold a knife like this," they told me. "You work a screwdriver from your shoulder, swing a hammer from your hip, and spread your fingers wide when you want to hold something safe."

Though half the county went in terror of them, my uncles were invariably gentle and affectionate with me and my cousins. Only when they were drunk or fighting with each other did they seem as dangerous as they were supposed to be. The knives they carried were bright, sharp, and fascinating, their toolboxes were massive, full of every imaginable metal implement. Even their wallets bulged with the unknown and the mysterious—outdated ID cards from the air base construction crew, passes for the racetrack, receipts from car repairs and IOUs from card games, as well as little faded pictures of pretty women who were not their wives. My aunts treated my uncles like overgrown boys—rambunctious teenagers whose antics were more to be joked about than worried over—and they seemed to think of themselves that way too. They looked young, even Nevil, who'd had his teeth knocked out, while the aunts—Ruth, Raylene, Alma, and even Mama—seemed old, worn-down, and slow, born to mother, nurse, and clean up after the men.

Men could do anything, and everything they did, no matter how violent or mistaken, was viewed with humor and understanding. The sheriff would lock them up for shooting out each other's windows, or racing their pickups down the railroad tracks, or punching out the bartender over at the Rhythm Ranch, and my aunts would shrug and make sure the children were all right at home. What men did was just what men did. Some days I would grind my teeth, wishing I had been born a boy.[11]

The details here—from what the men had in their wallets to how they swung a hammer to how the women, with their tired shrugs, responded to their antics—testify to Allison's intimate knowledge of the world she depicts. But what is more impressive is how these details of her characterization inform the plot. Perhaps the most harrowing (and finely handled) aspect of *Bastard Out of Carolina* has to do with the failure of the Boatwright family to deal adequately with Daddy Glen's abuse of Bone. Their response, a common one, is to ignore the outward signs, pretending that it isn't happening; all they can think to say to Bone is, "Oh, honey, what are we gonna do with you?" Even Anney, Bone's mother, responds this way. Though Anney knows she should leave Daddy Glen, she is never able to break away, and in the end she chooses him over her own daughter. Gradually, as a result of her family's response to her abuse, Bone comes to believe that it is her fault, that she has somehow "asked for it," and her mother does nothing to dispel the idea. As for her uncles, when finally confronted with the truth, they respond in the only way they know how—with violence. Yet so perfectly is this novel realized, so fully developed are its characters, that when this terrible beating of Daddy Glen finally does take place, the reader is forced to feel sorry for him and to want the beating to stop.

One of the more interesting things about a book like *Bastard Out of Carolina* —and this could be said about most so-called hick chic writing—is the full and complex way in which the characters respond to their position in society, their designation as "poor white trash." While most of the older characters in the novel, especially Anney Boatwright and her sister Raylene, attempt to deny this position or to make excuses for it, insisting that "people are the same" and "everybody just does the best they can," Bone, as a child, is acutely aware of "what the neighbors called us, what Mama wanted to protect us from[,] . . . who we were" (82). "Other people don't go beating on each other all the time," she tells Raylene. "They don't get falling-down drunk, shoot each other, and then laugh about it. They don't pick up and leave their husbands in the middle of the night and then never explain" (258). When Bone reads *Gone with the Wind,* she has no trouble recognizing herself and her family: "Emma Slattery, I thought. That's who I'd be, that's who we were. Not Scarlett with her baking-powder cheeks. I was part of the trash down in the mud-stained cabins, fighting with the darkies and stealing ungratefully from our betters, stupid, coarse, born to shame and death" (206). The thought fills her first with shame, then with anger, and finally with hate. "Anger was like a steady drip of poison into my soul," Bone observes, "teaching me to hate the ones that hated me" (262). By the middle of the novel, she has come to accept Daddy Glen's characterization of her as "cold as death, mean as a snake, and twice as twisty" (111). It is only after surviving the novel's horrible climax— in which she is brutally raped by Daddy Glen and then has to watch as her mother leaves with him—that Bone comes to her final conclusion: "It wasn't God who made us like this, I thought. We'd gotten ourselves messed up on our own" (306).

Such a message, with its overtones of neoconservative ideas about responsibility, would scarcely be palatable (and perhaps not even possible) coming from a novelist who did not share with his or her characters the same class or ethnic origins. Yet this is precisely the realism underlying almost all hick chic writing. Take, as another example, some of the stories in Chris Offutt's first short story collection, *Kentucky Straight* (1992), which earned Offutt the 1993 Jean Stein Award for fiction. The collection opens with a story about a young man in the Appalachian hill country of eastern Kentucky who decides, for private reasons, that he wants to take the GED high school equivalency exam. The exam is given in the local VISTA office, which is presided over by outsiders come "to help you people."[12] From the first, everyone on the young man's "home hill" is against the idea, including his own brother, who ridicules him by saying he's been "eat up with the smart bug" (9) and that GED really stands for "Get Even Dumber" (10). "Not a one on this hillside finished high school," the narrator observes. "Around here a man is judged by how he acts, not how smart he's supposed to be" (3). In these hills, people are held down not only by "outside forces" but by their own families and neighbors. Yet far from making the small, stunted lives of the people Offutt writes about seem to be ultimately their own fault, this admission actually makes the very real, "outside" oppression they suffer all the more convincing. In another story, "Horseweed," a hill man named William is determined to make a better life for himself and his family, yet when he saves his pay from a construction job for three months and buys his own tools instead of getting drunk every night with the other men, the foreman on the job responds by laying him off with the excuse that "he didn't mix well" (63). The message he receives from this, that "trash" does not rise, is the same message his father and grandfather, both miners, had received before him. William's grandfather had reacted to his situation by making moonshine. William's father had worked an illegal mine and died doing it. William grows pot in a hollow abandoned by the mining companies, and guards his plants with the same rifle his grandfather and father had used.

Offutt's theme here—that some things don't change—would seem commonplace were it not for the fact that the *method* for such a theme in fiction has itself changed dramatically, particularly with regard to character. If Bone sees herself and her family in Margaret Mitchell's characterization of Emma Slattery, that is not because she *is* Emma Slattery any more than her uncles could be contemporary Snopeses in some late Faulkner novel. Characters like Emma Slattery and the Snopes family were conceived from the outside and *above,* by authors from a very different social class than their characters. Bone, and in their own ways Sam in Mason's *In Country* and William in "Horseweed," are neither Slatterys nor Snopeses but contemporary renderings of Twain's Huckleberry Finn. They speak to us directly, in their own voices, and the tales of survival and development they tell are "triumphs of vernacular voice and tone" (77), as Fred Hobson has noted about a number of other "contemporary Huck Finns" in southern fiction, from Carson McCullers's Mick Kelly to the eleven-year-old narrator of Kaye Gibbons's *Ellen Foster* (1987). For Hobson, writers like Mason, Allison, and Offutt are themselves Huck Finns of a sort, "finding it difficult to accept received values, old notions of honor and hierarchy, or—as Huck called Tom's romantic ideas and schemes—'Tom Sawyer's lies'" (77–78).

Ultimately, writing of the sort I've been discussing above relies on the authority of its narrative voice and the power of its rendered details, which is why hick chic fiction that goes astray goes so far astray. Only consider a book like Dale Peck's *Now It's Time to Say Goodbye* (1998). Peck's first two novels, the highly acclaimed *Martin and John* (1993) and *The Law of Enclosures* (1996), were both highly autobiographical, took the form of coming of age narratives, and dealt with the highly charged subjects of gay love and AIDS.

Born on Long Island in 1967, Peck lived there until he was seven years old, at which time his abusive, alcoholic father packed up a family already devastated by the death of Dale's mother three years before and moved them out from under the cultural canopy of New York City and, horror of horrors, onto the harsh, exposed plains of western Kansas, where in time the boy would discover that he was different, gay and talented, a born outcast, all against the violent backdrop of Dale Peck Sr.'s subsequent marriages and divorces and drunken rampages. It was the kind of story that played well back East, as Dale Peck discovered when he returned there (first to Drew University, then to Columbia) and made himself into a writer who demanded the attention of publishers and the gay press and, eventually, a world eager to show its good will in the face of the AIDS epidemic.

After *Martin and John*, which mixed the unvarnished details of the author's early life with the story of a lover dying of AIDS, Peck turned his attention to his father's tormented life and the lives of the four women foolish enough to marry him. The result was *The Law of Enclosures*, which critics praised as an even greater feat of virtuosity than the first book. As the first flush of praise faded, however, one began to hear whispers that gradually turned into questions. What would happen after Peck had raided every detail of his emotional and sexual history, when he had exhausted autobiography? What would he write about then? Would it be any good?

Now It's Time to Say Goodbye, Peck's answer to these questions, attempts to paint the portrait of an entire town, and to do so from multiple points of view. As Justin Time, one of the book's multiple narrators, puts it, "[T]he story you are about to read is the story of a place, not a person. It is like a parade: though one marcher after another will step forward and claim to be the star, it is, in the end, the spectacle of stardom itself that lingers in the memory."[13] This is a tall order, to be sure, and Peck's failure in this book demonstrates, if nothing else, how easily shoddy hick chic writing can fall into just those stereotypes Dorothy Allison so skillfully avoids in *Bastard Out of Carolina.* Compared to Allison, Dale Peck comes across in this book as the worst kind of hack, a writer who not only gets the individual voices in his story hopelessly wrong, but also manages to give a false impression of an entire region.

The novel concerns the past and present life of two small towns in Kansas, one populated entirely by blacks and bearing the name Galatia, the other populated entirely by whites and bearing the name Galatea. The two are divided by a highway, but also by history. Galatia, the older of the two, was founded before the Civil War by free blacks who hoped to bring Kansas into the union as a free state. Galatea, by contrast, was not incorporated until 1976, in the aftermath of a grain elevator explosion that leveled a nearby town and caused three hundred of its former inhabitants to relocate onto land owned by a transplanted southerner named Rosemary Krebs. From the first, the two towns live in uneasy proximity to each other, a situation that is only made worse when, in 1984, an albino black boy named Eric Johnson is accused of molesting a seven-year-old white girl named Lucy Robinson—and is subsequently lynched by a group of masked white men. It's ten years later when a couple of refuges from the AIDS epidemic, the New York writer Colin Nieman and his lover Justin Time, wander into town, take up residence in an old limestone house, meet most of the towns' quirky inhabitants (including, improbably, a gay painter named Painter and a black male prostitute named Divine), and are thus present for the book's second horrific event and principal plot engine, the brutal rape and kidnapping of Lucy Robinson, now a high school cheerleader.

If any part of this sounds oddly familiar or like a cartoon version of the whole southern Gothic line of Faulkner, Carson McCullers, Tennessee Williams, and others, that's because *Now It's Time to Say Goodbye* is nothing so much as a pastiche of different styles and influences, a strange brew of farm novel clichés (MAN EATEN BY HIS OWN HOGS!), Deep South plot machinery (ALBINO NEGRO RAPES WHITE GIRL, GETS LYNCHED!), and, above all, different voices, for Peck has taken Faulkner's *As I Lay Dying* as his chief model here, employing over a dozen different narrators—none of them to much effect. However, the biggest influence on this novel by far is not literature or even film but television—and very lowbrow TV at that. Sheriff Eustace Brown, who muddles through his investigation of the book's multiple murders without ever thinking of calling the Kansas Bureau of Investigation, resembles no one so much as Deputy Roscoe from *The Dukes of Hazzard*, just as rich Rosemary Krebs comes across as a kind of female Boss Hogg. As for the book's dialogue ("Sheriff! This here man done hit my Charlene!" "Fraid there ain't much I can do for you, Howard. People done told you time and time again, busy street's no place for a napping hog"), it's *worse* than *The Dukes of Hazzard*, if that's possible.

There are other problems with the book, too—problems with the plot, problems with the prose, and so on. It would take more pages than the book is worth to list them all. In the end, one simply wonders how, given his years growing up there, Peck could have gotten his former state so wrong? Or why, faced with representing its people, he instead imports southern stereotypes? Has he been gone that long? On one level, of course, this book and its failures mean very little. After all, Dale Peck is still young, barely thirty years old, and obviously has many more books in him. But on another level, the failure means a lot. Nicodemus, the very real town upon which Galatia is based, deserves better—as does Kansas itself, which still quietly awaits, Dale Peck or no Dale Peck, its first true voice since Truman Capote.

Which is but another way of saying that there are no shortcuts to doing regionalism right.

Taken as a whole, the work of these writers demonstrates not only a persistent hick chic impulse in recent American writing but also the general direction of contemporary American fiction as a whole, which by the end of the 1980s was developing in a way that recalled past traditions even as it broke new ground. Regional in subject matter and realist in bent, this fiction was also somewhat minimalist in style, especially in its attention to the surface details of prose. Written by a new breed of writers, who were often from humble origins (and also very highly educated), it took seriously its representations of locale and work and sought to accurately portray a changing America as seen through the example of small, forgotten places. No longer could it be said, as Tom Wolfe had complained of both postmodernism and minimalism, that the characters in the new fiction had "no backgrounds," that they "came from nowhere," that they "didn't use realistic speech," or that nothing they "said, did, or possessed indicated any class or ethnic origin."[14] Instead, this fiction often displayed precisely the kind of meticulous research and reporting Wolfe called upon for the new social novel.

A good example of the kind of novel I'm thinking of is E. Annie Proulx's *The Shipping News,* which in 1994 won the Irish Times International Fiction Award, the Pulitzer Prize, and the National Book Award. Proulx had begun her career very much in the hick chic mode with the story collection *Heart Songs and Other Stories* and the novel *Postcards,* which won the 1993 PEN/Faulkner Award. In preparing to write *The Shipping News,* the story of one man's return to his ancestral Newfoundland, Proulx visited the island eight times over a six-year period, staying for a month or longer on each visit. To get the speech patterns of Newfoundlanders right, Proulx read the entire *Dictionary of Newfoundland English.* "I literally slept with that book for two years," Proulx has said. "I'd fall asleep while I was reading it. This is the point in the work. You get it right, or you don't do it. Everything depends on your getting it right."[15]

Such attention to detail is a trademark of much contemporary American fiction and one of the more enjoyable things about it. Read Cormac McCarthy's *Blood Meridian* (1985) and you'll see how gunpowder is made from a mixture of nitre, saltpeter, charcoal, brimstone, and sulfur. Read Barbara Kingsolver's *Animal Dreams* (1990) and you'll not forget how a train is taken over a mountain pass. Read Proulx's *Postcards* (1992) and you'll understand the pains that must be taken to remove human scent from fox traps. Read Charles Frazier's *Cold Mountain* (1997) and you'll learn why firewood should be cut in the old of the moon and why corn should be planted "when the poplar leaves are about the size of a squirrel's ear."[16]

For Proulx and writers like her, the accumulation of such detail is just one part of a process that is ultimately aimed at depicting change, the lifeblood of all fiction. "There's a particular kind of personality and social situation I'm attracted to," Proulx has said, "and that is the individual, or group, or region, or place, or time that's caught in change, that's caught in flux, that balances on some kind of edge that's either disintegrating or coming together or both."[17] This idea, which echoes those expressed in Wolfe's essay, harkens back to theories of the novel developed by Sir Walter Scott and Balzac, among others, and might also be taken as the mantra of much American fiction after postmodernism, which is in the process of returning to its roots.

5 / Return of the Native

5 / Return of the Native Native

In the great "Custom-House" section of *The Scarlet Letter,* Nathaniel Hawthorne wrote movingly of what he called the "strange, indolent, unjoyous attachment" of dust for dust, the irresistible pull, from the author's point of view, of the native place.[1] Hawthorne marveled that, although he had often "dwelt away from" his ancestral home of Salem, Massachusetts, and indeed was "invariably happiest elsewhere," there remained in him a feeling of "affection" for "Old Salem," a desire not only to return there but also to make it the subject of his fiction (40). For one under the pull of the native place, Hawthorne wrote, all other considerations simply do not avail: "It is no matter that the place is joyless for him; that he is weary of the old wooden houses, the mud and dust, the dead level of site and sentiment, the chill east wind, and the chilliest of social atmospheres;—all these, and whatever faults besides he may see or imagine, are nothing to the purpose. The spell survives, and just as powerfully as if the natal spot were an earthly paradise. So it has been in my case. I felt it almost as a destiny to make Salem my home" (42–43). The feeling is remarkably consistent among writers of regional origins and tends to show up as well in the characters they create. What else did Faulkner's Quentin Compson agonize about at Harvard but the South and Yoknapatawpha County, "site and sentiment" of both ancestral guilt (shades of Hawthorne) and incestuous desire? What did Hardy's Clem Yeobright dream of in Paris— disastrously, as it turned out—but a return to Egdon Heath? What did Thomas Wolfe's George Webber feel in New York but the magnetic pull of home? In these stories and many others, the pull of the native place is a subject of much ambivalence. Haunted, bedevilled, bedazzled by the past, these characters long for what has been lost, long to return; yet they know that little in the way of happiness awaits them back home.

What Hawthorne discovered by returning to Salem was that the imagination, to steal a phrase from Flannery O'Connor, is not free but bound. Of the three major elements that go into the writing of fiction—desire, talent, and material—only material comes under the direct control of the writer, and even this is in some sense God-given, both a blessing and a curse. Most young writers, O'Connor wrote in her essay "The Catholic Novelist," feel that "the first thing they must do in order to write well is to shake off the clutch of the region."[2] They want to set their stories elsewhere than on their home ground, "in a region whose way of life seems nearer the spirit of what they think they have to say," or better, "they would like to eliminate the region altogether and approach the infinite directly" (503). However, O'Connor warned, this "is not even a possibility": "The fiction writer finds in time . . . that he cannot proceed at all if he cuts himself off from the sights and sounds that have developed a life of their own in his senses. The novelist is concerned with the mystery of personality, and you cannot say much that is significant about this mystery unless the characters you create exist with the marks of a believable society about them" (503). O'Connor wrote these words in the late 1950s, a time when, to her way of thinking, the "larger social context [was being] left out of much current fiction" (503). For someone like Flannery O'Connor, the loss or diminishment of a vibrant sense of place in American fiction must have seemed like a loss of nerve, a false step at the very least. Eudora Welty, a contemporary of O'Connor's, felt much the same way. "The truth is," Welty wrote, "fiction depends for its life on place. . . . Every story would be another story, and unrecognizable as art, if it took up its characters and plot and happened somewhere else."[3]

But place is not merely a formal element in literature. As Leonard Lutwack argues in *The Role of Place in Literature* (1984), the twentieth century "evidences a new interest in place as an important issue in general":

> This is a result of widespread public recognition that earth as place, or the total environment, is being radically changed and perhaps rendered uninhabitable by more and more pervasive and powerful technologies. . . . An increased sensitivity to place seems to be required, a sensitivity inspired by aesthetic as well as ecological values, imaginative as well as functional needs. In so far as the representation of place in literature has an important influence on how people regard individual places and the whole world as a place, it may be concluded that literature must now be seen in terms of the contemporary concern for survival.[4]

As Lutwack notes, the contemporary concern with place is dictated by a series of "values" or "needs": aesthetic, ecological, imaginative, functional. But it is also informed by a "concern for survival." Nowhere, perhaps, is this more evident than in the various "renaissances" that collectively make up so much of our current American fiction. Contemporary American fiction takes up the issue of cultural survival in a number of different ways: critiques of the popular culture's leveling of regional distinctions, worries about what is lost through assimilation and affirmative action, ecological themes that tend in the direction of conservation, the use of languages other than English. "Native American survivance is a sentiment heard in creation stories and the humorous contradictions of tricksters and read in the tragic wisdom of literature," Gerald Vizenor writes in his introduction to *Native American Literature: A Brief Introduction and Anthology*. "Cultural survival is nothing new in Latino culture," write Delia Poey and Virgil Suarez in their introduction to *Iguana Dreams: New Latino Fiction* (1992). "How much of our culture should we be willing to lose or suppress in order to participate in mainstream society? The answers to this important question vary, yet it is an issue that all Latino writers must tackle either directly or in more subtle ways."[5]

In our time, writing about place has most often meant an exploration of the imagination's ties to place, whether literally, in the case of the native writer who returns home to find his material, or figuratively, in the case of the outland writer who appropriates the narrative of return as his material. Chris Offutt, whose work I discussed briefly in the previous chapter, is a good example of the first kind of writer, one who works, as it were, from the inside out. Offutt was born in the Appalachian region of eastern Kentucky in 1958. At twenty, he lit out for the city, Joe Buck–like, to become an actor on the New York stage. He washed dishes, scribbled in his journal, and for the better part of the 1980s drifted across the American landscape like a tumbleweed before a tornado, turning up finally, in the early 1990s, at the Iowa Writer's Workshop. By this time he had acquired a wife who encouraged him, a few workmanlike short stories, and about a thousand pages of journal notes. He was ripe for the return to regional consciousness then sweeping the workshop scene.

The Same River Twice (1993), Offutt's account of his life on the road and his struggles with vocation, traces the curious process by which one becomes a writer about place: How one must first break free of place, becoming a sort of prodigal son, a person made alien to his home territory through the experience of books and cosmopolitan values; how one steadily comes to devalue this education, longing for a lost childhood rooted in the land; and

Garland's story "The Return of the Private" or Hemingway's "Soldier's Home." (Faulkner's first novel, *Soldier's Pay* [1926], is a muddled version of the same strategy.) More recently, this narrative has played a part in some of our most profound Native American fiction, including N. Scott Momaday's *House Made of Dawn* (1968), Leslie Marmon Silko's *Ceremony* (1977), and Louise Erdrich's *Love Medicine* (1984). The question, in these narratives, is whether the native place and the community it implies can heal the psychic wounds of the hero. Momaday's Abel, Silko's Tayo, and Erdrich's Henry Lamartine are all wounded men who must choose between a twentieth-century culture defined by its corruption (especially in the form of alcohol and drugs) and an older, land-based culture that offers salvation through ceremony. This is also true of most of Hemingway's veterans, who typically seek solace, whether as spectators or participants, in blood pursuits such as bull fighting, boxing, hunting and fishing—all "ceremonies" with links to a pre-modern time and an ancient "home."

In much of the fiction of the post-Vietnam era, home is a place with possibilities for healing, but it is up to the individual to make the ceremony of return work. This idea is most often demonstrated through the use of a doubling motif in which two wounded heroes return to the same place, where their separate struggles can be conveniently played off of one another. Richard Ford's novel *A Piece of My Heart* (1976), for example, tells the story of two men, Robard Hewes and Sam Newel, who return to their Mississippi roots after years in the West and North. At the beginning of the novel it is Hewes, a man hopelessly in love with his own married cousin, who seems most sure about his return. Hewes has few illusions about his homeland's ability to heal or change him, but he does believe that the place will "hold him up long enough to do what he came to do, pay him, in a sense, for having been born there and having put a good-hearted attempt into staying when it was clear nobody like him ever *should* stay."[10] In other words, Hewes expects that the South will somehow authorize his illicit affair, or if not that, at least protect those involved while he carries it out. Sam Newel, by contrast, leaves Chicago for Mississippi with no expectations and for no reason he can understand other than boredom and the feeling that "everything is the same." It is not even his idea, but his girlfriend Beebe's, and she is the one person in the novel who doesn't believe in return, arguing that the "stupidest" and the "strongest" urge animals have is to "remain faithful to their own wretched unpromising territory—past when the food had depleted and they were impoverished and falling over to predators" (185). Yet in the end, it is Newel who profits most from his return, if only because he finally comes to realize that the problem is not with where he is but *who* he is. Robard Hewes comes to no such realization, denying that he is in trouble right up to the point where his friend and adversary W.W. dies because of his actions. "I ain't in no kind of fix at all," Hewes tells Newel, "though if I was to try to pin together my past and make something intelligent out of it I'd damn sure be in one then. I'd either get bored to tears or scared to death" (230).

Madison Smartt Bell's *Soldier's Joy* (1989) is a good example of a post-Vietnam novel that combines the narrative of the soldier's return home with the doubling motif of Ford's *A Piece of My Heart*. Bell's fifth novel but his first set in his home state of Tennessee, *Soldier's Joy* tells the story of Thomas Laidlaw, a wounded Vietnam veteran who returns from the war to his family's hill-country farm outside Nashville. His father dead, the old homestead burned down, Laidlaw moves into a ramshackle cabin and begins the process of recovering from the war. As a narrative of return, *Soldier's Joy* is concerned with the possibility of healing and redemption for its wounded protagonist. As a southern novel set in the early 1970s, however, it is also concerned with the region's history of troubled race relations and with the legacy of Vietnam. The respective wounds of nation, region, and self must be healed before any real social progress can be made. This theme is played out through a classic doubling structure: also home from the war is Rodney Redmon, the black son of the hired man who once occupied Laidlaw's cabin. Laidlaw and Rodney grew up together "almost as brothers" (shades of Faulkner here); they even served together in Vietnam; as doubles, therefore, the redemption of both is required before either can be well.

The first half of the novel takes up the question of Laidlaw's recovery, and it does so in a fascinating way. Laidlaw has no interest at all in cultivating his farm or returning it to its prewar grandeur. Instead, he lets it fall into even further disrepair, spending all of his time—literally from sunrise to sunset—sitting on the porch of his cabin trying to learn the complicated and old-fashioned "drop-thumb" method of banjo picking. In perfecting this particular banjo style, Laidlaw is looking forward to the day when his veteran's benefits run out and he'll have to make a living for himself as a professional bluegrass musician. But he's after something else as well, something that balances his need for self-expression with his need to follow the traditional forms and folkways of his region. He chooses the drop-thumb method of playing because "the style had evolved organically, in winterbound shacks up in the mountains."[11] For Laidlaw, there is a deep connection between bluegrass music and the actual landscapes it comes out of, and by practicing this music's most difficult and hallowed techniques, he hopes, in one sense, to make himself one with landscape:

> While his hands went up and down the banjo, Laidlaw's eyes wandered from spot to spot, fixing on one thing and then another. There were always birds busy in the yard, and he had fallen into the habit of tossing out breadcrumbs for them. He enjoyed their light movements, something to look at. There was no use looking at his fingers. The left hand already knew what it was doing and the right hand would have to teach itself. In the mornings before the coffee got through him, Laidlaw could fancy it was someone else trying to play, awkwardly framing the one-to-one clawhammer beat, the sound of it coming back to him from some distance, while his intelligence drifted elsewhere, above and beyond the body. His thought and senses wound into the landscape while his hands went on their way, chopping steadily at the banjo, lifting the coffee cup, lighting cigarettes. In time, however, he'd come back to himself, the parts of him pulling together. Just short of noon most days there came a kind of melding, so that he knew that it was he who made these exact movements, produced these sounds. Fully awakened, he looked all around himself and saw that he was here, and was amazed all over again at his presence. (5–6)

By melting into his native landscape and then "melding" back into himself, Laidlaw hopes to cleanse himself of the Vietnam experience. At this early stage in his recovery, the music he plays—old-time folk numbers like "Cripple Creek" and "Soldier's Joy"—is meant to enter his body and mind and change him, cure him, even as later, after he has mastered his own personal style, the music that pours out of him is meant to soothe and cure his people.

The second half of *Soldier's Joy* takes up the question of racial hatred in the South and Laidlaw's friendship with Rodney Redmon. Here the desire is for a community of black and white that is symbolized, for Laidlaw, by the brotherhood of soldiers in Vietnam. That this part of the novel fails so miserably (in a scene straight out of *Rambo,* Laidlaw, Redmon, and another Vietnam vet take on the Ku Klux Klan with the aid of a stash of M-16s) shows, if nothing else, that it is much easier to imagine one man's recovery than it is to bring about the recovery of an entire region, especially one as fraught with problems as the American South. Nevertheless, in the narrative of return as we have it in much contemporary American fiction, the individual's attempt to redeem the region is ultimately as important as the expectation that the region will somehow cure the individual.

Perhaps the most profound and fully formed example of the narrative of the wounded soldier's return home in our recent fiction can be found in Charles Frazier's novel *Cold Mountain* (1997). Set in the autumn and winter of 1864, at the tail end of the Civil War, the novel concerns the long walk home made by an AWOL confederate soldier named Inman. Drawing on years of research, Frazier takes great pains, early in the novel, to describe the fighting Inman has seen at Petersburg and elsewhere, and this fighting in no way resembles the sabre-drawn, horseback charges one often associates with sentimental depictions of the Civil War. It is trench warfare, pure and simple. Men huddle like animals in holes in the ground while bombs explode all around them. In the process, a "new landscape of pure force" is created.[12] The soldiers themselves are described either as body parts ("All underfoot were bodies and pieces of bodies, and so many men had come apart in the blowup and the shelling that the ground was slick and threw a terrible stink from their wet internalments" [124]) or as animals awaiting slaughter ("a pen of shoats waiting for the hammer between the eyes" [124]). Having experienced such fighting, and having witnessed so much death "that it seemed no longer dark and mysterious" (180), Inman comes away a mere shell of a man whose "spirit" had been "burned" and "blasted out of him so that he had become lonesome and estranged from all around him" (16). He is man hollowed out, "brooding and pining for his lost self" (16), for like his fellow soldiers on both sides of the trenches "he had seen the metal face of the age and had been so stunned by it that when he thought into the future, all he could vision was a world from which everything he counted important had been banished or had willingly fled" (2).

Shell-shocked in this "new landscape of pure force," Inman walks away from a field hospital and attempts to cure himself by returning to another landscape, that of home. Walking west from the lowland battlefields of Virginia toward his native Cold Mountain in North Carolina, Inman reads "the third part of Bartram's *Travels*" (10), a book filled with dense descriptions of mountain landscapes. "Such images made Inman happy," we are told,

> as did the following pages wherein Bartram, ecstatic, journeyed on to the Vale of Cowee deep in the mountains, breathlessly describing a world of scarp and crag, ridge after ridge fading off blue into the distance, chanting at length as he went the names of all the plants that came under his gaze as if reciting the ingredients of a powerful potion. After a time, though, Inman found that he had left the book and was simply forming the topography of home in his head. Cold Mountain, all its ridges and coves and watercourses. Pigeon River, Little East Fork, Sorrell Cove, Deep Gap, Fire Scald Ridge. He knew their names and said

them to himself like the words of spells and incantations to ward off the things one fears most. (11)

It is this "topography of home in his head" that is meant to cure Inman, if anything can. As in the earlier example from Bell's *Soldier's Joy,* Inman is "melding" himself back into his native landscape, in memory at first, later in actual sight. Meanwhile he must plunge through the hated lowlands of "planed-off, tangled pinebrakes," a "flat land" full of "red dirt" and "mean towns" that for Inman is "nothing but the place where all that was foul and sorry had flowed downhill and pooled in the low spots," a country of "swill and sullage, sump of the continent" (53). In opposition to this hell, Inman imagines a heaven high atop Cold Mountain, a place he will escape to with Ada, the woman he left behind in going to war, there to live a life "so quiet he would not need ears," where "there might be the hope . . . that in time his despair might be honed off to a point so fine and thin that it would be nearly the same as vanishing" (65).

Meanwhile, back in North Carolina, Ada awaits Inman's return, surviving as best she can by living off the land. Unlike Inman, Ada is not a native of the region, but rather an outlander from Charleston who "had been educated beyond the point considered wise for women" and was "filled with opinions on art and politics and literature," possessing, however, very little in the way of practical knowledge. After her father dies, Ada discovers herself to be "frighteningly ill-prepared in the craft of subsistence, living alone on a farm that her father had run rather as an idea than a livelihood" (23). Thus Frazier will come at the idea of place from both ends, as it were: the wounded son's return to the native place, and the outsider's initiation into the significance of place.

Ada's teacher in the ways of mountain survival is the illiterate hill woman Ruby, a kind of female Huck Finn and jack-of-all-trades for whom "all the actual facts and processes connected with food and clothing and shelter" are "concrete" and nonmysterious, "falling immediately and directly to hand, and every one of them calling for exertion" (80–81). Ruby's knowledge is vast and impressive, gained both by watching and asking questions of experts ("grandmother knowledge") and by simple observation and "puzzl[ing] out in her own mind how the world's logic works" (106). From Ruby, Ada learns that place is particular. Ruby puts her hands over Ada's eyes and asks her what she hears. Trees, Ada replies.

—Trees, Ruby said contemptuously, as if she had expected just such a foolish answer. Just general trees is all? You've got a long way to go.

> She removed her hands and took her seat again and said nothing more on that topic, leaving Ada to conclude that what she meant was that this is a particular world. Until Ada could listen and at the bare minimum tell the sound of poplar from oak at this time of year when it is easiest to do, she had not even started to know the place. (228)

As Ada will discover in the course of the novel, the process of coming to know a particular place is a lifelong process that begins with the big picture and then slowly moves in for the details: "General to particular. Everything had a name. To live fully in a place all your life, you kept aiming smaller and smaller in attention to detail" (307).

As Frazier's novel progresses toward its inevitable conclusion, we come to understand that it will be enough for Inman to reach Cold Mountain one last time. Achieving this, he will have "achieved a vista of what for him was homeland" (281). Ultimately, the novel will belong to Ada, who by its end has progressed to a point beyond even Ruby, a point at which she is able to locate herself so precisely in relation to both time and place that the resulting foothold is her first complete identity:

> This evening she marked where the sun dove to the horizon, for over the weeks she had made a practice of noting its setting point on the ridge. She had watched it march southward as the days snuffed out earlier and earlier. Were she to decide fully to live here in Black Cove unto death, she believed she would erect towers on the ridge marking the south and north points of the sun's annual swing. She owned the entire span of ridge where the sun set through the year, and that was a thing to savor. One had then just to mark the points in December and June when the sun wrenched itself from its course and doubled back for another set of seasons. Though upon reflection, she decided a tower was not entirely needed. Only clear some trees to notch the ridge at the turning point. It would be a great pleasure year after year to watch with anticipation as the sun drew nigh to the notch and then on a specified day fell into it and then rose out of it and retraced its path. Over time, watching that happen again and again might make the years seem not such an awful linear progress but instead a looping and a return. Keeping track of such a thing would place a person, would be a way of saying, You are here, in this one station, now. It would be an answer to the question, Where am I? (260)

Which question, this novel attempts to show, is only another version of the question, Who am I? By the end of Frazier's novel, Ada has become a placed person. By dint of hard work and close observation, she has made herself a calendar and a map *out of trees,* and by doing so has connected herself completely to landscape.

As the example of Ada in *Cold Mountain* suggests, regional identity today can be as much a matter of choice as an accident of birth or a true representation of a writer's origins. These days, the very idea of "material" is mobile; it can be discovered *on the road.* Madison Smartt Bell is a case in point. Before writing *Soldier's Joy,* he set novels in New York, England, Italy, and other venues. *Save Me, Joe Louis* (1993) is a tour de force in this respect, moving effortlessly from Hell's Kitchen to Baltimore to the same Tennessee county featured in *Soldier's Joy,* while *All Souls' Rising* (1995), perhaps Bell's most accomplished novel to date, is set in Haiti in the late eighteenth century. After writing *A Piece of My Heart,* Richard Ford set novels in New Jersey and Mexico, while the story collection *Rock Springs* is set in Montana. With *Independence Day* (1995), winner of the 1996 Pulitzer Prize, Ford returned to suburban New Jersey for his material. Thomas McGuane and Barbara Kingsolver, two writers whose work I will discuss at length in the pages to come, each made several significant moves within the United States (and even abroad) before settling in and writing about the regions for which they are now famous. McGuane, born in Michigan, set novels in his native state (*The Sporting Club*) and Florida (*Ninety-Two in the Shade, Panama*) before writing *Nobody's Angel,* his first Montana novel. Kingsolver began her career writing about her native Kentucky (in *Homeland and Other Stories*) but is now thought of primarily as a Southwestern writer. As Ford has remarked in an interview, "I'll try to exhaust my interest in a place, and then I'll just move on. I think the ways in which people accommodate themselves to a place is a lot of what stories of mine are about."[13]

One would think, given the mobility of these authors, that they would write primarily about characters much like themselves, people new to a place, just beginning to figure it out. What we often find, however, is just the opposite. As Kingsolver has said in an interview, "The people of the West I write about are the rooted people—the people who belong here."[14] Even Quoyle in Proulx's *The Shipping News* is a native of sorts; his family's roots in Newfoundland run as deep as the island's rocky soil allows. Similarly, the characters in a book like Ford's *Rock Springs* are Montana *natives* who are either in the process of leaving their hometown (or state) or, just as likely, returning to it after a time away. The opening paragraph of "Winterkill" is typical of this second scenario: "I had not been back in town long. Maybe a month was all. The work had finally given out for me down at Silver Bow, and

I had quit staying down there when the weather turned cold, and come back to my mother's, on the Bitterroot, to lay up and set my benefits aside for when things got worse."[15]

Ford's entire book, in fact, can be read as an extended meditation on the limitations of the native place as a sanctuary. The bitterness we detect in the above passage comes in part from this narrator's realization that returning home is as much an admission of failure (things will undoubtedly get "worse") as it is a search for shelter when the "weather turn[s] cold." The narrator of "Children," like many in *Rock Springs,* is a man who looks back on his youth in Montana and wonders what effect place has had on his subsequent life. He prefaces the story by describing the "empty, lonely place" where he grew up, because, as he says, "I have thought possibly it was the place itself, as much as the time in our lives or our characters, that took part in the small things that happened and made them memorable" (69–70). In this passage, and in many others like it in books of a regionalist bent, place becomes almost a character in its own right, something that "takes part" in all that happens and is later personified. At the end of "Children," Ford's narrator returns to the idea of place, this time to a vision of the world outside Montana as terrifying and meaningless: "Claude and I couldn't see the world and what would happen to us in it—what we would do, where we would go. How could we? Outside was a place that seemed not even to exist, an empty place you could stay in for a long time and never find a thing you admired or loved or hoped to keep" (98). The world of Montana is a huge, heartless, yet familiar stage on which one's life is played out to neither laughter nor applause but only a kind of silent judgment. The native landscape is epic, threatening always to diminish the individual actor, while all that lies outside it is both unknown and terrifying in its indifference. In such a world, departure is imminent, return inevitable.

Writers like Ford, Kingsolver, and McGuane bring to the story of the native's return an emotional and aesthetic distance some have criticized as the mark of the outsider. For a fourth-generation westerner like Russell Martin, a novel like McGuane's *Nobody's Angel* (1982) succeeds in defining "the essential concern of the region's new fiction—rural people searching for a safe place" even as it fails to give us much in the way of a convincing native protagonist. "In the end," Martin writes, "although [McGuane's lead character] is superbly shaped and sustained, he still seems much more like a Montana immigrant—someone like McGuane himself . . . than a native son who almost certainly would have grown up apologizing for the place."[16] Yet it is just this quality of ambivalent distance that makes an exploration of place interesting. Books like *Nobody's*

Angel or Kingsolver's *Animal Dreams* (1990) tread the line between insider and outsider status, creating a conflict out of which the meaning of place itself is generated.

Jane Smiley opens her *New York Times* review of Kingsolver's *Animal Dreams* by questioning the political and aesthetic possibilities of a regionalism grounded in the specifics of place. "Have American novelists," Smiley asks, "especially younger ones, abandoned a larger political and cultural vision in favor of a narrow domesticity? Or have critics who make these charges failed to see a new vision emerging in the place of outmoded forms?"[17] Smiley goes on to remark how difficult it is to create anything new in a world where so many of the old forms and systems "have turned out to be either ineffectual or bankrupt." Her answer, as we might expect from the author of *A Thousand Acres,* is that writers such as Kingsolver have not abandoned the world at large but have in fact been rethinking it at a grass-roots level: "Barbara Kingsolver is one of an increasing number of American novelists who are trying to rewrite the political, cultural and spiritual relationships between our country's private and public spheres. The traditional approach has been to use small figures on a large canvas to demonstrate social theories or patterns. But those theories and patterns seem to have failed, sometimes spectacularly. Like others who are looking for a new approach, Ms. Kingsolver prefers to concentrate upon particulars."

Ursula Le Guin, reviewing the novel for the *Washington Post,* called *Animal Dreams* part of "a new fiction of relationship, aesthetically rich and of great political and spiritual significance."[18] The imagery underlying the novel, Le Guin wrote, is "of networks, bonds, patterns, connections, bodies, the body politic, the web, the weft." The key word in both reviews is *relationships.* It is only by coming to terms with our origins, our ancestry, our relationships with others and the environment that we achieve happiness—what we might call, in the world of fiction, "selfhood" or "development." The vehicle for such a statement, in Kingsolver's novel and others like it, is the prodigal's return home.

Early in *Animal Dreams,* we are introduced to Codi, or Cosima Noline. Her name means "order in the cosmos," but her life is far from being in order. She is a lost soul, someone whose method of living has long been, by her own admission, the way of the open road, "the familiar tug of [the] brand-new place" that might, "this time, turn out to be wonderful."[19] "I get lost a lot," she says. "I keep hoping some guy with 'Ron' or 'Andy' stitched on his pocket and a gas pump in his hand will step up and tell me where I'm headed" (184). For fourteen years—ever since she left her hometown of Grace, Arizona, in fact— she has been "running, forgetting what lay behind and always looking ahead for the perfect home, where trains never wrecked and hearts never broke, where no one you loved ever died" (236). Deep in a crisis that begins with her sister's departure for Nicaragua, Codi returns home, where all the ghosts of her past still reside and where her father, Doc Homer, is being slowly consumed by a degenerative brain disease.

The initial return home is a failure, of course. Codi feels no more connected in Grace (or to grace, as Kingsolver's sometimes blunt symbolism would have us believe) than she did on the road; in fact, she feels "disoriented and disgraced, a trespasser on family rites" (16): "I was *here,* after all, with no more mission in life than I'd been born with years ago. The only difference between then and now was wardrobe. . . . Under my picture in the yearbook it said, 'Will Go Far.' . . . You could accept this as either prophecy or a bad joke. I'd gone halfway around the world, and now lived three-quarters of a mile from the high school" (28). Her desire had been to "step off the bus and land smack in the middle of a sense of belonging" (12), but even she can see this is a "hopeful construction" (149). Though she declares herself willing to sell her soul and all her traveling shoes just to "*belong* some place" (30), the fact is she is now "a stranger to Grace" (12), and, as always, "[i]t's tough to break yourself as news to a town that already knows you" (13).

As is often the case in these novels, Codi's feelings of estrangement from her hometown begin with her estrangement from her family. Her father, the town doctor, had raised Codi and her sister Hallie to think of themselves as somehow above the other town residents. They differed from their peers "in ambition, native ability, even physical constitution" (46). Whereas everyone else in Grace is descended directly from "the nine blue-eyed Gracela sisters" who "came over from Spain to marry nine lucky miners" (14), Codi and her family are outlanders, people who arrived in Arizona much later from somewhere in Illinois. However, none of this keeps Codi from dreaming. "More than anything else," she says, "I wished I belonged to one of these living, celebrated families, lush as plants, with bones in the ground for roots" (165).

The Nolines, by contrast, are a dysfunctional family, having never recovered from the early death of Codi's mother. As a single parent, Doc Homer has not been the sort from whom one can "expect hugs and kisses" (72). Codi's relationship with her father is a distant one, and even with her sister Hallie, whom she loves deeply, there is the feeling that their paths will always be different, "divergent," true to the end to "the laws of family physics," which call for the "equal" yet "opposite" reaction of different members (8). Ultimately, the Noline family is uncommunicative, a family of secrets. Codi herself keeps the fact of a stillborn pregnancy in adolescence from both her father and sister.

Among the other ghosts from her past Codi must confront upon her return to Grace is Loyd Peregrina, the Pueblo-Apache-Navajo Indian who unwittingly fathered the lost baby of Codi's teenage years. Much of the success of Codi's return must be measured by what happens in her relationship with Loyd, who, with his deep roots in the Southwest, represents the "new" (though by Indian standards, quite old) idea that man is a "houseguest" on this earth, not the endowed consumer of Anglo belief. For Loyd, "[t]he important thing isn't the house. It's the ability to make it" (235). "We're like coyotes," he tells Codi. "Get to a good place, turn around three times in the grass, and you're home. Once you know how, you can always do that, no matter what. You won't forget" (235).

Thus the ultimate question in this novel becomes: Can Codi, who has proven herself no "nester," in fact the very "opposite of a 'homemaker'" (77), discover the sense of place, of belonging, she has missed all her life? The answer to this question is foretold, at least in part, by Codi's discovery that her lifelong fear of blindness has less to do with a loss of personal vision than with a loss of *relation* to place. "What you lose in blindness," she discovers, "is the space around you, the place where you are, and without that you might not exist. You could be nowhere at all" (204).

Many of these same themes may be observed at work in Thomas McGuane's first Montana novel, *Nobody's Angel,* only this time the outlook is far less hopeful than in *Animal Dreams.* Perhaps this is because McGuane himself is more ambivalent about the idea of place than either Kingsolver or Charles Frazier. In his essay "Roping, from A to B," McGuane praises Jack Kerouac as the writer who "trained us in the epic idea that the region was America."[20] But he also has this to say by way of distancing himself from Faulkner and other "regional" writers: "The vulgarity we call the 'sense of place' is a fairly nelly sub-instance of schizophrenia, saving up facts, preferably inherited, about locale. It's like when Southerners talk about losing the war; you want to puke. It always made me very suspicious that *no one* from Yoknapatawpha ever went to Miami. Faulkner certainly left no stone unturned for himself; but the denizens of his books he locks up in this morbid Cloud-Cuckoo-Land where everybody has mule trouble while the author rides up and down Sunset Strip in a convertible" (221). McGuane, it would seem, has no truck with "place." Yet at other times he has admitted to having "struggled to have a sense of place"; while expressing no interest in "replicating Montana or rendering landscapes in a recognizable way," McGuane has felt "something forceful about these landscapes" that should, if nothing else, "turn up in language."[21]

Part of McGuane's ambivalence about place must be traced to the fear, shared by many writers, that being identified as a "regionalist" will necessarily diminish his stature as a writer of national importance. "It's getting worse and worse," McGuane has complained. "Now at *The New York Times* when I have a book come out they'll assign it to some minor western writer to review. And they'll call me from time to time and want me to review some western book. I say, gimme Philip Roth! Gimme the new Updike!"[22] McGuane's ideas about western writing echo Richard Ford's about another famous region of the country. "Personally, I think there is no such thing as Southern writing or Southern literature or a Southern Ethos," Ford has written. "What 'Southern Writing' has always alibied for, of course, is regional writing—writing with an asterisk. The minor leagues."[23]

Also present in McGuane's attitude, as can readily be seen in the above comment on Faulkner, is the idea that too much striving for an "authentic" sense of place necessarily leads a writer to fake what he actually sees around him—for example, to add more cowboy hats (or mules) than are actually there. Speaking of his novel *Nothing But Blue Skies,* McGuane said, "I was interested in the discrepancy between the official West and the West we were all living in. Instead of cowboys and ranchers, a lot of the people I knew had car lots and drove Toyotas."[24] Ultimately, McGuane embraces the idea of place, but qualifies it according to the tenets of realism. "I feel strongly," he has said, "that writers need to be some place. The real thing, the real job of artists of any kind is to somehow seize the life you're living in an unrelinquishing grip."[25] His often-stated choice of epitaph, "No stone unturned—except this one," humorously realigns him with that side of William Faulkner that surely did drive down Sunset Strip with the top down.

Nobody's Angel concedes place as the site of a personal struggle with issues of selfhood and development but stops well short of the affirmation we find in Kingsolver and Charles Frazier. According to Dexter Westrum, McGuane wrote the novel "out of the ache created when his father, mother, and sister died"; McGuane now sees in the book a "depressing fatalism" he attributes to that time in his life.[26] Like *Animal Dreams,* the book concerns the return home of a dissatisfied drifter, Patrick Fitzpatrick. But whereas Codi Noline came home to a place called Grace, Patrick returns to the ominously named Deadrock, "a modest place of ten thousand souls" wholly given over to a "sad and irresolute boosterism." The novel begins, "You would have to care about the country," an ambiguous statement that immediately calls into question Patrick's ability to make this place his salvation; but even before this, in an epigraph to the novel taken from Malcolm Lowry, McGuane hits the representative chord: "I love hell. I can't wait to get back."[27]

Patrick, like Codi Noline, is initially thrown off balance by his return home. While serving as an Army tank captain in Germany, Patrick had invested his family's Montana ranch, the Heart Bar, with the mythic status of sanctuary from all trouble. Once home, however, he has no idea what to do with this "beautiful ranch he would someday own, land, homestead, water rights, cattle and burden" (65). Though he wants desperately for "his heart to seize the ancient hills, the old windmills and stock springs" (86), he instead feels trapped and confused, "like someone out of stir, trying to establish a pattern in a new world" (10). He loves the place but can't help but feel that it is all "edges and no middle" (61). When asked if he is home to stay, he can only respond by saying, "Trying to be" (9). Finally he is forced to admit that living on the ranch, "which from his tank had seemed a series of bright ceremonies, was now more like entrapment in a motel on the interstate" (142). The bottom line, for Patrick, is the state of feeling *burdened*: burdened by the ranch and its responsibilities, burdened by his hometown—which, both he and his sister agree, is only good "for supplies" (106)—and, especially, burdened by his family and its history.

Like the Nolines, the Fitzpatricks are a dysfunctional group. Patrick's father, a Boeing test pilot with whom Patrick never got along, died in a plane crash in Oregon, leaving Patrick to wonder, "[I]f my father is dead, how can I be alive?" (21). His mother has remarried an undistinguished man and moved to California. Thus Patrick's Montana family consists only of his sister Mary, a sad young woman plagued by mental illness, and his grandfather, a distant and bitter man who hates the contemporary West and longs for the days when Montana was "a real stockman's country" (55). Though the family has lived in Montana since 1884, they still "did not fit or even want to fit or, in the words of Patrick's grandfather, 'talk to just anybody'":

> They would bear forever the air of being able to pick up and go, of having no roots other than the entanglement between themselves; and it is fair to say that

they were very thorough snobs with no hope of reform. They had no one to turn to besides themselves, despite that they didn't get along very well with one another and had scattered all over the country where they meant nothing to their neighbors in the cities and suburbs. Only Patrick and Mary with her hoarding mind and their insufferable grandfather were left to show what there had been; and when they were gone, everyone would say in some fashion that they had never been there anyway, that they didn't fit. (104–105)

Isolated from their neighbors and separated from one another, the Fitzpatricks as a Montana phenomenon face almost certain extinction. As with the Cheyenne, who are said to have been "very thoroughly kicked out" of Montana, it will soon take a shovel to find that the Fitzpatricks had ever been there at all (3). As a group, they suffer from "the connection they never had," an "absence that was perilously ignored" (86), and much of Patrick's searching in the novel is for another kind of connection, any kind, to replace this missing one.

Unlike *Animal Dreams, Nobody's Angel* does not figure this connection as a rekindling of a former, high school romance. McGuane would save that story for his next two novels of return, *Something to Be Desired* (1984) and *Keep the Change* (1989). In *Nobody's Angel,* Patrick's romantic interest is an outlander, the Oklahoma-born Claire Burnett. Claire's outsider status, together with the fact that she is already married to an ersatz good old boy named Tio, signal to the reader just how doomed the pairing is. For his part, Patrick can't help but think that "Claire could change it all" (137). What he wants is a "big simp love story," a kind of big-screen romance wherein his job "would be to save the ranch" and Claire's job would be to save him. Claire, however, has her own problems—namely, Tio, who is something less than stable—and anyway, as she puts it, "I don't want to be in a big simp love story" (147). Naturally what this leads to, as Patrick must come to find out, is "nothing eventual" (171), which, in a sense, has been his problem all along.

Thus Patrick must confront the ghosts of his past alone, something he proves himself hopelessly unable to do. He had returned to the ranch "hoping to learn something from his grandfather," but "the old man was still too cowboy to play to nostalgia for anyone" (61). The most he will do is talk about an older, better West, a time and place that Patrick's sister Mary ridicules as "[k]ill, shoot, whack, stab, chop" (55), but that Patrick himself still struggles to believe in. Listening to the old man's stories, he wonders, "Had all this really disappeared?" His answer is the closest McGuane comes in this novel to affirming place as a kind of salvation:

As then, when he felt the old man's past, or when he went among the ancient cottonwoods that once held the shrouded burials of the Crow, Patrick felt that in fact there had been a past, and though he was not a man with connections or immediate family, he was part of something in the course of what was to come. None of which meant he'd failed at ambition, but only that its base was so broad he could not discover its final curves, the ones that propelled him into the present, or glory, or death. (63)

In the end, however, simply being part of something "in the course of what was to come" cannot cure Patrick Fitzpatrick. In the novel's last few lines he retreats into the old pattern of escape, rejoining the Army and buying a flat in Madrid, where he lives essentially by himself, "a blackout drinker" who "never came home again" (227).

The narrative of the prodigal's return home articulates a series of quasi-mythic themes that are indeed a part of what Jane Smiley calls a "new vision emerging in the place of outmoded forms." Among the themes one encounters again and again in books like *Animal Dreams* and *Nobody's Angel* are the search for the lost father, the search for vocation, the search for a viable connection with the natural world, and the encounter, held over in many ways from an earlier literature, with the ghosts of a Native American past.

In the work of women writers like Kingsolver, Smiley, and Louise Erdrich, the presence of such themes has led some reviewers and critics to speak of a new subgenre in American literature, so-called eco-feminist fiction. "The plot of this evolving genre has become reasonably clear," wrote one reviewer of *Animal Dreams*. "Women, relying on intuition and one another, mobilize to save the planet, or their immediate neighborhoods, from the ravages—war, pollution, racism, etc.—wrought by white males."[28] Alternatively, when seen in the work of male writers like Thomas McGuane, these tendencies have often been lampooned as a doomed masculinity's search for the "wild man" within. "Thomas McGuane's men would like to be Hemingway heroes—if they could," wrote the *New York Times*'s Michiko Kakutani. "But while the America they inhabit still boasts patches of pristine wilderness, it's hardly the testing ground for manhood that it was in simpler times."[29]

Regardless of how we interpret or assess these themes, however, there is no denying their persistence. Take, for example, the theme of the "search for the father." In her review of *Animal Dreams*, Ursula Le Guin noted the recurrence of this theme in contemporary fiction, wondering offhand "why so many sons seem to mislay Pa somewhere, and then have epiphanies when they find him."

We might answer Le Guin's question, at least in part, by noting that this theme is almost always tied to a search for personal identity. The symbolism inherent in such a theme is often simplified by the absence or death of other family members—mothers and siblings. For example, Codi Noline's mother died when Codi was still a girl; her sister Hallie is murdered. In *Nobody's Angel,* Patrick Fitzpatrick's mother is conveniently relocated to California, safely out of the novel's domain; his sister, Mary, commits suicide halfway through. In both books, this leaves the field open for a more streamlined confrontation between the protagonist and a distant father figure who is also shrouded in death.

As Le Guin notes, this confrontation usually does involve an epiphany. The search for the father reveals the father's own mortality, his status as a mere mortal after all, and not the looming presence remembered from childhood. The confrontation and epiphany in Kinglsolver's *Animal Dreams* is especially striking:

> For the first time in my life then, and just for a few seconds, I was able to see Doc Homer as someone I felt sorry for. It was a turning point for me, one of those instants of freakishly clear sight when you understand that your parent might have taken entirely the wrong road in life, even if that road includes your own existence. I pitied Doc Homer for his slavish self-sufficiency. For standing Hallie and me in the kitchen and inspecting us like a general, not for crooked hems so much as for signs of the weakness of our age: the lipstick hidden in a book satchel, the smoldering wish to be like everyone else. Being like no one else, being alone, was the central ethic of his life. Mine too, to some extent, not by choice but by default. My father, the only real candidate for center of my universe, was content to sail his private sea and leave me on my own. I still held that against him. I hadn't thought before about how self-sufficiency could turn on you in old age or sickness. The captain was going down with his ship. He was just a man, becoming a child. It became possible for me to go back to Grace. (69)

Codi's confrontation with the mortality, the simple humanity, of Doc Homer is indeed "the turning point" in her life. Seen in his final illness, Doc Homer no longer looms as the "general" who ruled over Codi's childhood. Nor is he the "captain" or seasoned navigator of life's waters; instead, he is simply another flawed human being. The "central ethic of his life"—the ability to remain alone—is found to be hopelessly inadequate, and as such, is no real inheritance (or burden) after all. Far from being the "center" of the "universe," the father is "just a man," and a dying one at that. Discovering this is what allows Codi to finally "go back to Grace."

In *Nobody's Angel,* Patrick's father is already dead, but this in no way excuses Patrick from having to face the meaning of his father's mortality. Shortly after Patrick's return to Montana, he spots with his binoculars a wrecked airplane in the mountains above his ranch. All winter long, he must wait for the snow to thaw so that he can get a horse up there to "look into the pilot's eyes" (5). His going to see the dead pilot operates as a delayed confrontation with his own father's death in a plane crash in Oregon:

> Then in May Patrick walked up the endless sloping nose and saw the pilot quite clearly. He climbed past him to the copilot's seat and found fractured portions of granite, parts of the mountain that had poured like grapeshot through the fuselage clear into the tail section, leaving the copilot in innumerable pieces, those pieces gusseted in olive nylon, and the skin of the aircraft blood-sprayed as in a cult massacre. Farther aft in the tapering shape where the beating spring sun shone on the skin of the plane and where viscera trailed off in straps, fastening and instruments, it stank. Arms raised in uniform, the pilot seemed the image of a man in receipt of a fatal sacrament. The oxygen hose was torn away, and beyond the nautiloid effigy, Patrick could see his mare grazing on the alpine slope. Unable to differentiate flesh and electronics, he was avoiding the long-held notion that his father had died like a comet, igniting in the atmosphere, an archangelic semaphore more dignified than death itself. For Patrick, a year had begun. The inside of the plane showed him that life doesn't just always drag on. (5–6)

As with Doc Homer, Patrick's father is figured here as a kind of navigator, a "pilot" whose job it was to lead one safely through life. But upon seeing the aftermath of a real plane crash, Patrick can no longer maintain the illusion that his father was "an archangel more dignified than death itself." Instead, he was a real man dependent upon oxygen for life, a man whose corpse, strewn across an aircraft's instruments, "stank" like anyone else's. The effect of this realization, for Patrick, is that "a year had begun." Once the presence of the father has been eliminated, the home place can be seen for what it really is—either the "Grace" of Kingsolver's novel or the "Deadrock" of McGuane's. In both books, the search for the father turns out to be really about the search for a space (or place) in which to live one's life. What is required for such a space to exist, in these novels at least, is the removal of the father as pilot or navigator. The father must be killed off, as it were, so that the son (or daughter) can take to the air.

In both of these novels, the death of the father represents a kind of required demise of old ways of thinking—especially the time-honored American tradition of individualism—so that a new way can emerge. Part of Codi Noline's problem has been her inability to decide what to do with her life. Trained as a doctor, she dropped out of her residency just short of certification when she failed in the delivery of a breach birth. Since then, she has drifted between safe research jobs and stints working as a night clerk in convenience stores. As Codi explains it, "I'd discovered there was something serious, mainly a matter of nerve and perhaps empathy, that stood in my way" (107). Her return home has been in part an attempt to rediscover her vocation. It was prompted not so much by Doc Homer's illness as by her sister Hallie's decision to run off to Nicaragua to help the Sandinistas, a move the preachy Codi figures as "saving the world." Even the locals in Grace see Codi's return as part of a plan to take over Doc Homer's medical practice, to "save the town," as it were. Yet part of Codi's problem is her inability to admit any of this to herself. When she takes a job teaching science at the local high school, she insists to everyone that it is only short term—a year taken out of her rolling-stone existence to recharge her batteries. It is only with time that she begins to see her work at the high school as "saving" work, meaningful to both herself and those around her. From here it is but a small step to her later involvement in a grass-roots effort to defeat a powerful mining company that has been polluting the town's river and orchards.

In McGuane's novel, Patrick Fitzpatrick fails to save himself, in part at least, because he cannot find a vital connection between place and vocation. The ranch he sees himself as "saving" needs to be farmed more and grazed less, but to Patrick farming is just a highly evolved form of mowing the lawn. An adept trainer with great feeling for horses, Patrick is nevertheless unable to turn even this into meaningful work. It is too isolated, like the ranch itself, "all edges and no middle," with no possibilities for meaningful connection to others. There remains only the possibility of a connection to landscape, but in the end Patrick must admit that his grandfather is the only person who has ever done a good job running the ranch; his own attempt has been half-hearted at best.

The search for vocation in these novels mirrors, in many ways, the search for meaning in the writing life. This is particularly true for a writer like Kingsolver, who sees the act of authorship as "a way to live in an imperfect world without having to suffer in silence," as a "little shot at changing the world."[30] But even for Thomas McGuane, who has been known most of his career as a kind of "language star," the vocation of writing becomes with each successive book more of an attempt to come to grips with "a larger piece of territory, a larger slice of humanity."[31] For both of these writers, the crucial issue becomes finally the environment, the search for a meaningful and responsible connection to the natural world.

In both *Animal Dreams* and *Nobody's Angel*, this search comes about through a crucial encounter with an American Indian. The encounter in *Animal Dreams* is a sexual one. Loyd Peregrina is Codi's lover as well as her teacher. According to Loyd, Man's proper relation to Mother Earth is that of a "houseguest," not an exploiter of natural resources. In *Nobody's Angel*, the encounter is more complex. Playing opposite Patrick's cowboy is the Cheyenne David Catches, sometime hired hand on the Heart Bar and Mary Fitzpatrick's former lover.

Catches, unlike most Native Americans in our literature, is an "educated man," a thoroughly modern Indian who nevertheless retains a strong sense of his people's history. After Mary's suicide, and before his own showdown with Catches, Patrick asks his grandfather to tell him about the former hand. He was some use, the old man allows; he worked a long day; but then, "after that was done, he'd try to tell you how it was" (123). Already having Mary "about half made over," Catches sets out to "make an Indian" out of her grandfather by giving him "the feeling he'd know where Mary had gone" in her fits of depression (123–24).

To Patrick, who doesn't share his grandfather's respect for the "Old Ones," this is all part of "the world-wide aborigine credit bureau," the tendency among whites to think that Indians "are the only ones with coherent attitudes" on subjects like the earth or "doom" (120). When Catches arrives at the ranch after Mary's funeral, he and Patrick face off in a mock duel that has more in common with a drinking bout than an actual fight. Each man carries a knife, but the real contest involves words. At issue, as Catches points out, is Mary:

> "Do you think you helped Mary an awful lot, being an Army officer who kind of looked down on her no matter how much she thought of you?"
> They drank another glass of whiskey before Patrick answered: "Is that what happened?"
> "You didn't save her. I'm saying that."
> "Maybe *you* should have saved her," said Patrick. "And I didn't look down on her. I neglected her. It's different."
> "You didn't do jack shit."
> "This is a pretty state of affairs," said Patrick. "Who's to pour our whiskey?"
> "I'll do it." Catches refilled the glasses.

"I have something you can take to the powwows," Patrick said. "You'll be the talk of the town." He left the room for a moment.

It was the sheet Mary had painted of herself and the baby. He draped it over the shoulders of David Catches.

"This was Mary's way of saying, '*Adios, amigos.*' I want you to have it for whatever gala occasions you chaps have down on the reservation, social events that inevitably produce the Budweiser flu and well-known Cheyenne jalopy crashes. Having said that, we will now drink heap more deathbed whiskey. You didn't take care of her."

"What care could you take of her? She was a grown woman." Catches stopped. "Besides, we are now to the point where one of us is inclined to kill the other." (126–27)

Mary, as we know, is the victim of "the connection [the Fitzpatrick family] never had," the "absence that was perilously ignored" (86). David Catches, who understands this all too well, stands in judgment of the entire family. As a Plains Indian, a Northern Cheyenne, Catches symbolizes the importance of the group over the individual, and as Mary's lover and the one person who tried to save her, he is the only character in the novel who stands on moral ground. Patrick's only defense in such a situation, as in so many other situations in the novel, is whiskey and the solipsism it implies. He will outdrink David Catches, and by doing so will prove himself equal to him in other matters: "Patrick thought, This Cheyenne is going to buckle under the sour mash. He thinks he's got something for me to buckle under; but it's going to be a cold day in hell. I'm going to ice this redskin" (128–29). But when this ploy fails, as it ultimately must, Patrick is forced to admit that it was Catches who had the more real connection with Mary. "She was more to me than she was to you," Catches claims. "Do you deny that?" "I don't deny it," Patrick says. In doing so, he "absolutely let something break in the name of some small, even miserable decency, something in its way perfect and unmissed by David Catches" (137).

In his encounter with David Catches, Patrick is made to come face to face with what is missing in his own life. Like Loyd Peregrina in *Animal Dreams,* Catches is "of the land"; he belongs in Montana whether he has a ranch to run or not. The ancient bones both Patrick and his grandfather unearth at different times in the novel are Cheyenne bones, the bones of David Catches's people. Patrick Fitzpatrick, despite his family's history in the region, will never be anything more than what he is at the beginning of *Nobody's Angel,* "a fourth-generation cowboy outsider, an educated man, a whiskey addict and until very recently a professional soldier" (4). His inheritance is one of isolation, not community, nor "connection," nor even, as it turns out, love. For the one thing that most haunts Patrick after his encounter with his iconic adversary is "the impact of Catches' love of Mary": "Even after Mary's death, it meant more than anything he had. Patrick was closest to it with Claire, and that was not very close" (141).

For Codi Noline, things turn out differently. She discovers her deepest connection with the land through her marriage to Loyd Peregrina, but even before this, she unearths the secret that has been kept from her all her life: that she does in fact descend from one of the nine original blue-eyed Gracela sisters, and hence belongs to a living, celebrated family "with bones in the ground for roots" (165). Knowing this, all is changed. She is even ready, after a few short discussions with Loyd, to participate in the Pueblo worship of Mother Earth:

> It was a new angle on religion, for me. I felt a little embarrassed for my blunt interrogation. And the more I thought about it, even more embarrassed for my bluntly utilitarian culture. "The way they tell us Anglos, God put the earth here for us to use, westward-ho. Like a special little playground."
> Loyd said, "Well, that explains a lot."
> It explained a hell of a lot . . .
> I remembered Loyd one time saying he'd die for the land. And I thought he'd meant patriotism. I'd had no idea. I wondered what he saw when he looked at the Black Mountain mine: the pile of dead tailings, a mountain cannibalizing its own guts and soon to destroy the living trees and home lives of Grace. . . .
> To people who think of themselves as God's houseguests, American enterprise must seem arrogant beyond belief. Or stupid. A nation of amnesiacs, proceeding as if there were no other day but today. Assuming the land could also forget what had been done to it. (240–41)

It is but one short step from here to burying Doc Homer for good and giving birth to a child of her own, one to replace the baby lost in adolescence. By the end of the novel, Codi has come full circle, earned her name of "order in the cosmos." She has returned home for good. Two years after the mining company is defeated by a group of townspeople of which Codi is a fundamental part, the earth itself makes a comeback, with gold flowers beginning to grow "like a renegade crop in the long, straight troughs of the old irrigation ditches" (341).

The narrative of return as we have traced it in these two novels tells the story of coming home to a new sense of the self. It is not about returning to childhood, the lost father, or, as Thomas Wolfe once wrote, those "old forms and systems of things which once seemed everlasting but which are changing all the time."[32] Patrick Fitzpatrick's return is doomed from the start for just these reasons. It is the dark side of return, return as regression, going backward. Codi Noline's return, by comparison, seems hopeful in the extreme, reflecting what novelists like Kingsolver would like to believe about our possibilities for the future, both in terms of our society and our literature. It will be a future, Kingsolver implies, that we will make for ourselves.

6 / New West, or, the Bo

6 / New West, or, the Borderlands

Aside from being narratives of return, books like Kingsolver's *Animal Dreams* and McGuane's *Nobody's Angel* are also westerns or, in the parlance of the region they depict, "new westerns," novels of the "New West." As such, they are part of one of the most exciting developments in contemporary American fiction—one that in many ways epitomizes the general direction American literature itself has taken in the wake of postmodernism.

The current renaissance in western writing dates back at least to 1978, when Elliot Anderson, editor of the literary magazine *TriQuarterly,* asked William Kittredge and Steven Krauzer to select writers for a special issue on western stories. Kittredge and Krauzer solicited work from a number of prominent writers, including Dorothy Johnson, Thomas McGuane, Richard Ford, Ivan Doig, Leslie Marmon Silko, and Cormac McCarthy, declaring in their introduction to the issue that western writing circa 1978 was at a point "similar to that of southern American writing in the early 1930s when a major regional voice, in the persons of William Faulkner, Robert Penn Warren, Eudora Welty, Andrew Lytle, and Katherine Anne Porter, was beginning to be heard."[1]

This was a daring comparison, to say the least, but Kittredge and Krauzer believed that the genesis of both movements was remarkably similar. "Just as the old south was gone," they wrote, "the old west is gone. Free of the need to write either out of the mythology or against it, the writers of the new west, responding to the variety and quickness of life in their territory, are experiencing a period of enormous vitality" (12).

Several of the claims made by Kittredge and Krauzer in their introduction were picked up in a long article Russell Martin published in the *New York Times* in December 1981. Martin, a fourth-generation Coloradan then completing the first of two New West anthologies, expanded the growing western canon to include writers like N. Scott Momaday, James Welch, John Nichols, and Rudolfo Anaya, arguing that the most distinctive thing about the new writing was its diversity, its attempt to "represent all of the region's ethnic and social variety."[2]

The cowboy novel, once thought to be gone forever, had in recent years returned, dressed this time in the robes of literature instead of the rags of pulp fiction. But alongside it had arisen something altogether new, the Native American novel as written by Native Americans. Meanwhile, with influences from both north and south of the border, came the Nuevo Mexicano novel as fathered by Rudolfo Anaya. Each of these subdivisions of the new western had something different to say about the history, the mythology, and what Kittredge and Krauzer had called "the quickness of life" in the New West.

For Martin, however, the New West's relationship to myth was somewhat more complicated than Kittredge and Krauzer, in their enthusiasm, had implied. Far from being "free" of mythology, new western writers had to take the lingering mythology of the Old West head-on, "or at least get it out of their way," before they could "take a critical view of a region that had become, in many ways, a parody of itself." Beyond this, the writing of the New West was "focused on the landscape," just as Old West tales had been, although that landscape was no longer a pristine wilderness but "shaped by the West's modern mix of gaudy rhinestone pretensions and grand energy-rich aspirations."

Taken together, Martin's three main points about the writing of the New West—its diversity, its complicated relationship with myth, and its focus on the land—describe a literary situation that is at least as rich as that inherited by the southern writers of the 1930s. But it is also quite different. The authors of the southern renaissance were writing in the aftermath of a crushing military defeat and humiliating occupation that was complicated by the region's collective guilt over slavery. The historical background of the New West renaissance is not so clear-cut, including pseudo-military success for some, defeat and near-annihilation for others, and a lingering feeling of loss felt by most (but not all) for what had been done in the process to the western landscape.

These differences are perhaps best illustrated by the central images or motifs we associate with traditional southern and western writing. The central image in southern writing, as Leslie Fiedler argued in *The Return of the Vanishing American* (1968), is the ruined or decaying plantation house—

Sutpen's Hundred, for example, in Faulkner's *Absalom, Absalom!* or Tara in *Gone with the Wind*. The classic southern story is about the fall of this house, which is to say, the ultimate failure of plantation society to live up to its pretensions as "the family writ large," to use a phrase popularized by Richard King in *A Southern Renaissance: The Cultural Awakening of the American South, 1930–1955* (1980). Although they were treated as children and frequently called "Aunt" or "Uncle," African slaves rarely received recognition as family members, even when, as was frequently the case, they were related to their owners by blood.

The central image in western writing, by contrast, is the lone rider traversing the western landscape. The classic western story, told from the perspective of this rider, is about the moment when he discovers that he is not alone: cresting a nearby ridge is a group of dangerous aliens or, in the parlance of the Old Western, "hostile Indians." Just as old as this story, although never as popular, is its reverse: the moment when a group of Indians, going about the age-old business of hunting, suddenly encounters the white man in their territory, and through this encounter begin to understand everything that he portends. Henceforth all will be changed, for if the plantation house in southern literature represents the idea of society as the family "writ large," the lone rider in western literature represents all of western expansion "writ small." Southern literature is about the family—who is in it, who is not; western literature, at its heart, is about landscape—who it belongs to, how it should be lived in—and the encounter in that landscape with an alien "other."[3]

By making landscape the yardstick against which all western writing was to be judged, Martin was echoing what might be called the gospel of the western form. "The Western novel," wrote John R. Milton in *The Novel of the American West* (1980), "to be authentic, must be honest with the region which gives it birth, must . . . be a novel of the land, a novel in which the land actually becomes a character, a force to be reckoned with, part of the conflict as well as the background."[4] Seen from this perspective, contemporary western writing springs, at least in part, from a concern with place.

If the literature of the Old West, essentially about conquest, begins in the fine memoirs and autobiographies of the late nineteenth and early twentieth century—books like Mark Twain's *Roughing It* (1872), Charles A. Siringo's *A Texas Cowboy* (1885), Andy Adams's *The Log of a Cowboy* (1903) and Teddy "Blue" Abbott's *We Pointed Them North* (1939)—the literature of the New West, about survival and preservation, begins in such haunting, poetic works of nonfiction as Ivan Doig's *This House of Sky* (1978), Gretel Erhlich's *Solace of Open Spaces* (1985), and William Least Heat-Moon's *PrairyErth* (1991). In these works and others like them, the western landscape is the first thing brought to life. The world of Doig's book starts, quite precisely, along the "south fork of Sixteenmile Creek," under "the fir-dark flanks of Hatfield Mountain," far back "among the high spilling slopes of the Bridger Range of southeastern Montana." Out of this exact and exacting environment Doig spins a story of a family half at odds and half in harmony with the elements. Gretel Ehrlich begins her book five days out in the Badlands of Wyoming, a hailstorm coming on, proceeding from there to consider how living and working in such a place, with its hundred mile views, "is to lose the distinction between foreground and background." William Least Heat-Moon begins his monumental work, the *Moby-Dick* of all writing about place, at sundown in the middle of the Flint Hills of Kansas—where the West itself begins—"in quest of the land and what informs it."[5]

In books such as these, the western landscape rises above mere setting, as John R. Milton required, to become a character in its own right, an overwhelming influence on the lives of men and women. Out of the immensity and omnipresent threat of the western land come a predictable array of desires: to know it, tame it, own it, exploit it. But also these: to live in it, to worship and preserve it. "The West is less a place than a process," Wallace Stegner wrote in *Where the Bluebird Sings to the Lemonade Springs* (1992). "And the western landscape that it has taken us a century and three quarters to learn about, and partially adapt our farming, our social institutions, and our aesthetic perceptions to, has now become our most valuable natural resource, as subject to raid and ruin as the more concrete resources that have suffered from our rapacity."[6]

The new western takes up the exact rendering of landscape as we have it in Doig, Erhlich, and Least Heat-Moon, and adds to it the drama of the West's teetering between rapacity and preservation, the challenge (often the failure) of its diverse peoples to live together.

Beyond this, contemporary fiction of the New West, like contemporary American fiction more generally, is characterized by its hybrid nature, its exploration of a series of "borders" that exist in the authors themselves, the society they live in and attempt to depict, and especially in the work they produce. Contemporary New West writers are typically "breeds," to use an Old West expression. They are transplanted southerners (Cormac McCarthy, Richard Ford), or easterners come West (John Nichols), or westerners educated in the East (Louise Erdrich). Most of them have passed through academia on their way to a world view that is often a sophisticated form of primitivism. This is especially true of Native American authors, many of whom are literally "breeds": part Laguna Pueblo, part Mexican, part white, in the case of Leslie Marmon Silko; part Chippewa, part French and German, in the case of Louise Erdrich; part Blackfeet, part Gros Ventre, part Irish, in the case of James Welch. The New West these writers depict is indeed "diverse," as Russell Martin notes, but it is also "divided," a place of divisions and borders, and not merely in terms of geography, such as mountain ranges, deserts, and rivers, but also in terms of neighborhoods—Anglo farming and ranching communities, Spanish pueblos, Indian reservations—and languages.

Formally, the new western explores the borders between realism and modernism, the *Bildungsroman* and the picaresque narrative, Old West mythology and New West revision, the oral tradition and the written tradition, English and Spanish and any number of Native American tongues. The characters in New West stories, when they are nominally Indians or Hispanics, often exhibit a duality of blood and consciousness that forces them to choose between assimilation and tradition. They are "coyotes," "half and half," and mostly uncomfortably so. Even when New West characters are nominally "white," they must choose between the old, land-based way of life represented by the horse and ranching, and a new way of life represented by the automobile and oil production. They become "renegades," identifying with the great Horse Culture of the Plains Indians, or, in the most visible form of selling out, they become car dealers or real estate executives. On a broad, metaphorical level, the choices these characters face represent not only the current array of choices faced by the West as a region, but also those faced by America as a society, for as Frederick Turner once wrote, "The meaning of America still resides, somehow, in the West."[7]

Old-style, "horse opera" westerns began to be declared dead at about the same time the novel was declared dead, which is to say sometime between the end of World War II and the beginning of America's involvement in Vietnam. There were plenty of reasons for the demise of the western, particularly in its film version: overproduction by Hollywood; the advent of television; new ratings systems based on demographics, which revealed that upscale viewers, and hence advertisers, were no longer interested; the reexamination of cultural myths occasioned by the war in Vietnam; the feeling, declared by academic critics, that the genre had exhausted its possibilities as myth.[8] Looked at from a twenty-first-century perspective, however, the so-called death of the western, and more particularly of the cowboy novel, seems more like a pause—and a pregnant one at that.

Despite untold efforts to kill him off, the cowboy, America's dominant mythic figure, has already passed his hundredth birthday. Charles A. Siringo's autobiographical account of his life on the range, *A Texas Cowboy* (1885), was published while the West was still full of real or would-be cowboys, and many of them, including Teddy Roosevelt himself, read the book. By the time Roosevelt's friend Owen Wister published *The Virginian*, in 1902, the cowboy was already firmly in place in the American consciousness as a stoic, brave man who paved the way for the "taming" of the West even as he himself, like Huck Finn, resisted civilization. The first western movie, *The Great Train Robbery*, had already been made (in New Jersey) by 1903, and one of this film's stars, Gilbert B. Anderson, went on to become the first cinematic cowboy hero in the 1910 movie *Bronco Billy's Redemption*.[9]

To get where he is in of our pantheon of heroes, the cowboy beat out an entire gallery of western types—the mountain man, the forty-niner, the pony express rider, the buffalo skinner—most of whom came before him and many of whom better represented the virtues we associate with heroism. As Walter Van Tilburg Clark observed in his introduction to A.B. Guthrie Jr.'s novel *The Big Sky* (1947), it was the mountain man, not the cowboy, who was the direct descendant of Cooper's backwoods Leatherstocking, the only earlier candidate for the pantheon, "and he was a more complete representative of the type, because he moved in a much vaster and more dangerous wilderness, and separated himself much more completely from every manifestation of unheroic civilization."[10]

Since his unlikely canonization, the cowboy has survived attacks from realists who point out his obvious inadequacies and from pop culture critics who argue that his obvious attractions have been exploited beyond recuperation. "The cowboy in practice," wrote Wallace Stegner, "was and is an overworked, underpaid hireling, almost as homeless and dispossessed as a modern crop worker, and his fabled independence was and is chiefly the privilege of quitting his job in order to go looking for another just as bad."[11]

"The cowboy hero has always been a commodity," wrote William Savage Jr., author of *The Cowboy Hero* (1979). "He may be part of a mythic construct of the American past, and his image in popular culture may be rife with sociological and psychological implications, but he exists in the first place because of a superior act of marketing."[12]

More recently, the cowboy has been taken to task by New Historicists who complain that his WASP persona leaves out entire groups and ideologies. The cowboy, like Christopher Columbus, is an insult to women and minorities. Finally, the cowboy has become the favorite punching bag of environmentalists who argue that his connection to the land is skewed in favor of production. "Today," writes Sharman Apt Russell in her book *Kill the Cowboy: A Battle of Mythology in the New West,* "there is much more to say about the cowboy. Dreams, as we discover again and again, are half seduction. And the cowboy, the seductive cowboy, has a dark side."[13]

What is it about the cowboy that makes him, even today, such a seductive figure? To begin with, he is an equestrian, a man on a horse moving restlessly through a massive landscape. The horse gives the cowboy mobility, the most persistent trait of the American in the twentieth century. Cowboys famously shun the idea of going on foot, where they are lesser men somehow, and certainly more in danger, than they are when mounted. On the other hand, and despite his mobility, the cowboy remains connected to the land. He lives close to the earth and is constantly in the presence of animals. The earth is his bed, we are told in the dime novels, the sky his blanket. Thus the cowboy represents the best of both worlds: the rambling instinct Americans have demonstrated since at least the early nineteenth century and a countervailing desire to remain connected to the land, the single good place.

The cowboy, then, is the ultimate border figure. Everything about him is a contradiction, albeit usually a pleasing one. On the one hand, he is a knight errant, an embodiment of the medieval chivalry southerners picked up from reading too much Sir Walter Scott; on the other hand, he is an outlaw and a drifter, a man thoroughly at home in a world filled with violence.

If the "horse opera" died a slow death in the mid-1960s, its resurrection took place in the mid-1980s—23 June 1985, to be exact. On that day, a single page of the *Los Angeles Times'* book review section carried news of two important developments on the horizon of western literature.[14] The first of these was publication of Larry McMurtry's long-awaited trail-drive novel, *Lonesome Dove,* which would go on to win the Pulitzer Prize for fiction and become one of the most successful westerns ever written. The second was publication of a strange, blood-soaked tale of western expansion called *Blood Meridian, or The Evening Redness in the West,* which announced, in quieter fashion than *Lonesome Dove,* the arrival of a new talent in western writing. Like the legions of Civil War–era southerners before him, Cormac McCarthy, the author once called the "ghost of American letters," the "best American writer nobody ever heard of," had moved west into new territory.[15]

Both novels were based on a panoply of sources—historical accounts,

Hollywood westerns, the nineteenth-century American novel—and both attempted to revise the western myth, though in doing so they often simply intensified or reinforced it. *Lonesome Dove,* for example, owed as much to *Red River,* Howard Hawks's 1947 trail-drive film, as to Teddy "Blue" Abbott's *We Pointed Them North* or J. Evetts Haley's biography of Charles Goodnight, *Charles Goodnight: Cowman and Plainsman* (1936). *Blood Meridian* drew on various historical accounts of the American Southwest, especially Samuel E. Chamberlain's *My Confession,* from which the characters of both John Joel Glanton and Judge Holden were taken.[16]

By investing a modicum of realism into his portrait of the trail herder, McMurtry sought to revise two equally absurd versions of the cowboy hero, one of which tended to portray the cowboy as a guitar-picking "natural man," the other of which tended to make him out to be a gunslinging outlaw. Yet the result was far from being purely revisionist. "All of Mr. McMurtry's anti-mythic groundwork," wrote one critic, "his refusal to glorify the West, works to reinforce the strength of the traditionally mythic parts of *Lonesome Dove,* by making it far more credible than the familiar horse operas. These are real people, and they are still larger than life."[17]

Indeed, if the success of *Lonesome Dove* proved nothing else, it proved that realistic, historically researched cowboys are *more popular* than the gunslingers and guitar pickers of the dime novel and B western, and this is in part because McMurtry's characters expand, rather than level out, the contradictions of the border figure. They are good and evil, lovers and killers, homesteaders in both Texas and Montana and relentlessly driven to the road.

Cormac McCarthy's treatment of western myth in *Blood Meridian* displayed a similar mixture of debunking and intensification. Calling the book "the bloodiest novel ever written," Jonathan Yardley questioned McCarthy's graveyard vision of the nineteenth-century West, his nonstop depiction of blood and gore. "If what McCarthy is up to is demythologizing the Old West," Yardley wrote, "then it can only be said that he has taken the myth from one extreme to the other."[18] Yet in the character of Judge Holden, McCarthy created a figure of extreme violence who was also highly educated and whose tastes in music and literature were classical.

Aside from its status as a western, *Blood Meridian* powerfully demonstrates how the best contemporary American fiction situates itself among the great books in the tradition. For his part, McCarthy believes in what he calls an "ugly fact": "books are made out of books." "The novel," he declared in a rare interview, "depends for its life on the novels that have been written."[19]

This statement seems to me a good place to begin thinking about a book like *Blood Meridian,* which comes so clearly out of the books that came before it. On the one hand, and exactly one hundred years before *Blood Meridian* (1985), we have *The Adventures of Huckleberry Finn* (1884), which, like McCarthy's novel, features a fourteen-year-old "kid" who leaves an alcoholic father and strikes out for a territory where he will confront the evil, ignorance, and violence of man's most basic condition. The time frame of the two novels is nearly identical, *Blood Meridian* beginning in 1849 and *Huckleberry Finn* taking place "forty or fifty years" before 1884, which is to say, sometime between 1834 and 1844. On the other hand, and published precisely fifty years after *Huckleberry Finn* and fifty years before *Blood Meridian,* we have Faulkner's *Absalom, Absalom!* (1936), a book that also features a fourteen-year-old protagonist (Thomas Sutpen) who also abandons an alcoholic father to strike out on his own in dangerous territory. Like *Huckleberry Finn* and *Blood Meridian, Absalom, Absalom!* is set almost entirely in the mid-nineteenth century, hovering around the crucial decade before the Civil War. This time period (1849–50) takes on an additional importance when we consider the other book that has influenced *Blood Meridian* in a profound way, namely, Melville's *Moby-Dick* (1851). From the single interview we have with McCarthy, we know that *Moby-Dick* is his favorite book. We also know that Faulkner thought highly of *Moby-Dick* and was in fact in the process of reading it aloud to his daughter during the composition of *Absalom, Absalom!*

These somewhat touristic remarks take on a new meaning when we consider that *Blood Meridian* belongs to a long line of American novels that in one sense or another meditate upon the moral consequences of American power, especially in the crucial decade of the nineteenth century. *Huckleberry Finn* and *Absalom, Absalom!* are both concerned with the historical signi-ficance of slavery and the broader issue of race relations, and *Absalom, Absalom!* especially figures these as the result of an Ahabian will to power. Thomas Sutpen, it is often remarked, is a wronged Huckleberry Finn who grows into a kind of Ahab, seeking the obliteration of past wrongs through an explosive will to power that ignores all moral consequences. The downfall of his "design," which stands as a metaphor for the "design" of the South, comes about when his *sons* rise up against him. From here, it is only a small step to the last text that figures into all of the above, namely, the King James Version of the Bible, which supplies the names of both Ahab and Absalom, the theme of sons rising against their fathers, and indeed, the peculiar linguistic force we find in all of these authors.

Blood Meridian bears the marks of its inheritance in a number of ways, many of which I have already alluded to. In the first place, there is the texture of McCarthy's prose, a tapestry of all that is good (and bad) in the Bible, Melville, and especially Faulkner. The tortured syntax and nineteenth-century rhythms are alleviated only occasionally by the tight, beautiful, bare-bones descriptions of the natural world we see coming out of Twain. The echoes of Faulkner are everywhere. "A legion of horribles, hundreds in number, half naked or clad in costumes attic or biblical or wardrobed out of a fevered dream," begins a sentence that spans two pages in the novel.[20] The strings of adjectives following the few, spare nouns in this is typical of the homage McCarthy continually pays Faulkner. But then there is also writing like this to consider: "He rose and turned toward the lights of town. The tide-pools bright as smelterpots among the dark rocks where the phosphorescent seacrabs clambered back. Passing through the salt grass he looked back. The horse had not moved. A ship's light winked in the swells. The colt stood against the horse with its head down and the horse was watching, out there past men's knowing, where the stars are drowning and whales ferry their vast souls through the black and seamless sea" (304). Pure poetry—and of all things, most reminiscent of Huck's raptures on his raft in the Mississippi. It is interesting that to achieve this effect McCarthy turns not only to the natural world—the site of nearly all his most lyrical passages—but also to water, the sea, and, quite ominously, when you think about it, a *whale*.

This brings us to the second, most obvious, influence on *Blood Meridian*—the presence of something decidedly Ahabian in the figure of Judge Holden. As Vereen M. Bell has written, "To point out that the one articulate spokesman of this novel, Judge Holden, is a direct descendent of Melville's Captain Ahab is to summon up an American tradition—the compulsion to make war upon the unknown, to challenge destiny itself. . . . To add that he is perhaps even more like Conrad's Kurtz is to fix [the book] in a moral category that deals with the psychopathology of conquest." Ultimately, Bell concludes, the Judge is "a more terrifying figure than either Ahab or Kurtz because his madness is wholly under control and because he rather than justice—divine or social—prevails."[21]

In *Moby-Dick,* Melville unfolds his allegory of man's confrontation with evil on the high seas—long associated in the western tradition with the desert, the site of McCarthy's book. In both of these novels, a ragtag group of men made up of many races and creeds becomes involved in a hunt led by a madman. And both Ahab and Judge Holden know without asking who among their men fails to join the hunt wholeheartedly. As the Judge says to the kid, "Did you think I could not know? You were mutinous. You alone reserved in your soul some corner of clemency for the heathen" (299). The one word—mutinous—a word we normally associate with the order of ships on the sea, brings all the difficult questions raised by *Moby-Dick* to bear on *Blood Meridian*.

The third major aspect of *Blood Meridian* that brings it clearly into the tradition I have been discussing is its use of the narrative of fathers and sons. Of all the abstract discussions initiated by Judge Holden—discussions that recall, at different times, Voltaire, Kant, Nietzsche, Heidegger—the most interesting, from my point of view, is the one in which the Judge explains, by way of parable, which tribe of Indians built the ruined dwellings his men come to in their scalp hunting. The story might be called the parable of the lost father, since it deals with, as the judge says, "a son whose father's existence in this world is historical and speculative even before the son has entered it" (145). This son, who, we later find, "went away to the west and . . . himself became a killer of men," is "in a bad way. All his life he carries before him the idol of a perfection to which he can never attain" (145). Likewise, the Indians the Judge and his men hunt "wander these canyons to the sound of ancient laughter" (146). "The tools, the art, the building" of the ancient Pueblo ancestors—"these things stand in judgment on the latter races" (146). And so it is also with the Judge's men, many of them descendants of Europe's most advanced civilizations, who now wander the deserts of the American West, little more than primitives. And so it is finally with McCarthy himself, who would appear to understand how the great books of the past stand in judgment on the works of all later writers, even as the best work of later writers alters all that came before.

As treatments of Old West subject matter, *Lonesome Dove* and *Blood Meridian* have little to say in a direct way about specific New West themes such as the westerner's relationship to his environment. Nevertheless, by presenting a history of the origins of the contemporary West, especially the origins of its myths, these novels do tell us something about how the New West came to be what it is today.

Lonesome Dove was McMurtry's first novel set in the nineteenth-century West. His first westerns had been set in twentieth-century Texas and had dealt with the closing of the range, the end of the cattle empire just in its infancy in *Lonesome Dove*. In this early work, McMurtry has written, he was trying to deal "in a small way with a large theme: the move from the land to the cities" that characterized so much western life in the postwar years. "The cattle range had become the oil patch," he writes, "the dozer cap had replaced the Stetson almost overnight." Yet, as McMurtry goes on to observe, even as this change took place, "the myth of the cowboy grew purer every year because there were so few actual cowboys left to contradict it."[22]

It is just this paradox that informs McMurtry's border novels. Both his Thalia trilogy of novels—*Horseman, Pass By* (1961), *Leaving Cheyenne* (1963), and *The Last Picture Show* (1966)—and the later *Lonesome Dove* (1985) are structured by an archetypal journeying motif that works, as Janis P. Stout has noted, as both an invitation to adventure and a metaphor for cultural loss. In the early novels, Stout writes, the impulse to journey is "chiefly a desire for experience, and the more fully a character identifies himself with the ranching way of life the less he travels." In McMurtry's later work, journeying becomes "a metaphor for modern life itself, which is seen as being impoverished by the demise of the old traditions and the lack of new structures of meaning and allegiance."[23] In each case it is the cowboy, in his various incarnations as trail herder, rancher, Texas Ranger, and rodeo performer, who demonstrates the paradoxes inherent in the border figure.

In *Horseman, Pass By,* the old, ranching way of life is represented by the cowman Homer Bannon, the protagonist's grandfather, who despises oil wells and vows that as long as he's alive "there'll be no holes punched in this land."[24] Modern life is represented by Homer Bannon's stepson Hud, a Cadillac-driving cowboy who wants the old man gone so he can turn the ranch over to oil exploration, thus freeing himself from its constant demands.

The old way of life is defined by its independence and freedom, its lack of—indeed, contempt for—contact with the outside world. The costs of this freedom, however, are high. When ranchers brag, as they sometimes do, about putting one hundred thousand miles on a pickup "without ever leaving the place," they are doing more than talking up the size of their spreads. They are also expressing how little real mobility they have, how tied they are to the land. Cattle must be looked after constantly, summer, spring, fall, and winter, which is why farmers, in their longstanding feud with ranchers, often refer to their rivals as "babysitters."

Oil wells, McMurtry's symbol for the modern age in Texas, don't require this kind of attention, and the profits they generate offer one a different kind of freedom than that offered by ranching. (When told he should stay home in case it rains, Hud, who hates to be tied down, replies, "If I sat around an' waited for ever little piss cloud to turn into a tornado, I'd never go anywhere"

[12].) Yet if the old way of life ties one to the land, the new way only leads one into exile. "That's no way of life," says Jesse, the ex-rodeo performer who works on the Bannon ranch. "You boys think stayin' in one place is tiresome, just wait till you see that goddamn road comin' at you ever morning. And still comin' late that evenin' and sometimes way into the night. I run that road for ten years and never caught up with nothin'" (79).

Lonnie Bannon, McMurtry's protagonist in *Horseman, Pass By,* is caught in the borderland between these two worlds. On the one hand, he identifies almost entirely with his grandfather and fears and distrusts Hud. On the other hand, he is drawn to movement, listening wistfully to the cars that pass by the ranch on a nearby highway, wondering, each time he sees a train pass at night, "where in the world the people . . . were going night after night" (6). To Lonnie, "it was exciting to think about a train" (6), whereas the nightly Zephyr only makes Homer Bannon feel tired. In the struggle between Homer and Hud that drives the plot of the novel, Lonnie stands firmly with his grand-father's moral code, but he is also attracted by Hud's restlessness and recognizes an element of it in himself.

In the end, however, Lonnie never gets a chance to decide between the two; the decision is made for him by a changing world. After the death of his grandfather signals the end of the old way of life, Lonnie has no choice but to be swept into the new. By the novel's final pages he has become its most footloose character, hitching a ride away from the ranch without even knowing where he is going or if he is ever coming back. McMurtry universalizes the border condition with the novel's final line, when Lonnie says of the truck driver who picks him up, "he reminded me of everyone I knew" (143).

Although Cormac McCarthy's foray into the western was formally announced with *Blood Meridian,* it actually began ten years earlier, when the author pulled up stakes in Knoxville, Tennessee, and started spending most of his time in the American Southwest, especially El Paso, Texas. General notice of McCarthy's defection from southern letters was given at the end of *Suttree* (1979), when McCarthy's semiautobiographical protagonist, Cornelius Suttree, hitches a ride out of Knoxville and into "the vectors of nowhere," leaving behind him "the sad purlieus of the dead immured with the bones of friends and forebears."[25] Before *Blood Meridian,* McCarthy was identified as a southern writer, a rather self-conscious carrier of the Faulkner tradition whose novels, mostly rural in setting and gothic in character, were acclaimed without ever reaching a wide audience. No more, McCarthy seemed to be saying at the end of *Suttree,* would he be concerned with the specific burdens of southern history.

Not everyone was happy about McCarthy's change in locale. Southern and eastern critics worried that he had abandoned the country he knew intimately to try his hand at myth. "McCarthy should go home [to the South] and have another, closer, look," declared Terence Moran in his review of *Blood Meridian.* "He'll find the real devil soon enough there."[26] Western critics, meanwhile, were slow to admit that an outsider could do much of importance with the cowboy myth. There's a longstanding tendency in criticism of the western to separate writers into two distinct groups: those who were born and raised in the region (the "natives") and those who moved there or merely happened upon it (the "immigrants"). The distinction is so important, and so finely drawn, that even as thoroughly western a writer as Walter Van Tilburg Clark is considered "an adopted westerner rather than a native" simply because his family didn't arrive in Nevada until Clark was nine years old.[27] As for Owen Wister, author of the first cowboy novel, or Zane Grey, whose *Riders of the Purple Sage* (1912) did much to establish the form of the horse opera, they are, respectively, a "Philadelphia lawyer" and "an Ohio dentist."[28] Judged by this standard, even James Fenimore Cooper, considered by many the father of the western, turns out to be little more than an imposter, for Cooper wrote *The Prairie* (1823) without ever having stepped foot in the West.

But these are academic concerns at best. Today it seems likely that McCarthy will be remembered more for his westerns than for the early work set in the South. If McMurtry's return to the western in *Lonesome Dove* brought him his biggest commercial success since the Thalia trilogy, Cormac McCarthy's adoption of western subject matter in the novels after *Blood Meridian* brought him his first wide notice. Whereas his southern novels, *The Orchard Keeper* (1965), *Outer Dark* (1968), *Child of God* (1973), and *Suttree* (1979), rarely sold three thousand hardcover copies, McCarthy's second western, *All the Pretty Horses* (1992), sold 180,000 copies in hardcover and won both the National Book Award and the National Book Critics Circle Award for fiction.

Set in the west Texas of 1949, a border of sorts between old and new worlds, *All the Pretty Horses,* volume 1 of McCarthy's Border Trilogy, deals with the same themes McMurtry had treated in *Horseman, Pass By*—the end of the cattle empire and the coming of the modern age of oil exploration on the southern high plains. As Gail Moore Morrison has noted, *All the Pretty Horses* is archetypal in structure, built around four basic movements: Dispossession, Wandering, Discovery of Paradise, and Expulsion. The novel begins, in other words, where *Horseman, Pass By* had closed: with the dispossessed son of rancher forebears taking to the open road.[29]

John Grady Cole, like Lonnie Bannon, has just buried his grandfather, the last Grady and the last of the old-time cowmen, and at sixteen is deemed too young to take over the family ranch. His father, traumatized by his imprisonment at Goshee in World War II, is no help to him, and his mother, an aspiring actress, has other plans—oil interests—in mind for the ranch. The first few pages of the novel, which give us a picture of John Grady Cole riding along "the old Comanche road," the western sun "coppering" in his face, inform us that this is "a man come to the end of something," a man who identifies more with the lost Horse Culture of the Plains Indians than with a modern, mechanized world that has left his father a shell of his former self and his grandfather on the brink of bankruptcy.[30] John Grady's way is the old way, and there's little room for that in a Texas on the brink of the oil empire. As the banker who informs John Grady of his parents' divorce explains to him, "Son, not everybody thinks that life on a cattle ranch in west Texas is the next best thing to dyin and goin to heaven. . . . If it was a payin proposition that'd be one thing. But it aint" (17). The end of the ranching empire is indeed "a sorry piece of business," but "the way it is is the way it's goin to be" (17). Like the Comanche warriors who died out before him, John Grady has no choice but to look "south across the plains to Mexico" (6), that borderland that in McCarthy's work as a whole is the last refuge of the old way of life.

As Gail Moore Morrison points out, the trip south into Mexico, which John Grady makes on horseback in the company of his friend Rawlins and the thirteen-year-old Jimmy Blevins, takes the three boys into progressively more rugged and elemental territory. The people and animals they meet along the way become steadily less "civilized," in the sense of attachment to the modern world the boys are fleeing, and the danger represented by Blevins, who appears to have stolen the thoroughbred horse he rides, becomes more and more ominous, leading finally to his separation from John Grady and Rawlins before they reach their destination. Yet we are never in doubt about what John Grady and Rawlins seek in their flight across the border. "Where do you reckon that paradise is at?" Rawlins asks at one point, to which John Grady replies, "That's what I'm here for" (59). On a metaphorical level, the boys are crossing the border between boyhood to manhood, a theme McCarthy will pick up at greater length in *The Crossing* (1994), volume 2 of the Border Trilogy.

The Hacienda de Nuestra Señora de la Purísima Concepción, the boys' ultimate destination, is, as Morrison's explication of the novel's structure implies, a kind of paradise, and their journey toward it is a classic western encounter with landscape. To get there John Grady and Rawlins must cross a desert, rise into the foothills and then the mountains, and come finally to a plateau from which they look down upon "the country of which they'd been told" (93), much as Moses had looked down upon the promised land, and Christ, during his temptation, looked upon all the kingdoms of the earth. This is a country of deep grass "of a kind they'd not seen before," full of fat cattle, wild horses, and waterfowl. Even the lakes and streams and shallow marshes of the valley are full of life.

Just as important, La Purísima is a working ranch, the title to which has been passed down from generation to generation. McCarthy's description of this ranch, with its lofty biblical tones and echoes of Hemingway, assures us that John Grady has traveled back in time to a better place and a more pure relationship between man and the land he inhabits:

> The Hacienda de Nuestra Señora de la Purísima Concepción was a ranch of eleven thousand hectares situated along the edge of the Bolsón de Cuatro Ciénagas in the state of Coahuila. The western sections ran into the Sierra de Anteojo to elevations of nine thousand feet but south and east the ranch occupied part of the broad barrial or basin floor of the bolsón and was well watered with natural springs and clear streams and dotted with marshes and shallow lakes or lagunas. In the lakes and in the streams were species of fish not known elsewhere on earth and birds and lizards and other forms of life as well all long relict here for the desert stretched away on every side.
>
> La Purísima was one of very few ranches in that part of Mexico retaining the full complement of six square leagues of land allotted by the colonizing legislation of eighteen twenty-four and the owner Don Héctor Rocha y Villareal was one of the few hacendados who actually lived on the land he claimed, land which had been in his family for one hundred and seventy years. He was forty-seven years old and he was the first male heir in all that new world lineage to attain such an age.
>
> He ran upwards of a thousand head of cattle on this land. He kept a house in Mexico City where his wife lived. He flew his own airplane. He loved horses. (97)

The story of La Purísima, like most western stories, begins with landscape and moves quickly to the details of ownership, ending finally with the man who now controls the land and the odds of his keeping it. The odds in this case are apparently quite good, insofar as Rocha has lived longer than any other man who tried before him. Contrast this with the situation John Grady has just left behind in Texas:

> The house was built in eighteen seventy-two. Seventy-seven years later his grandfather was still the first man to die in it. What others had lain in state in that

hallway had been carried there on a gate or wrapped in a wagonsheet or delivered crated up in a raw pineboard box with a teamster standing at the door with a bill of lading. The ones that came at all. For the most part they were dead by rumor. A yellowed scrap of newsprint. A letter. A telegram. The original ranch was twenty-three hundred acres out of the Meusebach survey of the Fisher-Miller grant, the original house a oneroom hovel of sticks and wattle. That was in eighteen sixty-six. In that same year the first cattle were driven through what was still Bexar County and across the north end of the ranch and on to Fort Sumner and Denver. Five years later his great-grandfather sent six hundred steers over that same trail and with the money he built the house and by then the ranch was already eighteen thousand acres. In eighteen eighty-three they ran the first barbed wire. By eighty-six the buffalo were gone. That same winter a bad die-up. In eighty-nine Fort Concho was disbanded.

His grandfather was the oldest of eight boys and the only one to live past the age of twenty-five. They were drowned, shot, kicked by horses. They perished in fires. They seemed to fear only dying in bed. The last two were killed in Puerto Rico in eighteen ninety-eight and in that year he married and brought his bride home to the ranch and he must have walked out and stood looking at his holdings and reflected long upon the ways of God and primogeniture. Twelve years later when his wife was carried off in the influenza epidemic they still had no children. A year later he married his dead wife's older sister and year after this the boy's mother was born and that was all the borning that there was. The Grady name was buried with that old man the day the norther blew the lawnchairs over the dead cemetery grass. The boy's name was Cole. John Grady Cole. (6–7)

Comparing the two ranches and the land they encompass, we see that in both cases ownership began with a land grant, and the holding of this land was a challenge one took on at the risk of one's life. Typically the heirs die early and violently. And insofar as neither Don Héctor nor John Grady's grandfather produce a male heir, the future of both ranches, by law of primogeniture, is in question. Here, however, the similarities end. La Purísima is by far the older ranch, having been in Don Héctor's family for one hundred seventy years, whereas the Grady ranch (which apparently doesn't even have a name) lasted all of eighty-three years before being sold to oil interests. Its decline began long before, with the first introduction of barbed wire in 1883 and the first major "die-up" in 1886. Even before this, it could never have rivaled La Purísima in either natural beauty or abundance of wildlife. The only large animals natural to its range, buffalo, died out only twenty years after the ranch was claimed.

The comparative barrenness of the Grady ranch is further indicated by the life of its owner. Whereas Don Héctor lives the life of a baron, with his house in Mexico City, his airplane, and the horses he loves, John Grady's grandfather dies knowing that his ranch has seen better days, and that it—and his name—will die with him. His daughter, who sells the ranch after abandoning both husband and son, cannot compare to Don Héctor's daughter Alejandra, who is not only beautiful and cultured but a gifted and passionate horsewoman as well. Given these differences and John Grady's own stature as a horseman, it is no wonder he regards La Purísima as a kind of heaven on earth. When Rawlins asks him how long he would like to stay, his answer—"About a hundred years" (96)—indicates what he has perhaps only unconsciously thought: that he'd like more than anything else to outlive Don Héctor and claim both Alejandra and La Purísima as his own.

In the world McCarthy creates in *All the Pretty Horses,* man's proper relationship to the land is represented by his primal connection to horses. In McCarthy's work as a whole, animals, especially of wild or half-wild species, represent the untamed element in nature in much the same way that Old Ben in Faulkner's story "The Bear" represents the vanishing woods of northern Mississippi. In *The Crossing,* for example, Billy Parham is told by an old hermit that the wolf he attempts, at great personal cost, to return to Mexico is like "the copo de nieve": "Snowflake. You catch the snowflake but when you look in your hand you dont have it no more. Maybe you see this dechado. But before you can see it it is gone. If you want to see it you must see it on its own ground. If you catch it you lose it. And where it goes there is no coming back from. Not even God can bring it back."[31] Similarly, when John Grady asks an old man on La Purísima "if it were not true that should all horses vanish from the face of the earth the soul of the horse would not also perish for there would be nothing out of which to replenish it," the old man can only reply by saying "that it was pointless to speak of there being no horses in the world for God would not permit such a thing" (111).

Obviously the pretty horses of La Purísima, after centuries of domestication, cannot represent the wild element in nature. They are instead powerful representatives of the *pastoral life,* which is what is finally at issue in this novel. The land of the West, as can be seen in the example of the Grady ranch, to say nothing of the traditional hunting grounds of the Plains Indians, is hard to hold. Of John Grady we are told that if he had been born, by "malice or mischance," into "some queer land where horses never were," he "would have found them anyway" (23). He would have "known that there was something missing for the world to be right or he right in it," and he would have "set forth to wander wherever it was needed for as long as it took until he came upon one" (23).

In a sense, this is just what John Grady is forced to do after the failure of his family's ranch in Texas. His search for the old ranching life in Mexico is a search for a world where it is still agreed upon by men, as it is by Don Héctor and John Grady, that "God had put horses on earth to work cattle and that other than cattle there was no wealth proper to a man" (127). To live off the land in any other way—for example, from the profits to be made in high-tech agriculture or oil revenues—is to deface the grasslands God put on the earth for man's good.

As we have seen in the case of *Animal Dreams,* and will see again in the work of writers such as Louise Erdrich, this Judeo-Christian view of the land has little in common with Native American belief. Even so, John Grady's job on the ranch, head horse trainer and breeder, does brings him as close as he has ever come to the elemental and the sacred in nature. As a trainer, he achieves a kind of immortality through his breaking of horses: his voice, through his constant commands, comes to "reside in their brains like the voice of some god come to inhabit them" (105). Even his dreams, particularly after he lands in a Mexican jail, are of horses "still wild on the mesa who'd never seen a man afoot and who knew nothing of him or his life yet in whose souls he would come to reside forever" (117). As a breeder, John Grady takes a further step toward immortality by breathing into the ears of stallions the "almost biblical . . . strictures of a yet untabled law":

Soy comandate de las yeguas, he would say, yo yo yo sólo. Sin la caridad de estas manos no tengas nada. Ni cominda ni agua ni hijos. Soy yo que traigo las yeguas de las montañas, las yeguas jóvenes, las yeguas salvajes y ardientes. (128)

[I am the commandant of the mares, he would say, I and I alone. Without the charity of these hands you would have nothing. Neither food nor water nor children. It is I who bring the mares from the mountains, the young mares, the wild and ardent mares.][32]

What John Grady seeks through his connection with horses is both a tapping into all that is "wild and ardent" in nature and, as his choice of the word "comandante" implies, control. And what greater control is there than immortality?

But as John Grady comes to find, his dream of immortality through the training and breeding of horses is an illusion at best. Don Héctor's breeding program is designed to produce a superior cutting horse through the crossing of wild, quarter horse mares with a thoroughbred stallion. But there is little hope of John Grady emulating this strategy—literalizing what he does not even see is a metaphor—through his covert courtship of Alejandra, Don Héctor's daughter. Both the Don and Alejandra's grand-aunt, the Dueña Alfonsa, oppose the match, and Alejandra, "wild and ardent" as she is, will not go against her father's wishes. To do so would be to jeopardize her own family's hold on the land.

Cast out of paradise by the failure of his courtship of Alejandra and by his association with Jimmy Blevins, who, according to the Dueña Alfonso, has killed a Mexican policeman, John Grady descends, along with his friend Rawlins, into the depths of a Mexican prison, where "in an egalitarian absolute every man is judged by a single standard and that was his readiness to kill" (182).

The world of the prison is the opposite of John Grady's dreams of control and immortality. He can neither control his own destiny nor own the space he occupies nor create life and extend his bloodline through procreation. Worse, before his release can be arranged by Alejandra, he is forced to take life. His killing of a young man who comes after him with a knife is the completion of his journey from innocence to experience. At novel's end, having returned to Texas to find his father dead and the ranch sold, John Grady becomes once again a drifter. His only consolation is his recovery of Blevins's thoroughbred horse (unspecified, as Morrison notes, as either gelding or stud). The last line of the novel, similar in many ways to the end of *Horseman, Pass By,* has John Grady passing and paling under a blood-red sunset "into the darkening land, the world to come" (302).

This image, the central one in all of McCarthy's work, is carried to its logical conclusion in the final two volumes of the Border Trilogy, *The Crossing* (1994) and *Cities of the Plain* (1998).

The Crossing begins in 1939, a decade before the events that will take place in *Pretty Horses,* and it does so with an entirely new set of characters headed up by the brothers Billy and Boyd Parham. In no way is this book meant to continue the story began in *Pretty Horses.* Instead, its action works as a kind of dark variation on already established themes. Again we are on the U.S.-Mexican border; again we have a series of literal crossings by midcentury, teenage boys; again we are to read these crossings as a metaphor for the borderline between adolescence and manhood, that crucial literary realm populated by neither man nor boy but "kid," as in Billy the Kid, Melville's Billy Budd, Twain's Huckleberry Finn, and Faulkner's Ike McCaslin.

The book opens with a brilliant set piece in which Billy traps a fierce she-wolf on his family's New Mexico ranch and then sets out to return the animal to its native range across the border in Old Mexico. Strongly reminiscent of Faulkner's story "The Bear," this opening section, parts of which were originally published in *Esquire* magazine, is certain to be amputated from the novel as a whole and excerpted in all future anthologies of American literature:

> That night from the edge of the meadow where he made his camp he could see the yellow windowlights of houses in a colonia on the Bavispe ten miles distant. The meadow was filled with flowers that shrank in the dusk and came forth again at the moon's rising. He made no fire. He and the wolf sat side by side in the dark and watched the shadows of things emerge on the meadow and step and trot and vanish and return. The wolf sat watching with her ears forward and her nose making constant small correction in the air. As if to make acts of abetment to the life in the world. He sat with the blanket over his shoulders and watched the moving shadows while the moon rose over the mountains behind him and the distant lights in the Bavispe winked out one by one till there were none. (93)

The situation, the sentiment, and especially the prose here shimmer with what we have long considered great in a certain kind of American writing. It is Whitman's open road, Melville's high seas, Huck and Jim's raft rapture magically transported to the high plains of fifty years ago. Reading the novel, we must work hard to remind ourselves that Billy and Boyd Parham are not nineteenth-century cowboys but in fact of the same generation that produced the beat characters in Kerouac's *On the Road*. At its most basic, *The Crossing* is a book about this open road—its lure, its perils, and, ultimately, its emptiness.

It goes without saying, however, that the road is about to close, if it has not closed already. The majestic wolf, whose "ancestors had hunted camels and primitive toy horses on these grounds," is now hard pressed to find anything to eat, for "[m]ost of the game was slaughtered out of the country" and "[m]ost of the forest cut to feed the boilers of the stampmills at the mines," and all that remains is a fenced range full of awkward cattle whose stupidity and bawling confusion is an affront to the wolves who "brutalize" as well as kill them, as if "they were offended by some violation of an old order" (24–25).

We sense from the outset that Billy's attempt to return the wolf to the mountains of Mexico, however noble, will be another of McCarthy's "doomed enterprises" (129). He returns to find both of his parents dead, and his later forays into Mexico in search of Boyd end in futility if not outright disaster. The picaresque structure of the novel puts Billy into contact with a huge cast of enigmatic characters, most of whom have some message to deliver about the novel's primary themes. There is the nihilistic old wolf trapper who tells him that "the wolf is a being of great order and that it knows what men do not: that there is no order in the world save that which death has put there" (45); the wandering Mormon who tells him that this world "which seems to us a thing of stone and flower and blood is not a thing at all but is a tale" (143); the prima donna from the traveling opera company who tells him that the "shape of the road is the road. There is not some other road that wears that shape but only the one. And every voyage begun upon it will be completed. Whether horses are found or not" (230).

Whereas John Cole Grady emerged from *All the Pretty Horses* as a seasoned yet still romantic adult—a hero if there ever was one—Billy Parham ends up as a man who has lost everything and learned little beyond the hard facts of the road. It is as if McCarthy weighed in his hands the two most persistent forms his recent writing has taken—the *Bildungsroman* and the picaresque narrative—and decided that, try as he might, he simply could not balance the impulse toward development in the one with the impulse toward movement in the other. He would have to choose the road, and in doing so, cast his hero out into a vagabond existence on the high plains, a place from which no man can return whole. As the Mormon hermit tells Billy early in *The Crossing*, "Such a man is like a dreamer who wakes from a dream of grief to a greater sorrow yet. All that he loves is now become a torment to him. The pin has been pulled from the axis of the universe. Whatever one takes one's eye from threatens to flee away. Such a man is lost to us. He moves and speaks. But he is himself less than the merest shadow among all that he beholds. There is no picture of him possible. The smallest mark upon the page exaggerates his presence" (146). The book ends on an apocalyptic note, with Boyd dead and Billy witnessing a blinding light that turns out to be the Trinity nuclear test explosion of 16 July 1945—which is to say, the ushering out of the old frontier and the ushering in of the nuclear age.[33]

Cities of the Plain brings together the separate stories of John Grady Cole and Billy Parham, simultaneously completing the Border Trilogy and, as several reviewers noted, revealing the "grand design" behind it.[34] It is the autumn of 1952, and John Grady, now nineteen, and Billy, now twenty-eight, are both working on Mac McGovern's Cross Fours Ranch in Alamogordo, New Mexico, where they have both landed after much wandering and disappointment. The book's title, an allusion to the Bible (also to C.K. Moncrieff's translation of Proust's *Sodome et Gomorrhe*),[35] refers literally to the nearby cities of El Paso, Texas, and Juarez, Mexico, and indeed much of the novel's action will take place in an urban atmosphere of back alleys and brothels. Unlike in the two previous novels, there will be no grand journey to anchor this book's action; in fact, John Grady and Billy spend as much time in taxi cabs as they do on horseback. Nor will there be the heroic and beautiful connections with animals the previous volumes exhibited (John Grady and the wild mustangs in *All the Pretty Horses,* Billy and Mexican wolves in *The Crossing*), all this having been replaced by a grimly ironic set-piece in which the two cowboys hunt down and kill a pack of feral dogs by roping them with their lariats ("John Grady dallied the home end of the rope about the polished leather of the pommel and the rope popped taut and the dog snapped into the air mutely").[36] Finally, the iconic romance of John Grady and Alejandra from *Pretty Horses* has been replaced by a more sordid and complicated affair: John Grady's love for an epileptic young prostitute named Magdalena who is being held against her will by an evil pimp. As Edwin T. Arnold has written, "This is a diminished world McCarthy creates in *Cities of the Plain,* a post-war West suffering through its final mockeries and subtractions, a world hard-pressed for heroics and depending instead on simple decency."[37]

Given such a situation, it is not surprising that the novel's primary theme turns out to be the question—a recurrent one in the trilogy—of man's relation to fate or destiny. Shortly after John Grady meets and falls in love with the prostitute Magdalena, Billy advises him that it's not "too late," he can always drop the girl, change his mind about what he has decided to do, since they both agree the whole affair is bound to turn out badly for everyone involved. But John Grady merely shrugs and replies, "There's some things you dont decide. Decidin had nothin to do with it" (121). Asked by Billy how he could have let things get this far, John Grady says, "I feel some way like I didnt have nothin to do with it. Like it's just the way it is. Like it always was this way" (121). The history of Magdalena would appear to confirm this idea. She did not "choose" to become a prostitute but "had been sold at the age of thirteen to settle a gambling debt" (139). She runs away from the brothel several times, once to a convent, but each time she is captured and returned against her will. Men only "imagine that the choices before them are theirs to make," an old man tells John Grady later in the novel. In fact, "we are free to act only upon what is given. Choice is lost in the maze of generations and each act in that maze is itself an enslavement for it voids every alternative and binds one ever more tightly into the constraints that make a life" (195).

Thus, once he has fallen in love, John Grady has no "choice" but to follow his passions, despite the near certainty that all will go terribly awry. Still, as the old man tells him, "A man is always right to pursue the thing he loves"—even if it kills him (199). Later in the novel, still trying to convince John Grady to give up his doomed love, Billy mouths the commonplace: "You cant tell anybody anything" and "You just try to use your best judgment and that's about it" (219). But as John Grady is quick to point out, the "world dont know nothin about your judgment," and finally Billy is forced to agree, adding, "It's worse than that, even. It dont care" (219). The world is not actively hostile to us and our desires, merely indifferent. Ultimately, despite our having to make all of our most important decisions in the dark, as it were, we are still responsible for the shape of our lives; and, like John Grady, we must follow our desires even if we know in advance we are destined to lose.

The final showdown between John Grady and the pimp Eduardo, in which both men are killed, has in a sense been in the cards ever since the first scene of *All the Pretty Horses,* when John Grady's grandfather is laid to rest and our hero rides out into a blood-red sunset. As with the ending of *The Crossing,* this one is also figured as the dying of one age and the dawn of another. Not only has John Grady, continually referred to in *Cities* as "the great american cowboy," passed on, but the very land where he once worked is being bought up by the government for construction of a cold war military base.[38]

In the epilogue that makes up the book's final twenty-seven pages, we see Billy leave the ranch for good as he once again takes to the open road, this time clearly in flight rather than in search of something. In the space of only a few paragraphs, the book warps forward through drought and economic depression to land Billy, now aged seventy-eight, square in "the new millennium," where the only work he can find is as a movie extra. His shoe leather is too thin to patch anymore and he has "long since sold his saddle" (265). Sleeping beneath a highway overpass in Arizona, Billy dreams "of his sister dead seventy years and buried near Sumner" (265) and wakes to think "of his brother dead in Mexico" (266). There follows a long, quasi-philosophical dialogue with a nameless man of "no determinable age" (267), the essence of which is that, while the events of our lives may be determined, controlled by what we call fate, we ourselves create the meaning by the stories we tell. We live our lives in retrospect, making sense of what happens only after it has happened, and assigning our own shape to the whole.[39]

Meditations on the meaning of the western land, the novels in McCarthy's Border Trilogy, like Larry McMurtry's early work, show how modern man has become separated from the earth by his exploitation of it and how he must now wander its surface in perpetual exile. As in McMurtry's work, journeying becomes a metaphor for a crossing over from innocence to experience but also for a loss of connection with place. The cowboy is a heroic, footloose character, but also a "dying breed," like the Plains Indians John Grady identifies himself with at the beginning of *All the Pretty Horses,* and, perhaps most of all, like the pathetic figure Billy Parham makes at the end of *Cities of the Plain.* As a whole, McCarthy's work in the western form and especially in the Border Trilogy explores the borders between past and present, Mexico and the United States, adolescence and manhood, the Old West and the New. Many of these same themes are present, in manifold and fascinating ways, in recent fiction by Native American and Hispanic writers of the New West, to whose work I will turn in the chapter that follows.

7 / Tribes and Breeds, Coyotes
and *Curanderas*

In his introduction to a special issue of the literary magazine *Ploughshares* devoted to the theme of "Tribes," James Welch tells the story of how, twenty-five years earlier at the University of Montana, an Irish poet who had come there to teach for a year expressed wonder that someone like Welch, who is of Native American ancestry and identifies himself as an Indian, could have come to "have a name like Welch," so obviously "an Irish name." Welch explained to the poet that while both of his grandmothers were Indians (one Blackfeet, the other Gros Ventre), both of his grandfathers were of mainly Irish descent (one of them, it was said, "had a Cherokee princess in his ancestry"). A week later, the poet showed up at a bar where Welch was relaxing with friends and spread a map of Ireland out before them and, as Welch recalls, "pointed to a spot along the southern coast and said, 'That's where you're from! That's where the Welch tribe originated!'"[1]

As this story so beautifully illustrates, the whole notion of "tribe" is as much about identification as it is about ancestry. For the Irish poet, who obviously identifies powerfully with his own Irishness, two Irish grandfathers clearly trumps a pair of Native American grandmothers: Welch, as his name indicates, is a member of "the Welch tribe." But this is not at all the way Welch himself felt about the matter at the time. "In truth I had never identified with the Irish," he writes. "I had grown up as an Indian, as a member of two Indian tribes. All my relatives were Indians" (5).

The experience with the map did little to change that, but it did lead the young Welch to have a revery, later that night, about "all the tribes in the world: European tribes, the Goths, the Franks, the Picts, Middle Eastern tribes, the Lost Tribes of Israel, Far Eastern tribes, desert tribes, the Ainus of Japan, Mongolians, Genghis Khan, the tribes of Africa, Watusis, Zulus, the tribes of Southeast Asia and South America, some of whom were still being 'discovered'" (6). In his "beery state," Welch found himself "thrilled by the notion of a world full of tribes" dependent upon "collective memory, spirituality, environmental lightness, and group loyalty to perpetuate their way of life" (5–6).

Twenty-five years later, pondering the twin notions of tribe and tribalism, Welch professes himself saddened "to think that one day there will be no more tribes as we know them" (6). The anthropologists and missionaries and multinational companies will have soon found all the tribes out and introduced them "to the luxuries of civilization," at which point the only question to be studied will be "why they were so happy then and so unhappy now" (6). But if this is a sad thought, Welch is more than happy, in choosing stories and poems for the issue of *Ploughshares* he will edit, to expand his own definition of tribe to include "other variations on the theme," including sexual orientation, religion, occupation, and so on. Because for Welch, finally, the notions of tribe and tribalism at the edge of the twenty-first century boil down to the experience of existing "on the edge of established society," commenting on it "from the fringes," and, above all, acknowledging the people outside its "cozy confines" and their "inalienable right to bang at the gates" (6–7).

Welch has come a long way from his original point about his own mixed ancestry, but his thoughts here foreground what is perhaps the most important question facing American fiction at the close of the twentieth century, namely, whether the rise of multiculturalism in our time will create what former New York City mayor David Dinkins once called a "gorgeous mosaic" of difference, a celebration of multiple points of view, multiple "connections," or whether it will instead lead to a disastrous fragmentation and breakdown of the whole idea of a national literature. As I hope to show in the pages that follow, in the case of the recent literature of the American West—the work of James Welch included—the answer to this question has been in for some time, and the literature itself is far richer for its having been raised.

Contemporary Native American literature, written in English and following European forms, has been big news in this country since at least 1969, when N. Scott Momaday's novel *House Made of Dawn* won the Pulitzer Prize for fiction. Since then, there has been a steady proliferation of authors and texts, increasing academic interest in the work, and a generally favorable publishing environment for Native American authors—all leading to what many have called the renaissance of Native American writing.

In fact, the tradition goes back much further. Aside from the many autobiographies written by boarding school–educated Indians of various tribes in the nineteenth century, the late nineteenth and early twentieth centuries saw the publication of a number of novels and short story collections, including *Wynema* (1891) by Sophia Alice Callahan, *Queen of the Woods* (1899) by Simon Pokagon, *Cogewea: The Half-Blood* (1927) by Christine Quintasket (who wrote under the pen name Mourning Dove), *Sundown* (1934) by John Joseph Mathews, and *The Surrounded* (1936) by D'Arcy McNickle. Many of the themes treated in contemporary Native American fiction were first explored by these authors. As Gerald Vizenor has observed,

> Archilde, the main character in *The Surrounded,* returns to the reservation and the mistrust of his father (who is himself an outsider), the silence of his tribal mother, and the burdens of his identities. He has been away at a boarding school; now, a clever mixedblood in a white shirt and blue suit, he returns at the end of the Depression. . . . Caught at the heart of family loyalties, burdened with the contradictions of federal policies of assimilation, and touched by tragic wisdom, he was displaced by the author in the transcendence of native reason on the reservation.[2]

The word "renaissance" thus turns out to be a good description for the works of contemporary Native Americans, whose characters are often updated versions of McNickle's Archilde—border figures through and through.

Among the writers represented in this renaissance are James Welch, author of such novels as *Winter in the Blood* (1974) and *Fools Crow* (1986); Leslie Marmon Silko, whose reputation was founded on *Ceremony* (1977) and later works; William Least Heat-Moon, author of *Blue Highways* (1982) and *PrairyErth* (1991); and, of course, Louise Erdrich, whose series of Dakota novels, beginning with *Love Medicine* in 1984, has come in for perhaps the highest praise. In the 1990s, this celebrated group expanded to include Sherman Alexie, author of the story collection *The Lone Ranger and Tonto Fistfight in Heaven* (1993) and the novels *Reservation Blues* (1995) and *Indian Killer* (1996), among other works.

At their best, these books represent a whole new line in American literature, something fresh and exciting to read, talk about, and include in an ever-expanding literary canon. At their worst, which is only to say their most suspect, they are the result of an affirmative action wave in publishing and academic circles that since the early 1970s has been ever on the lookout for authors from minority backgrounds. While many have praised Momaday's novel, often lavishly, others see its success as more a reflection of the political climate circa 1969 than of clear artistic merit.

The standard response to such a charge has been to say that books like Momaday's *Dawn* or Silko's *Ceremony* or *Almanac of the Dead* (1991) come out of both a European tradition of written literature and a more primitive, oral tradition many non–Native Americans have trouble understanding. Momaday, for example, believes that criticism of the artistry of his novel arises out of an ignorance of Indian myth and tradition, "a mystical culture of animal spirits, gourd dances, and creation rituals."[3] David Seals, author of *The Powwow Highway* (1979), has argued that Native writers can only be successful if they bend to white expectations concerning plot and prose. "I'm very pleased to see a few Indians breaking the barriers into New York publishing," Seals has written. "But the essential barriers of language are not tumbling down. If you want to get published, you had better write clean, clear, polished prose and tell a tightly constructed, tightly paced story. You had better, as my editor at Penguin/NAL explained, 'make it accessible to white Americans.'"[4]

There are real differences in the work as a whole. On the one hand are writers like Momaday and Silko, whose works tend to be less accessible, more focussed on specific Indian lore, and, many would argue, simply more flawed artistically. On the other hand are writers like Welch and Erdrich and Sherman Alexie, whose work is less influenced by a Native American artistic tradition and more focussed on modern Indians and their problems with isolation, assimilation, and alcoholism. Behind this difference, I would argue, is also a change in aesthetics generally in contemporary American fiction. Momaday and Silko had their heyday in the experimental 1970s, while writers like Erdrich, Welch, and Alexie have come to the fore in the 1980s and 1990s, a time of return to more basic models, especially realism; like most of their peers, regardless of ethnicity, they are at least in part the products of MFA programs. Then too, after the initial success of *House Made of Dawn* in the late 1960s, Momaday did not publish another novel until 1989's *The Ancient Child;* Silko's second novel, *Almanac of the Dead,* wasn't published until 1991, thirteen years after *Ceremony.* In the roughly twenty years between *House Made of Dawn* and *Almanac of the Dead,* contemporary Native American letters was dominated by the likes of Erdrich and Welch, both fairly traditional novelists whose works proved highly palatable to a general readership.

Welch's career is a case in point. After the initial, critical successes represented by *Winter in the Blood* and *The Death of Jim Loney* (1979), Welch's work became more expansive, more realist in tendency, and without doubt more commercial. *Fools Crow*, a historical novel about the Marias River massacre of 1870, won the American Book Award and *Los Angeles Times* Book Prize in 1986. *The Indian Lawyer*, published in 1990, took the form of a political thriller and featured as its protagonist an upwardly mobile Indian attorney preparing to run for Congress on the Democratic ticket. Erdrich has also widened her net. *The Bingo Palace* (1994) features as one of its main characters a successful Indian businessman who wants to bring full-scale gambling to the Chippewa reservation of North Dakota.

Another way of putting the above trend is to say that in the 1980s and 1990s, so-called Indian writing has become part of a general New West literary renaissance grounded in the specifics of place. As Robert F. Gish wrote in a review of Welch's novel, "*The Indian Lawyer*, to a much greater degree than Welch's other works, editorializes on the racial, cultural, political and ecological crises of the New West. . . . [B]etter than any other novel to date, *The Indian Lawyer* conveys the complexity and ferment, the social and racial eruptions and evolutions underway in today's multiple Wests."[5]

Books like *The Indian Lawyer* or *The Bingo Palace*—even Silko's *Almanac of the Dead*—are as much about the mix of life in the contemporary West as they are about Indians. These books confront the problems of an entire region, not just a people. Their characters, border figures both culturally and by blood, embody many of the same divisions that affect McMurtry's or McCarthy's Anglo protagonists—divisions between the past and the present, the individual and the community, the old way and the new—as well as divisions of special interest to Native Americans, such as the divide between traditionalism and assimilation, profit and environmentalism.

Sylvester Yellow Calf, the hero of *The Indian Lawyer*, is caught between two worlds, white and reservation. Though he grew up on the Blackfeet Reservation near Browning, Montana, an orphan abandoned by his alcoholic parents, Yellow Calf is also a graduate of Stanford Law School and a partner in a Helena, Montana, law firm. As a boy, he had excelled at two things: basketball and being the star minority pupil. Basketball got him a scholarship to attend the University of Montana, affirmative action his place at Stanford. Along the way, he made it a point to be nice to everyone, Indians and whites alike, and his rise to the top was almost effortless, capped off neatly by his new Saab, his wealthy blonde girlfriend, his position on the Montana State Board of Pardons, and his congressional campaign. Yet in assimilating so successfully into the white world, Yellow Calf has also lost a part of himself: "He had left so many people behind, so many friends and acquaintances, to live in a world that had little to do with his people. He had always been different, even back there on the reservation, and now he was different in a white man's town in a white man's world of briefcases, suits, law, and politics."[6]

Yellow Calf's dilemma resembles the experience of many minorities who succeed in the majority culture. On the one hand, he has more in common with his business associates and white friends than he does with his childhood friends from the reservation, many of whom he only sees in his position on the Montana parole board. On the other hand, he doesn't "feel particularly close to" his white friends and mentors, whom he sees as having "handed" him along (58). His oldest Indian friends are apt to think of him as a sell-out, while his white, liberal friends like him in part because he's a "good Indian," a token in their world. He can never be sure if his success is because of his own innate abilities or because he's useful politically. "I can't remember a time that I had to work hard, on my own, to achieve something," he complains to his girlfriend. "There was always somebody there to open another door, to say, 'Come on in, it's warm in here,' then they seem to shut the door on the faces of the people I came from" (58).

Welch's symbol for all that Sylvester Yellow Calf has left behind in his rise to the top is the ancestral war bundle his grandmother had tried to give him when he went off to college. This war bundle represents, among other things, Sylvester's Indian identity and his traditional role as a warrior for his people. Midway through the novel, his congressional campaign in jeopardy because of an affair he has been tricked into by the wife of a white prisoner to whom he has denied parole, Yellow Calf returns to the reservation and discovers this lost legacy among the abandoned things of his childhood:

He looked at himself in the mirror above the child's dresser. His black hair looked dull and his close-set dark eyes were foggy with fatigue. He knocked on the scratched, sorrel-colored dresser top and noticed the pouch. He picked it up and felt it. The covering was soft-tanned hide made hard by the years. The top was tied shut by a thin yellowing sinew. He held it before his eyes by the two rawhide strings. It was completely unadorned and heavier than Sylvester remembered. It was his great-great-grandfather's war medicine, the medicine his grandmother had tried to give him when he went away to college. He held it to his neck and looked at himself in the mirror again. He tried to see in the mirror a Blackfeet warrior, getting ready to raid the Crow horses, but all he saw was a man with circles under his eyes, a faint stubble of beard on his chin, a man whose only war, skirmish, actually, was with himself. He wasn't even a new warrior. He was a fat cat lawyer, helping only himself, and some fatter cats, get richer. He put the pouch carefully back on the dresser. (167–68)

In purely American terms, Yellow Calf is a stunning example of a rags-to-riches success story; but as an Indian, his success will always be muted by the fact that little of what he does with his life pertains to Native American reality as a whole. Though the plot of *The Indian Lawyer* is driven by Yellow Calf's dangerous fling with Patti Ann Harwood, and the consequences it will have for his political career, its most pressing thematic concern is Sylvester Yellow Calf's crisis of identity, a personal and professional crisis grounded in his need to find meaningful work. It is this aspect of the novel, more than anything else, that makes *The Indian Lawyer* a western novel rather than one concerned solely with the consequences of affirmative action and assimilation.

Yellow Calf solves his dilemma by pulling out of his congressional race, thereby nullifying all threats of blackmail, and returning to his ancestral home on the reservation. At the height of his legal career, Yellow Calf had driven regularly in his Saab through the plains of his homeland, regarding the landscape around him "as nothing but wheat fields and prairies" (342). But after his return to the Blackfeet Reservation, he comes to love the land once again, becoming "very attentive in it, as though a discovery would be made over the next hill, down in the next swale of wash" (342). His newly found connection to the land, and by extension to his people, is made clear by Yellow Calf's decision to sacrifice a large part of his lucrative legal career to devote himself to Indian water rights cases, arguing before the Montana courts, and the Supreme Court if necessary, that "the Winters doctrine and later court cases had established that the Indians could protect the amount of water necessary for future as well as current use" (343).

This issue is a small part of *The Indian Lawyer* as a whole, and is only taken up in its final pages, but to anyone familiar with past and current battles in the West, the mere mention of the Winters doctrine, the controversial 1908 Supreme Court decision confirming Indians' rights to water originating within or flowing through their reservations, is enough to transform the entire meaning of Welch's novel. For if there is one single characteristic that defines the West as a region, one issue that informs nearly all of its debates and divides its people more than anything else, it is the West's basic dryness and the complex issues surrounding the destiny of its water. As Wallace Stegner once wrote, "Aridity, and aridity alone, makes the various Wests one"; in the arid

West, "water is safety, home, life, *place*."[7] By working to protect his people's rights to this water, Welch's protagonist has returned home in one of the strongest senses possible. He has become "a new warrior" as surely as his great-great-grandfather was an old warrior.

The theme of the New West border figure rediscovering his identity through place is explored at greater length in Erdrich's *The Bingo Palace,* the fourth in an ongoing series of North Dakota novels that includes *Love Medicine* (1984), *The Beet Queen* (1986), *Tracks* (1988), and *Tales of Burning Love* (1996). In this group of novels, Erdrich undertakes the first major attempt since Faulkner to map out and populate an entire landscape. By concentrating so thoroughly on her own "postage stamp of native soil," as Faulkner described his Mississippi material, Erdrich has raised the stakes of contemporary writing about place and elevated the New West and Native American novels to a new level. Since Erdrich, there is less reason to cringe at statements, such as those made by William Kittredge and Steven Krauzer in the seventies, that compare the New West renaissance to southern writing of the 1930s. In its way, Erdrich's task in the North Dakota series has been no less daunting than Faulkner's in the Yoknapatawpha novels. Certainly it is more ambitious, and ultimately more interesting, than latter-day southern attempts to map out a territory—for example, James Wilcox's efforts in the Gladiola novels (*Modern Baptists* [1983], *North Gladiola* [1985], *Polite Sex* [1991]). Erdrich's cast of characters is huge, their individual histories and genealogies incredibly complex. Characters drop out of one volume only to resurface in another; births, deaths, marriages, and adoptions overlap one another. To be sure, it takes a dedicated reader to keep everything Erdrich is doing with her characters in focus, but the *payoff* to all this work, which in the end is the test of whether difficulty in a novel is rewarding or not, comes in the way Erdrich has subordinated all of her lesser themes to her main one: the "personal and communal connotations" of place, the interconnectedness of Indian history, tribal land, and family genealogy.[8]

"In a tribal view of the world," Erdrich wrote in a 1985 essay, "Where I Ought to Be: A Writer's Sense of Place," "where one place has been inhabited for generations, the landscape becomes enlivened by a sense of group and family history. Unlike most contemporary writers, a traditional storyteller fixes listeners in an unchanging landscape combined of myth and reality. People and place are inseparable."[9] The critical commonplace that western writing is always finally about the land takes on a whole new meaning when applied to the work Native American writers, latter-day descendants of entire peoples forcibly evicted from homelands they literally worshiped. Native

Americans are at once the most displaced of all twentieth-century persons and those to whom the concept of place is perhaps most vitally important. And Native American writers, Erdrich writes, "have a task quite different" from that of other writers. "In the light of enormous loss, they must tell the stories of contemporary survivors while protecting and celebrating the cores of cultures left in the wake of catastrophe." They must concentrate on the present without forgetting the past, representing place as both a contemporary home and the lost or wrecked homeland their ancestors once inhabited. Erdrich's choice of the word "catastrophe," which implies both the concluding action of a drama and a sudden, violent change in the earth's surface, underlines the complex ways in which the fate of Native Americans is intertwined with the fate of their land.

This idea is borne out in Erdrich's work, which is focused in large part on the relationship between people and landscape. "It is the land that first assails the reader," wrote one reviewer of *The Bingo Palace:* "The harsh, North Dakota landscape swallows June Kashpaw in Erdrich's first novel, *Love Medicine;* Lake Matchimanto, the spiritual center of the Chippewa tribe, tries several times to capture the body and soul of Fleur Pillager in *Tracks;* and in *The Bingo Palace,* the latest novel in Erdrich's series, the land, brooding, mysterious and threatened, once again dominates the lives of her characters and resists their attempts to control it."[10]

Landscape is both threatening and threatened, a common theme in New West writing. In truth, though, this is only half the picture of what Erdrich is doing in her fiction. The other half, as I've suggested, concerns the ways in which Native American lives are themselves intertwined.

Erdrich organized *The Bingo Palace* around a doubling motif involving two Chippewa Indians on a North Dakota reservation—Lipsha Morrissey and Lyman Lamartine. As doubles, the separate histories of these two men is "a twisted rope."[11] "His real father," says Lipsha of Lyman, "was my step father. His mother is my grandmother. His half brother is my father" (16). Despite their connections, however, the two men could not be more different. Lipsha is a dreamy, drifting young man who, despite high ACT scores, has never really amounted to much. His only valuable skill is his ability to cure small aches and ailments through the power of his touch, but even this flees him when he begins to charge a twenty dollar fee for his services. Lyman, on the other hand, is the reservation's "biggest cheese," a tireless entrepreneur with a hand in everything from cafes and gas stations to a tomahawk factory and a bingo parlor.

Erdrich's use of a doubling motif in *The Bingo Palace* is self-conscious and often the subject of inside jokes. "If you read about a thing like Lyman and me happening in those days," says Lipsha, referring the "plays of the old-time Greeks," "one or both of us would surely have to die. But us Indians, we're so used to inner plot twists that we just laugh" (17). The tragic connotations of classical doubling are muted in order to make an extended comparison: Lipsha and Lyman represent two different tendencies in the modern American Indian, the one toward a spiritual, vision-seeking side aligned with the Native American past, the other toward a pragmatic, assimilation-based model that argues for entrepreneurship and Native American success in business. At issue in such a comparison is the fate of both the Chippewa people and their land— a fate that, in Erdrich's time, has become inseparable from the whole issue of gambling on reservations. "Depending on whom you speak to," Erdrich has said in an interview, "[reservation gambling] is either the greatest thing that's ever happened to Native Americans or the worst. Some reservations are handling it with more ease and grace, while others have been devastated."[12]

Like Welch's *The Indian Lawyer* and Kingsolver's *Animal Dreams, The Bingo Palace* brings the reservation situation into focus through an archetypal narrative of return in service of an underlying theme of "connections." The novel opens with Lipsha's grandmother, Lulu Lamartine, going to the post office to mail a letter; yet as the narrator of chapter 1 says, "in her small act there was a complicated motive and a larger story" (3): "The story comes around, pushing at our brains, and soon we are trying to ravel back to the beginning, trying to put families into order and make sense of things. But we start with one person, and soon another and another follows, and still another, until we are lost in the connections" (5). As with all stories about people and the land, this one will turn on just this issue of connections. The envelope Lulu Lamartine mailed that day contained a single sheet of paper, a photocopy of a wanted poster of Gerry Nanapush, Lipsha's father. It is a summons of sorts, a subtle message that tells Lipsha he must turn his life around by returning to the reservation. But as Lipsha discovers, turning one's life around by returning to one's home is more easily contemplated than accomplished. "Lipsha," he tells himself, "you didn't have to come back" (19). Staring at his father's wanted poster, he had "the impulse to change [his] life," but he soon realizes that in this he is only "looking for a quick solution, as usual" (19). Once back on the reservation, Lipsha spends most of his time playing bingo, eventually winning a prize van that is later vandalized by a group of Montana "rednecks." The bingo life, like return, is also a "quick solution." And like reservation gambling as a whole, its rewards do not last.

The doubling, return, and gambling (or "luck") motifs of Erdrich's novel are brought together in the rivalry between Lyman and Lipsha for the love of Shawnee Ray Toose, a woman both men see as "the best of our past, our present, our hope of a future" (13). Lyman can lay claim to Shawnee Ray because she has already borne his son, and of the two men he is the most responsible and successful. Lipsha counters this with the greater physical passion he and Shawnee Ray share. In the end, however, Shawnee Ray will have neither of them—even after both men go on a vision quest in an attempt to purify themselves. In this she is like the land itself—difficult to approach, hard to hold—and beyond this triangular plot lies the real issue in the novel: Lyman's plan to develop some of the reservation land into a tourist resort and gambling casino.

For Lyman, reservation gambling is just one part of a development plan that begins and ends with land. Fleur Pillager, the old woman whose fortunes, especially with regard to land, mirror those of the Chippewas as a whole, comes to Lyman in a dream and gives him this advice: "*Land is the only thing that lasts life to life. Money burns like tinder, flows off like water, and as for the government's promises, the wind is steadier. . . . This time, don't sell out for a barrel of weevil-shot flour and a mossy pork. . . . Put your winnings and earnings in a land-acquiring account. Take the quick new money. Use it to purchase the fast old ground*" (148–49). With his investor's eye, Lyman sees "wheatland accumulating, a pasta plant, then sunflowers" (149). He sees a bright future for his people, wealth and acclaim for himself. And it all starts with bingo, money made from gambling.

To Lipsha, things look decidedly different. Having won and lost at bingo, he knows that "bingo money is not based on solid ground" (221). Bingo money "gets money, but little else, nothing sensible to look at or touch or feel in yourself down to your bones" (221). In the chapter called "A Little Vision," Lipsha finally gets the vision he has been searching for when the skunk who ruined his previous vision quest comes to him while he lies on his waterbed and begins to talk. "*This ain't real estate,*" the skunk says.

> And that's when I get the vision.
> The new casino starts out promising. I see the construction, the bulldozers scraping off wild growth from the land like a skin, raising mounds of dirt and twisted roots. Roads are built, trees shaved, tar laid onto the new and winding roads. Stones and cement blocks and wood are hauled into the woods, which is no longer woods, as the building is set up and raised. It starts out as revenue falling out of the sky. I see clouds raining money into the open mouths of the

tribal bank accounts. Easy money, easy flow. No sweat. No bother. I see money shining down into Lyman Lamartine's life. It comes thick and fast and furious. *This ain't real estate,* the skunk says again. (219)

For Lipsha, Lyman's relationship to Chippewa land is essentially that of a real estate developer's to investment property. Lyman wants to develop the reservation land so he can buy more land and develop that. The land Lyman has marked out for development—"partly Fleur [Pillager]'s land and partly old allotments that the tribe holds in common" (219)—is also a burial ground, and Lipsha is disturbed by the thought that parking lots and blackjack tables will soon be rolled out "over Pillager grave markers" (219). Yet for all the power of his vision, Lipsha himself has no plan for Chippewa land or for anything else. He is no real opposition to Lyman, but only a kind of ineffectual conscience of his people.

In the end, Erdrich leaves the issue of reservation gambling unresolved, but her implication is that unless some stronger opposition than Lipsha arrives on the scene, Lyman and the forces behind more widespread gambling will win. In the world of *The Bingo Palace,* as in the world of the contemporary West more generally, what is to come of the everpresent border between land as real estate and land as resource remains to be seen.

Contemporary Hispanic American writing finds its roots in two Mexican American novels from the late sixties and early seventies, Rudolfo Anaya's *Bless Me, Ultima* (1972) and Tomás Rivera's *. . . y no se lo tragó la tierra / And the Earth Did Not Devour Him* (1971). Both of these works, like most Hispanic fiction from the period, were published by small, grassroots presses, for example Houston's Arte Público Press or Pajarito Press of Albuquerque, New Mexico. Other writers, such as Rolando Hinojosa-Smith, began their careers in Spanish and then switched to English when publishing opportunities became available. Hinojosa-Smith's Klail City Death Trip series, a group of novels set in the Lower Rio Grande Valley of Texas, represents a Hispanic answer to Faulkner's Yoknapatawpha novels and Louise Erdrich's North Dakota series, but these books have never reached a wide audience. The real breakthrough for Hispanic American fiction came with Cuban American Oscar Hijuelos's novel *The Mambo Kings Play Songs of Love,* which won the 1990 Pulitzer Prize for fiction, proving that Hispanic writers could reach a wider audience. Hijuelos's novel ushered in a renaissance for Latino\a writing similar in size and scope to that of Native American and Chinese American literature in the 1980s.

As is the case with Native American writing, however, the roots of Hispanic American literature go much deeper. As Nicolas Kannellos points out in his introduction to *Hispanic American Literature: A Brief Introduction and Anthology* (1995), "[T]here was Hispanic literature in existence north of the Rio Grande before the United State was ever founded," although much of this literary tradition "was suppressed, has been lost forever, or remains inaccessible to most readers and educators."[13] Historical accounts of North America were being published in Spain as early as 1542; epic poems about the colonization of the Americas, written in Spanish, were in existence by the late sixteenth century. By the time the first English-language minstrels reached California, "there were already full-fledged Spanish-language theatrical companies performing the high drama of Spain and the Americas" (2). Spanish was also the language "of the first printing presses in the Southwest and of the first newspapers in Arizona, California, New Mexico, and Texas" (2). By the second half of the nineteenth century, Hispanics were also publishing in English, although as Kanellos points out, "Few of the works from this period in English or those many more in Spanish . . . are currently available" (2).

Among the new Hispanic writers are Chicago-born Chicana writer Sandra Cisneros, whose short, poetic stories and sketches include those published in *The House on Mango Street* (1985) and *Woman Hollering Creek* (1991); Ana Castillo, also from Chicago, whose novels include *The Mixauiahuala Letters* (winner of a 1987 American Book Award), *Sapogonia* (1990) and 1993's *So Far from God;* Dominican American Julia Alvarez, author of *How the Garcia Girls Lost Their Accents* (1991) and *In the Time of Butterflies* (1994), among other works; and Nueva Mexicana writer Denise Chavez, author of *The Last of the Menu Girls* (1986) and the novel *Face of an Angel* (1994). Nicknamed "Las Girlfriends" by Cisneros, these four women have quickly come to be the vanguard for a host of other writers, many of them featured in new anthologies devoted exclusively to Hispanic American writing.

What these writers share, most immediately, is a linguistic background that includes Spanish as well as English, and the feeling that their experiences are outside the American mainstream. Yet there are also important differences between, say, Cuban Americans, whose experiences are those of urban immigrants/political exiles with an island past, and Nuevo Mexicanos, whose experiences are largely rural, connected to a folk culture, and rooted in a land they have occupied for centuries. There is a problem of definition here. As Earl

Shorris, author of *Under the Fifth Sun: A Novel of Pancho Villa* (1980), has observed, "No one is really quite certain about who qualifies as a Latino—or whether Latino, Hispanic, Spanish, Mexican, Mexican-American, Chicano, Nuevo Mexicano, Puerto Rican, Neorican, Borinqueno or other appellations are proper names. Were John Dos Passos and George Santayana Latino writers? How shall the category be defined? By ancestry? Surname? Subject matter? Geography?"[14] Subject matter alone must be thrown out, especially after the fiasco created when Danny Santiago, the winner of a 1984 prize for fiction, turned out to be blacklisted Anglo screenwriter Daniel Lewis James.[15] An easier question is what qualifies as Hispanic writing.

Despite differences, there are some constants in the fiction, especially the use of Spanish phrases and a penchant for Gabriel García Márquez–style magic realism. Beyond these traits, one also finds heavy doses of Catholicism, revisionist history, women as important and strong characters, and the vexed question of cultural and personal identity as a major theme. Two typical paragraphs come from Cristina Garcia's novel *Dreaming in Cuban* (1992):

> After her sleepless night in the house on Palmas Street, Celia wanders to the ceiba tree in the corner of the Plaza de las Armas. Fruit and coins are strewn by its trunk and the ground around the tree bulges with buried offerings. Celia knows that good charms and bad are hidden in the stirred earth near its sacred roots. Tía Alicia told her once that the ceiba is a saint, female and maternal. She asks the tree permission before crossing its shadow, then circles it three times and makes a wish for Felicia.
>
> Celia rests in the interior patio of the plaza, where royal palms dwarf a marble statue of Christopher Columbus. Inside the museum there's a bronze weathervane of Doña Inés de Bobadilla, Cuba's first woman governor, holding the Cross of Calatrava. She become governor of the island after her husband, Hernando de Soto, left to conquer Florida. Doña Inés, it is said, was frequently seen staring out to sea, searching the horizon for her husband. But de Soto died on the banks of the Mississippi River without ever seeing his wife again.[16]

The spirituality, "earthiness," and, for lack of a better word, "knowingness" of the female characters are foregrounded here, especially in the image of the fruit-bearing ceiba tree as a female and maternal saint. The main line of human development is not the story of fathers and sons we see in so much in the work of male (and Anglo) writers, but instead a progression of mothers and daughters who for all practical purposes move in a world governed by a female god—Mother Earth or, quite often, the Virgin Mary. The world of men is one of violence, exploration, and death (the fate of both Columbus and de Soto), while women play a more healing, family-centered (and ultimately more important) role. As one female character tells another in Ana Castillo's novel *So Far from God,* "I think it has something to do with the unnaturalness of killing compared to the naturalness of childbirth."[17]

The image of the woman, the Mother, as healer is most often explored through the character of the *curandera.* Perhaps the most famous *curandera* in Hispanic American writing is the character of Ultima in Rudolfo Anaya's novel *Bless Me, Ultima.* But it may also be seen in the work of, for example, Ana Castillo. In *So Far from God* the *curandera* character is Doña Felicia, who serves as a mentor for the would-be healer Caridad. As Doña Felicia tells Caridad, who has been working in a hospital, "I believe you are meant to help people a lot more than just wiping their behinds as they make you do in the hospital. . . . [Y]ou are destined to help people as even those trained doctors and nurses down there can't do" (55). In *Dreaming in Cuban* this character is represented by Celia del Pino, grandmother and spiritual guide of the novel's most important character, Pilar Puente. In all these books the *curandera* is someone who stands for the mysterious earth, holistic and spiritual healing, and as a guide for the development of younger characters, men as well as women. In Anaya's 1992 novel *Alburquerque,* both the main character Abrán González, and his girlfriend, Lucinda Cordova, are guided by powerful *curanderas,* and both ultimately aspire to become healers themselves.

There is an important connection here between the idea of the *curandera* as spiritual and cultural healer and the role of the artist or writer in these works. The main character in Denise Chavez's *The Last of the Menu Girls* (1986), Rocio Esquibel, achieves her development by moving from the profession of nursing to the role of the artist in much the same way that James Joyce's Stephen Dedalus moves from the idea of becoming a priest to the idea of becoming an artist. As Anaya has written in his introduction to *The Last of the Menu Girls,* "At the beginning of the novel Rocio cries out against the tradition of serving roles which society has prescribed for women, and she opts for the life of the artist. By the novel's end she has found her calling, and that is to give meaning to the emotionally turbulent lives of the people she has known."[18] The mother-daughter connection is made clear by the fact that Rocio is supported in her decision by her mother, who tells her on the novel's last page, "Rocio, just write about this little street of ours, it's only one block long, but there's so many stories."[19]

In the work of Hispanic New West writers, these themes are both continued and intensified, most often in service of a plot that portrays Nuevo

.Mexicano characters as border figures in search of identity. Anaya's *Alburquerque* is a good example of a Nuevo Mexicano novel that deals with all the important New West themes: the son or daughter's search for the father and identity, the new concern for environmental issues, the necessity of community, and the importance of place, which touches all these issues.

Anaya is perhaps best known for his 1972 novel *Bless Me, Ultima,* a poetic, beautifully written story of one Chicano boy's coming of age in postwar New Mexico. Anaya followed *Ultima* with other novels published by the University of New Mexico Press, including *Heart of Aztlan, Lord of the Dawn,* and *Tortuga.* But it was *Ultima* that remained the quintessential work of the man called "El Jefe," the "father of Chicano literature." Though published by a small, California press, *Bless Me, Ultima* sold three hundred thousand copies through twenty-one printings before being reissued by the giant Warner Books in 1994.[20]

Alburquerque, which won a Pen Center West Award for Fiction, tells the story of Abrán González, a "homeboy from the barrio" and former Golden Gloves boxer who must discover his true identity in contemporary Albuquerque after being summoned to the deathbed of his biological mother, Cynthia Johnson, an Anglo artist whose ambitious, businessman father made her give up Abrán for adoption twenty-one years earlier. Having learned that at least one of his parents is white, Abrán must admit to himself what has been whispered about him all along, that he is a "coyote," one of the "new mestizos," not as Mexican as those he has grown up with.

Onto this basic, search-for-identity plot, Anaya has grafted a New Western subplot, the story of one man's attempt to win the race for mayor or "Duke" of Albuquerque by promising to turn the city into the New Eldorado, a "desert Venice with beltways of green, ponds, and small lakes, all connected by the waterways that crisscrossed the downtown area."[21] Through the diversion of Pueblo water and the legalization of gambling (shades of both James Welch and Louise Erdrich here), Frank Dominic, the mayoral candidate, wants to make the Albuquerque of the year 2000 "like the old Aztec capital of Tenochtitlan, the precolumbian Mexico City" (132). The problem with this grand scheme, which fails in the end, has to do with the whole vexed issue of water rights in the West, and specifically with the issue of water rights held by Native Americans. Dominic's plan is to privatize water, form a corporation and buy the rights of the Indian pueblos and the old Hispanic land grants. As Dominic knows well, in New Mexico and elsewhere in the arid West, "[w]ater and the right to use it were the most crucial problems for development" (122). Accordingly, "[t]he only way to handle water rights, and ensure water for the future, [was] to privatize it" (124).

Dominic's plan is opposed by Ben Chávez, a Mexican American writer living in Albuquerque (who is also, it turns out, Abrán's biological father); by Marisa Martinez, the city's progressive incumbent mayor; and even by Walter Johnson, Cynthia Johnson's father. But more to the point, it is opposed by Joe Calabasa, a "Santo Domingo man" and Abrán's best friend; by Lucinda Cordova, Abrán's girlfriend from the mountains north of Albuquerque; and finally by Abrán himself, who had initially supported Dominic after the candidate agreed to help him find his father.

At issue in all of this is not only the city and the land around it but also the whole question of regional and personal identity. Abrán González, it turns out, is not the only person trying to find out who he is. Joe Calabasa, as a Vietnam vet and a "coyote" himself—"half Santo Domingo man, half Mexican from Peña Blanca" (47)—must also discover his place in the world, which for Joe means choosing between being a modern, urban Indian and returning to the circle of the pueblo. Even Frank Dominic, who yearns to be a scion of the Spanish conquistadors and the old dukes of Alburquerque, is in the grasp of a search for identity. (As Ben Chávez muses, "The Spanish legacy was a vision that many grasped for, and many a nut in New Mexico had spent his life's earnings trying to find his link to a Spanish family crest" [72].) But more than anything, of course, the identity of "Alburquerque" itself is in question, and has been since 1880, when an Anglo station master removed the first "r" from its name "in a move that symbolized the emasculation of the Mexican way of life" (112).

Modern Albuquerque, Ben Chávez knows, is a city of borders, a city of class lines and ethnic lines, divided between Anglos, Hispanics, Indians, blacks, and the homeless in between. Whoever becomes mayor will have to deal with this fact:

> [T]he city was changing, the interest groups were more complex, the balancing act was getting harder. . . . Too many new people in the city, immigrants who didn't know the history of the place, new people who knew nothing of the traditional communities and who often stepped over the old people.
>
> Those with money built walls around their subdivisions, like Taoan in the Heights; others built expensive adobe homes with wide lawns and a view of the mountains in the valley. They organized car pools to deliver the kids to private schools, and they were great supporters of the City Symphony. They had all the amenities of Southwest living without ever having to meet the natives. (66–67)

This is exactly the situation described in Castillo's *So Far from God*: "[T]here were a lot of outsiders moving in, buying up the land that had belonged to the original families" (139). And yet, as in Castillo's novel, the real problem is not with "outsiders" but with "insiders" like Frank Dominic. Dominic's plan, if it works, promises to improve the failing economy and make Albuquerque an even more exciting place for these newcomers and their tourist brethren, but it also promises to ruin the "traditional communities" of "la raza," the people, and this is something New Mexicans like Ben Chávez cannot abide. As a writer at work on an epic poem that explores "the Mesoamerican mythic elements Chicanos had incorporated into their heritage," Chávez hopes to create "a new consciousness for the people," a "new identity for the downtrodden" (60).

True identity comes only from establishing a correct link to the land and the people. In the case of Ben Chávez, this means writing his poem about two homeboys from the barrio who take a journey into the Aztec past. In the case of Joe Calabasa, it means returning to the inner circle of the Santo Domingo pueblo and helping to protect the water and land rights of his people. For Abrán, it means becoming a *curandero*. On a literal level, he will attend the University of New Mexico and become a doctor, just as Joe will finish his degree and attend law school. But on a metaphorical level, Abrán will become a "curer," someone capable of keeping his people and their land healthy.

Set off in italics, in the very center of Anaya's novel, is a parable that in many ways encapsulates the extended comparison between old and new we see in so much New West fiction. It is the time of *la Matanza* in Los Padillas, a fiesta that has at its center the ritualistic slaughtering of a pig. The old men of the village, who have performed the ceremony with dignity many times, stand aside and let the next generation prove themselves. The young men performing the ceremony, an attorney and a "*computer man at Sandia Labs,*" are like "*other young men who had left the valley for a middle-class life in the city*" and only return "*once in a while to visit parents and grandparents*" or "*for the fiestas*" (97). They have "*almost forgotten the old ways*" (97). Drunk, using ropes and a rifle, the young men make a mess out of killing the first pig. The first rifle shot misses the pig completely, frightening the children. The second only wounds it, and the pig must be gored to death with a knife. Nearby, watching this, "*the old men stood quietly. They shook their heads; it was not good*" (101). The pigs that are sacrificed should be killed cleanly.

When he can take no more of the debacle, one of the old men, don Pedro, steps forward and calls his old compadres:

"Secundino," he said softly, "el martillo."

The old man Secundino thought he hadn't heard, then he smiled and nodded. It was the call to the matanza, an old calling, something they knew in their blood, something they had done surely and swiftly all their lives. The right way. He hobbled to the shed and returned with a ten-pound, short-handled sledgehammer.

"Procopio, ponle filo a la navaja," the old man said as he rolled up his sleeves.

"Con mucho gusto," Procopio spat a quick stream of chewing tobacco through yellow-stained teeth and smiled. He took the long knife and began sharpening it on a small whetstone. "Lana sube, lana baja," he whispered as the blade swished back and forth on the stone.

"Compadres," don Pedro whispered, "la marrana." The men ambled silently but quickly toward the pen. . . .

They needed no ropes to move the pig. Secundino slipped the big hammer into don Pedro's hand. Then Procopio handed don Pedro the sharpened knife, so now the old man balanced the hammer in one hand and the knife in the other . . .

Don Pedro moved in a circle, keeping his eye on the pig as it came closer and closer to him. There was no noise, no ropes, no fast motions to spook the pig, just the circle of men getting smaller.

The compadres smiled and remembered all the years of their lives when they had done this. It was a ceremony, the taking of the animal's life to provide meat for the family. The young men needed to be reminded that it was not sport, it was a tradition as old as the first Hispanos who settled along the river . . .

When don Pedro had come face-to-face with the pig, he raised his hammer, and with the speed of a matador, there was a brief glint in the sunlight, the arc of his arm, a dull thud, and the pig jerked back and stiffened. The kill was complete and clean. (103–4)

This is a remarkable passage for a number of reasons. In the first place, Anaya's deft intertwining of Spanish and English here teaches even the reader without Spanish the meaning of don Pedro's simple words. In a sense, the Spanish phrases *are* the old way, Anaya the old master still using them like don Pedro's hammer. More significant, the ceremony of killing the pig is enacted to *"provide meat for the family,"* and it must be done *"cleanly."* There is a sacred relationship between man and his environment, and the ceremony that stands for this relationship is meant to bring the community together. The young men's attempt, accompanied by whiskey, guns, and shouting, had threatened to tear the community apart. Through don Pedro's stepping forward, everything has at last been done "the right way," but over don Pedro's success hangs an ominous cloud. He is an old man, and "it had taken all the old man's strength to make the kill" (104). He will not always be able to come to the rescue in this way. "*We will die and all this will pass away,*" don Pedro says to his compadres, closing the episode (105).

As with most New West fiction, the divisions or borders here are quite clear: on the one hand, Frank Dominic and his policy of environmental exploitation in the service of profit and growth; on the other hand, the old way, *la Matanza,* a humble and sacred relationship between man and his environment. Between these two examples stands the border figure, Abrán González, a "coyote" who must choose between them, the fate of a people and a region hanging in the balance.

These are the themes and set pieces of the New West novel as a whole: the dispossessed, dissatisfied border figure searching for his identity in a divided land; the conflict between the old way and the new; the final calling to become a healer for the western land and its people. In a very real sense, the New West writers themselves—Cormac McCarthy, Louise Erdrich, James Welch, Rudolfo Anaya—are border figures. Their writing is a search for "connections," the proper relationship between themselves, their people, and a western landscape that in a larger sense has always stood for America itself.

8 / The White Prison Novel
as Bildungsroman
8 / The White Prison Nov

8 / The White Prison Novel
as *Bildungsroman*

Joe Speaker is a young, white, drug-addicted, dope-dealing, strip-show barker about to be sent off to the Big House for the first time. Whisper Moran is "head chingaso" of the San Quentin Aryan Brotherhood, a man so carved up with jailhouse tattoos that the only kind thing awaiting him in this world is the Big Eraser. Says Whisper to Joe, as the two of them await prison in a San Francisco felony tank, "Just remember, homeboy. Do your own time, hold your own mud. It's simple, just aint always easy."[1]

This advice, which comes toward the middle of Seth Morgan's *Homeboy* (1990), is just the sort of thing we expect to read in a prison novel. It fits our overall picture of prison life, a picture that, even at this late date, probably includes striped uniforms, balls and chains, and the turn-key asleep at the prison door. The old con, the chronic repeat offender, takes the younger man under his wing, shows him the ropes. *Do your own time. Hold your own mud.* Humphrey Bogart might have said that. But the San Quentin Aryan Brotherhood? The Nazi as mentor and father? Where, we might ask, does this come in?

The simple answer is to say in books like *Homeboy*—novels predominantly—written since the 1960s by white authors serving time in California prisons. In these, the Aryan Brotherhood is as much a part of the landscape as was the old Communist Party in the proletarian fiction of the 1930s; which is to say, not so much as a theme as a *fact* of prison life, like guards and heroin and homosexuality. And just as we once might have read a book like Henry Roth's *Call It Sleep* (1934) to witness for ourselves the squalor and beauty of immigrant life, we can now look into books like *Homeboy* or Malcolm Braly's *On the Yard* (1967) or Edward Bunker's *Animal Factory* (1976) to get a glimpse of what lies behind the bars of our maximum security prisons. But to get that glimpse, to get it truthfully, we must withhold all judgments about the value (or values) of these novels until their separate worlds have been unfolded before us.

The unfolding of prison as a separate world is of course one of the main tasks and themes of all prison literature. Prison novels, especially, attempt to educate us in the ways of the prison, and by doing so, to show us that anyone so educated is unfit for anything but prison.[2] In this sense, prison fiction is always tendentious, always a protest against the prison condition. The colors of prison, chiefly the blues and grays of concrete or rain-filled clouds, the sounds, such as the echoing slam of a steel door made of bars, the stale smells, like something sealed too long in a jar—these stay with one long after the "prison book" has been put down. One is both appalled and fascinated. Despite both its tendentiousness and its sentiment, the prison novel, especially as we know it today, is *art*. It has a logic, a language, and a symmetry all its own; it exists as a thing unto itself completely outside the sometimes wasted lives of its authors.

Beyond this, the literature of the prison offers a distorted and sometimes shattered reflection of contemporary literature more generally, as well as of the society in which both are produced. The idea, so peculiar to our times, that we are all members of a series of overlapping "tribes"—racial, regional, religious, and so on—and that we each view what remains of a center from our respective margins (or, as the hero of William T. Vollmann's *The Atlas* has it, that we are all, individually, centers) finds perhaps its most extreme and logical expression in the literature of our society's prisons, wherein the boundary between so-called mainstream and marginal is not metaphoric but on the contrary quite literal. And insofar as the world of the prison is a microcosm of our world (a flawed idea, to be sure), it, too, may be seen to be divided into different gangs or "tribes."

These two ideas—that prison is a separate world, and that prisoners, as a matter of survival, belong to individual and competing "tribes"—together make up the most persistent message prison literature has to offer. In this sense, the prison novel, especially in its white manifestation, is at once the ultimate minority or marginalized literature and the most extreme expression imaginable of the dark side of humanity and the majority culture.

The American prison novel is a hybrid form with origins in prisoner autobiography, documentary naturalism, protest fiction, and the old-fashioned crime novel. Indeed, inasmuch as both prisons and novels developed at approximately the same time (the late eighteenth century), the prison novel itself can be said to be as old as either.[3]

More properly, however, the form as we know it begins with the rise of the proletarian novel and the hard-boiled fiction of the 1930s. Chester Himes's *Black Sheep,* written in the thirties but not published for another fifteen years (as *Cast the First Stone* in 1952), is the first American novel of any importance written by an actual convict. Himes, an African American writer best known for his detective novel characters Grave Digger Jones and Coffin Ed Brown, was influenced by both the activism of Richard Wright and the tough-guy style of Dashiell Hammett. Most subsequent prison fiction has reproduced this dual mark of inheritance—in the first place, by working to expose "prison conditions," and in the second, by focusing on underworld characters involved in almost nonstop conflict and action.

The most important and best known prison novel to date is Malcolm Braly's *On the Yard.* A thief and chronic repeat offender, Braly was also a novelist of considerable skill and resources, publishing in his lifetime on every aspect of the criminal justice system and in every major prose form, including autobiography. First published in 1967, *On the Yard* set the standard for all subsequent prison fiction, as well as establishing its basic plot, cast of characters, and chief areas of concern.[4]

In *Doing Time in American Prisons: A Study of Modern Novels* (1989), Dennis Massey identifies the three basic plot sequences of the modern prison novel as Entry, the World of the Prison, and Crisis.[5] In a typical Entry sequence, the reader is made to experience the initial shock of the prison experience through the consciousness of a "fish," or new inmate. Superior prison novels, such as *On the Yard,* cut back and forth between this fish experience and a day-in-the-life sequence featuring an experienced con, typically a long-termer who functions well in the prison environment. For example, in *On the Yard,* the severe jolt Will Manning feels upon first entering San Quentin is played against the extreme boredom of long-termers Society Red and Chilly Willy. Where Manning sees everything—and especially San Quentin's Big Yard—as total chaos, an arena of almost unlimited danger, Chilly Willy (so called because he remains so "cool") sees it as a more predictable "jungle" ecosystem, filled with predators, prey, and one or two "players," like himself, who exploit the situation in equally predictable ways.

The second sequence, the World of the Prison, typically takes up these different slices of prison life, concentrating especially on the prevalence of cliques, gambling, prison-style homosexuality, and a detailed inmate power structure determined by gang affiliation and access to such "juice" jobs as clerk for someone high in the prison administration. In *On the Yard,* for example, Chilly Willy's "juice" comes from his position as Lieutenant Olson's clerk, his gambling book, and his control of traffic in nasal inhalers and other drugs. Chilly's profits—sometimes cash, more often cigarettes—allow him to buy influence, friends, and the few material comforts available in prison, such as a single cell. The new prisoner, such as Will Manning, has no "juice" in the institution and so is in constant danger of becoming another man's prey.

The Crisis sequence in these novels reinforces the absolute *danger* of the prison situation by confronting one of the main characters (usually a fish) with some form of prison trouble. Whatever form the trouble takes—pressure about a gambling debt, gang trouble, the threat of homosexual rape—one thing is certain: the convict's name, his reputation, and thus his life as a man among men is in jeopardy. The choices in such a situation are few, and often revolve around the dilemma of whether to kill, and thus add years to one's sentence, or accept protective custody and a "jacket" as a punk or snitch. The overall message of the sequence, as one would expect, is that there is no easy "out" in the modern prison experience.

To Massey's basic structure for the modern prison novel must be added the genre's most durable set pieces—death by stabbing, homosexual rape, and the riot and/or race war. (This last is especially important in the post-1960s prison novel, in which racial warfare as a theme is second only to imprisonment itself.) Survival in the face of these individual threats is the basic theme of almost all prison fiction. In the parlance of the prison circa Braly, the new prisoner is in constant danger of getting "shanked," "turned out," or "caught in a shitstorm."

Edward Bunker's *The Animal Factory* is the best gang-era example of the modern prison novel. It begins not with a crime, nor even with a trial, but with Ron Decker's sentencing, the true beginning of his journey to the prison world. The novel then moves through Entry, the World of the Prison, and finally to Crisis, where Ron is required to brutally stab another inmate in order to ensure his own survival. This in turn creates a situation in which Ron is no longer "short" (i.e., a short termer), and so moves the novel into its fantasy of escape phase, in which Ron finally leaves the prison by hiding inside a garbage truck.

In recent years, prison literature, like the prison itself, has become split along racial lines, with the so-called black version finding its roots in the slave narrative (and African American autobiography more generally), the so-called white version finding its roots in the proletarian "tough-guy" novel of the 1930s. The reason for this split is nothing less than a fundamental difference in each group's view of imprisonment. As H. Bruce Franklin writes in *The Victim as Criminal and Artist* (1978), "To the Black convict or peon, imprisonment [does] not mean becoming an alien being isolated from the rest of his people but rather becoming the typical representative of his people."[6] The white prisoner, by contrast, can sustain such an illusion only by mouthing the sort of petrified, otherworldly communism one finds in Jack Henry Abbott's *In the Belly of the Beast* (1981); surely a difficult task for anyone to keep up for very long.

In a 1972 *Harper's* essay on the race wars then raging inside San Quentin, Edward Bunker delineated this difference from the specific point of view of the white inmate. Black inmates, Bunker wrote, have "decided they are political prisoners":

> The black realizes that he has committed a crime, or has acted against the statutes. However, the claim of "political prisoner" comes from the argument that he was formed by a corrupt system, that his acts are a result thereof, and therefore he cannot be held responsible. Secondarily, he feels that he has never been a part of this system, but is still in slavery, and consequently the white laws do not apply to him. Such personalities are often found in prison, where the flower of black racism is blossoming, virulent and paranoid. Many white convicts are equally dangerous and intractable, but they at least intellectually accept that their acts are wrong.[7]

For a critic like H. Bruce Franklin, who tends to view all convicts as victims of society, Bunker's views "do not reflect the political reality of today's prisons" (267). Yet even Franklin admits that these views do "unconsciously reveal the psychological core" of most white prison writing (267). Thus while a book like *The Autobiography of Malcolm X* (1965) must be taken as a sort of paradigm for the post-1950s black prison narrative, inspiring such lessor works as Eldridge Cleaver's *Soul on Ice* (1968) or George Jackson's *Soledad Brother* (1970), its impact on the white prison narrative has been largely limited to the section—anthologized in a thousand freshman composition readers—in which Malcolm teaches himself to read and write by copying out the entire Webster's dictionary.

Franklin's point about the lack of *alienation* in the black prison narrative would appear to hold true for the black prison *novel* as well. Passages such as the following, in which the hero of Nathan C. Heard's *To Reach a Dream* (1972) considers his prison experience, are common if not representative:

"The whole period of incarceration was nothing more than an extension course of his street education. He learned nothing new, only refinements of what he'd known all along from the life that helped to form him. He was black; he was prepared, therefore, for coping with jail, since his life style had so closely resembled prison. The methods of operation altered but not the madness."[8] But this is neither the attitude nor the message of the white prison novel, which represents prison as a place of overwhelming difference from the "outside." The lessons one must learn in order to survive in prison are of a different order entirely than those one must learn to succeed in society. Rather, these lessons form the mysterious code of a separate world; and the danger is not only that one should learn them improperly, and hence perish in prison, but also that one should learn them too well, and by doing so unfit oneself for ever living in the free world again.

When initially reviewed in the *New York Times, Homeboy* was compared not only to the work of William Burroughs and Henry Miller (both giants in the tradition of underworld realism), but also to that of Charles Dickens and Henry Fielding. Likening Morgan's Joe Speaker to such characters as Pip and Tom Jones, the *Times* reviewer saw *Homeboy* as a "classic coming-of-age novel" in which the hero "accrues character, nuance and compassion" from adventures "strongly informed by issues of patrimony."[9]

Morgan, who died in a motorcycle accident in New Orleans shortly after his novel was published, was not a career convict like Edward Bunker or Malcolm Braly, but in fact the ne'er-do-well son of Frederick Morgan, a minor New York poet and founder of the *Hudson Review*. Heir to a soap fortune, Frederick Morgan could afford to send his son to rich-kid schools like Hotchkiss and the American School in Switzerland, both of which Seth Morgan was kicked out of for various infractions before finally graduating from Butler Institute in Mexico. From there it was off to 1967 Berkeley, where Morgan discovered heroin and dated Janis Joplin. He was to have seen Joplin on the night she overdosed in October 1970. By 1977, after more drugs and booze and a muddled career in armed robbery, Morgan had wound up in Vacaville State Prison. Sober for the first time in a long time, Morgan took writing classes, and in 1978 he won the PEN American Prisoners' Writing Contest with a story about Janis Joplin and cocaine. Out on parole, Morgan mixed bouts of drug and alcohol abuse with writing, and eventually he managed to finish a 1,000–page manuscript, which editor Jason Epstein helped him cut to 390 pages.[10]

This difference between Morgan and most prison writers is reflected in his novel, which differs from the classic prison novel in that it begins with Joe Speaker on the street in his profession of drug dealer and strip-show barker, saving the prison sequences for the book's second half. *Homeboy,* that is to say, is in certain important respects a hybrid: half underworld crime novel, half prison novel. Be that as it may, once its prison sequence gets rolling, *Homeboy* centers itself around the same father-son, mentor-protégé relationship almost all prison novels make use of, this structure serving to facilitate the "lesson," or window-on-a-world format of the classic *Bildungsroman.*

Both *The Animal Factory* and *Homeboy* feature a central relationship between a young, relatively innocent first offender and an older, "state-raised" convict.[11] In *The Animal Factory,* the relationship between Ron Decker, a twenty-five-year-old drug dealer, and Earl Copen, a thirty-seven-year-old three-time loser, is complicated by homosexual overtones. Everyone in San Quentin, including Earl's closest friends, take his concern for the younger man to be a "jocker's" interest in the "punk" he's about to "turn out." Only Paul Adams, Earl's oldest prison associate, recognizes the relationship as one of friendship. In *Homeboy,* Morgan pushes the father-son analogy to a literal conclusion; late in the novel, Joe Speaker discovers that Earl Fitzgerald, his Coldwater mentor, is also his biological father. In both books, the father figure teaches the younger man everything he knows about prison survival, eventually even sacrificing himself so that the "son" might go free (Ron through an implausible escape, Joe through a bought, "coffee-break" parole).

The importance of the father-son theme lies in the "lessons" about prison it allows the writer to present directly to his reader. The first of these is that survival is dependent upon being good at the prison game. As Earl in *The Animal Factory* explains, "Prison is a separate world and you have to build a life separate from the world outside."[12] This means, among other things, that those who do best in prison are those who become, as Joe in *Homeboy* finally does, "accomplished convict chamberlain[s] . . . adept at negotiating official channels" (317). A man's "juice" in the institution determines what he eats, where he lives, and who his friends are. The irony, of course, is that those who become *too* good at the prison game never get out; or if they do, simply return again and again, making parole a sort of vacation from their true lives in the institution. Earl in *The Animal Factory* recognizes this about himself. When he fails to escape with Ron at the novel's end, he simply "snort[s] an ironical laugh" and says, "Aw, fuck it. I run something around here. I'd probably starve to death out there" (202). Hence, overadaptation to the prison environment is as deadly as underadaptation.

The second lesson has to do with image. As Earl Copen explains it to Ron Decker, "All a man in prison has is his name among his peers" (110). In other words, in prison a man can't afford *not* to care what people think about him; it is the key to his survival. As with many of the other lessons in *The Animal Factory,* Ron must learn this one through observation. Early in the novel, Ron isn't worried that other inmates take him to be Earl Copen's "punk": "As long as he himself knew the truth, it didn't matter what ignorant convicts thought. In the coming months, his attitude would change. He learned that a good name was important, critically so. He saw a man with friends get slapped and do nothing about it. The friends turned their backs and the man was thereafter made to pay his canteen for protection until he finally checked into protective custody and got transferred. Any sign of weakness invited aggression" (110). Besides showing how crucial the whole issue of image is, this passage further demonstrates the need for friends in prison. In many ways, Whisper Moran's old-time convict code, *Do your own time, hold your own mud,* is complicated by the contemporary prison's warring factions of cliques and gangs, which create an atmosphere where a man must choose sides in almost every prison dispute. As San Quentin old-timer Paul Adams remarks, things were different in the "old days": "[N]o big gangs, no race trouble. If a youngster would stand up, they'd pretty much leave him alone. Now if he doesn't have friends, they just rape him and it doesn't matter how mean he is. King Kong can't stand up to fifteen or twenty men with knives who not only don't care about killing, but want to kill" (120–21). The problem, of course, is knowing who your friends are. When Joe asks Whisper, in *Homeboy,* if he can trust another con, Whisper answers, "Not unless you trust your worst enemy. You dont front off friends with secrets they dont need to know. I seen bocco dudes shanked for being talked to out of school" (151).

Whisper's advice here leads us to the third general rule for successfully surviving a term in prison, namely, that no one is immune from trouble. As Earl Copen tells Ron after they both witness a shanking on the big yard, "Everybody can die. Everybody bleeds. And everybody can kill in the right situation" (114). Earl is the best-adapted prisoner in *The Animal Factory,* but even he is "at home" in prison only "in the way that the jungle animal is at home—cautiously" (25). Ron himself proves the maxim "everybody can kill" in his showdown with Buck Rowan, a new prisoner who makes the mistake of pressuring him for sex. Whereas the Ron of the early chapters has an aversion to violence, the Ron of nearly a year in prison has no trouble "burying fourteen inches of steel" in Buck Rowan's back (140).

Of course, while no one is immune from all trouble, there are ways to avoid the most stupid kinds. Whisper's general rule number one—never owe anyone anything—certainly applies to most of the killings in *Homeboy* and *The Animal Factory:* "Dont fuck with sissies, they'll put you in a cross every time. Dont gamble, you end up unable to cover your losses and stone cold dead. Same for narcotics, you'll dig your own grave. Ditto borrowing. I've seen dudes gutted for a pack of cigarets paid back a day late" (151). And Chilly Willy's demise in *On the Yard* is the perfect illustration of Whisper's rule. After having Paul Juleson murdered over little more than a pack of cigarettes, Chilly is himself done in by his involvement with the "sissie" Candy Cane.

The last and most problematic "lesson" expounded by the father figures of both *The Animal Factory* and *Homeboy* has to do with the necessary development of racial consciousness. Here the rule is, Remain loyal to your own race and don't mix unnecessarily with those of other races, even if they were friends on the outside. In each novel, the reason given for the rule is the spread of gangs throughout the California prison system in the mid-sixties and early seventies; and in each case, the existence of these gangs is blamed on the rhetoric and practices of sixties-era black revolutionaries—Muslims and Black Panthers. The similarities in story between the different novels is striking. *Homeboy:*

> The way Whisper ran it down, before the midsixties, there were no racial gangs in California's penitentiaries. Every joint had its tips for controlling dope and prostitution and gambling. But they weren't coordinated throughout the system, nor racially based. Yet within prison populations, blacks protected blacks and Hispanics looked after their own. It was an instinct brought out of the ghettos and barrios. The whites, accustomed to their majority in the real world, lacked this instinct. No white stood up for another simply because he was white. (152)

Earl in *The Animal Factory:*

> When I came here, a beef was a personal matter. It might involve a couple of friends, but even that was unusual. Then came the Black Muslims and the Nazis, and as long as they just fucked each other up, it still didn't bother me. Then *they* started stabbing white convicts indiscriminately whenever one of them got stabbed, even if it was over dope or a sissy. A lot of dudes don't know when it started, but I was here. I *know.* I don't like it, but I like it a lot better than what would happen if we didn't get down. (125)

For Ron, in *The Animal Factory,* this is a hard lesson to learn. He comes to San Quentin with a learned and felt sympathy for the plight of blacks and other minorities. He is angry when he witnesses the almost total segregation of the prison environment, even when he learns that this segregation is enforced by the convicts themselves, not the prison administration. He cannot understand why a man he might talk to in the education building cannot even be acknowledged with a wave or a nod on the prison yard. Earl tells him, "You think it doesn't involve you. It involves everybody, both sides. When the war starts, you'll be as potential a victim as anyone" (125). The convict who would ignore these racial codes is in danger from *both* sides, but especially his own because, as Earl tells Ron, "the dudes who do the fighting on your side don't dig fraternization" (125).

The "dudes who do the fighting" on the white side, are, of course, the Aryan Brotherhood or "Nazis." Far from being presented as a racist white power group, this gang is said to be "just a bunch of lowlife bikers and white trash" who have decided, for reasons of racial survival, that "whites [have] to start watching white backs" (*Homeboy* 152). Their reasons are given by Whisper Moran in the form of a primal scene of white fear:

No white stood up for another simply because he was white. . . . That's the way it was when I first came in on a burglary. They carried me to the Glass House, the old L.A. County jail. The second night they brought in a pretty young whiteboy. Right at the gate, the niggers took his cigarets. He asked the other whiteboys for help, they told him to cover his own ass. When he made the canteen cart, the beaners ripped off his zuuzuus and whamwhams. The rest of the whiteboys just watched. That same night the niggers and chilichokers dragged that boy back to the showers, gagged him with a sock, and ran a train on him all night long. Left him half dead. . . . And what did the other whiteboys do? Pretended to sleep through it. I was a firsttermer, young and scared, but half them guys were career cons . . . And here's the kicker. Along about dawn, this Arkie bohunk named Hutchinson actually got up and went back there and helped himself to some of that boy's butthole. Actually stood in line with niggers and chokes to rape his own kind. . . . Well, I guess you could say the Aryan Brotherhood was born that night in the Glass House. (152)

If we accept that all of the "lessons" we've seen so far operate on the principle of what a newcomer should most *fear* from the prison environment, then it is clear that this terrible scene is the culmination of them all. What it all boils down to is this: prison is a different world; forget what you learned on the outside; a man's image and friends are all important; any sign of weakness is exploited, and the biggest sign is to be raped; given the ongoing race war, the only protection a man really has against rape is solidarity with his own race, represented in this case by the Aryan Brotherhood.

This, above anything else, is the message of the contemporary white prison novel. That it is so stark and, ultimately, so frightening, should probably not surprise us. For that is precisely the stark reality of the prison itself.

Is such a message racist? I'm not so sure. The tone a book like *The Animal Factory* takes toward all prison problems, but especially the prison racial situation, is one of unmitigated sadness. A character like Earl Copen continually laments the fact that racially motivated attacks on both white convicts and guards has led to an "unholy alliance" between the two. Such an alliance is "alien to all of Earl's values" (42). Likewise, in *Homeboy,* Whisper Moran is presented as a wasted but wise character whose last advice to Joe is, "Aint no security in clicking up. If you got a problem inside, joining a prison gang only gonna make it worse" (152). In the end, even the head chingaso of the San Quentin Aryan Brotherhood argues against racism. His reasons for doing so, however, amount to little more than the simple survival of the individual in a hostile environment. Thus the ultimate irony of the prison novel is the same as the irony of the prison itself: that something so paltry as mere survival takes the place of what, in a better world, we might call development.

Conclusion

Conclusion
Conclusion
Conclusion

In the preceding pages I've tried to point out and describe some of the principal strengths of a continuing tradition in American fiction that began, as Hemingway once observed, with Mark Twain's *Adventures of Huckleberry Finn*—the first major American novel to combine realism with local color and sophisticated social commentary. American fiction at the end of the millennium embraces past traditions and forms even as it remains resolutely *topical,* both in the sense of belonging to a particular location or place, and in the sense of being of current interest, contemporary. This topicality, largely absent from the work of the postmodernists and only marginally there in minimalism, accounts for the wide interest readers outside the university have shown in the new fiction, but it also brings up the question of whether this fiction will last, stand the test of time, as *Huckleberry Finn*—in its own way, a relentlessly topical novel—has stood that test for more than one hundred years.

One of the books I used as a model for this one was Marcus Klein's *After Alienation* (1965), which took as its subject a period in American fiction beginning about 1950 and extending, as Klein noted in his preface, "to just this moment," that is, February 1964. One of the remarkable things about *After Alienation* is the way it has stood the test of time. The authors Klein regarded as important in the early sixties, most of them barely at midcareer by then, are by and large still the authors we would consider important today. All of them, that is, but one. Along with chapters on the works of Saul Bellow, Ralph Ellison, James Baldwin, and Bernard Malamud, Klein also included a full chapter on the novels of Wright Morris, about whom he writes, "No American of these years has been more deliberately or more consciously American than Wright Morris, and no novelist of this time has been more certainly in touch with American surfaces, with such things and such voices as seem to concentrate precisely a sense of the national uniqueness."[1] Where, we want to ask, is Wright Morris now? Who reads his novels? Who teaches them? And yet, at the time Klein wrote his book, there was very general agreement about Morris's importance.

The example of Wright Morris is a chilling reminder that any one of the writers whose work I have treated in this book could easily be forgotten and out of print thirty years from now. Despite this danger, however, which is perhaps inherent in a project such as this, I believe that the fiction I have discussed in this book, and of the last two decades of the twentieth century in general, will continue to be important for a long time to come, and I would like to take the space I have remaining to offer a few reasons for this belief.

To begin with, much contemporary American fiction published between 1980 and 2000 concerns itself with forgotten regions and explores marginal characters left largely untouched, or treated only as stereotypes, in previous American writing. Examples, in terms of place, include Erdrich's Chippewa Reservation in North Dakota, the mythic Southwest of Anaya, Kingsolver, and Cormac McCarthy, Richard Russo's New York, and the Louisiana of Ernest J. Gaines. The characters these and other writers create are as rich and diverse—and, quite often, as unprecedented—as the places they depict. They stick in the mind long after the books in which they appear are put down. I'm thinking in particular of Dorothy Allison's "Bone" Boatwright, McCarthy's John Grady Cole, and the unnamed narrators of Denis Johnson's *Jesus' Son* or William T. Vollmann's *The Atlas*. These characters come at the reader seemingly out of nowhere, but to follow their separate lives is to learn something new about human beings and their relationships with each other and the lands they inhabit.

Perhaps the perfect example of what is so new about the place and characters of contemporary American fiction comes in Robert Olen Butler's short story collection *A Good Scent from a Strange Mountain,* which won the 1993 Pulitzer Prize and the Richard and Hinda Rosenthal Prize issued by the American Academy of Arts and Letters. Each of the collection's fifteen stories is told from the point of view of a Vietnamese émigré transplanted from the Mekong Delta to the Bayou villages of Gretna and Versailles, Louisiana. Butler, an army linguist during the Vietnam War, has lived for some time in Lake Charles, Louisiana, where he has discovered, as Madison Smartt Bell wrote in his review of *A Good Scent from a Strange Mountain,* "a pocket of cross-cultural peculiarity, which has become, for him, a sort of writer's paradise." Butler's achievement in this book, Bell wrote, "is not only to reveal the inner lives of the Vietnamese but also to show, through their eyes, how the rest of us appear from an outside perspective."[2]

Vince Passaro for his part has remarked how thoroughly Butler has managed to avoid "the documentary tendency that many another writer would have applied" to this subject matter. In *A Good Scent,* Butler is not out to "show us what the Vietnamese eat or wear or how they worship or what, politically, they believe," although, as Passaro observes, "all of those things quite properly can be found in his stories"; instead, Butler delivers what every writer of "serious fiction" knows to be "his primary obligation," namely, a fascinating revelation of "the inner lives of his characters."[3]

These characters—a bar girl remembering what a delicacy apples were in Saigon, a successful businessman driving to Houston to pick up his wife's grandfather, just arriving from Vietnam, an old man preparing for death who is visited in a dream by the ghost of Ho Chi Minh—are something altogether new in American fiction; we glimpse through their eyes a different America, one still recognizably our own yet irrevocably altered.

Part of Butler's accomplishment in the collection can be traced to the fidelity with which he delivers these Vietnamese voices—his thorough, insider knowledge of the Vietnamese language and Vietnamese customs. Just as impressive, however, is the narrative technique Butler employs in the stories, which quickly draws the reader into a foreign world, then slowly goes about making complete sense of it. The story called "Mr. Green," for example, begins with the following enigmatic sentence: "I am a Catholic, the daughter of a Catholic mother and father, and I do not believe in the worship of my ancestors, especially in the form of a parrot."[4] The story concerns a married Vietnamese woman who has brought with her to America a parrot that had belonged to her grandfather, a "believer in what Confucius taught about ancestors" (17). Through this parrot, which speaks in the Vietnamese voice of her grandfather, the narrator is made to confront both the love and the resentment she felt for the man, who had denied her the respect he would have given a grandson. Another story, "Love," begins with these sentences: "I was once able to bring fire from heaven. My wife knew that and her would-be lovers soon learned that, though sometimes the lesson was a hard one for them. But that was in Vietnam, and when the need arose once more, here in America, I had to find a new way" (73). The exact meaning of these words, which initially sound like something out of a fairy tale, only becomes clear later in the story, when we learn that the narrator was once a spy for the American forces in Vietnam, and as such had the power to call in air strikes—

"fire from heaven"—on any coordinates he chose. In essence, these and the other stories in Butler's collection, especially the title story and "The Trip Back," do precisely what Frederick Karl, in *American Fictions,* had argued that the postmodern novel of the sixties and seventies did so well: they "defamiliarize the familiar," and while moving the America we know so well to the margins, move the margins of American experience to the center.

Indeed, the important fiction of our time is as likely to be set in Montana or South Carolina as in New York or Los Angeles. It is as likely to portray the lives of so-called marginalized people—reservation Indians, recent immigrants, crack-addicted prostitutes, prisoners—as it is to portray the familiar world of the suburbs. In these ways the new fiction operates as a window on a series of separate and yet intricately related worlds; taken together, it describes not a monolith but a web.

Contemporary fiction also impresses on a purely technical level. If we tend to think of previous periods of American literature in terms of the technical advances they embodied—for example, the flowering of the short story during the time of Poe and Hawthorne, or the more sophisticated direction the novel took during the time of Henry James—then in our own time, contemporary American fiction has embodied several similar breakthroughs, most notably the renaissance of the short story in the work of Raymond Carver and others, but also the rebirth of the story collection itself as a work of art.

As Vince Passaro observed in an essay on recent short fiction in the August 1999 *Harper's,* "Today's American short fiction is more various, more successfully experimental, more urbane, funnier, and more bitingly ironic than that written in the Hemingway tradition. It is also more idiosyncratic in its voices, less commercial, and more expansive in its approach to the requirements of art. . . . Quietly—indeed, almost invisibly, with little popular or critical recognition—the 1990s have presented us with some of the best and formally most innovative short fiction in our literature."[5] Passaro singles out a number of the form's contemporary practitioners, including Lorrie Moore, Denis Johnson, Thom Jones, William T. Vollmann, David Foster Wallace, George Saunders, Mary Gaitskill, Rick Moody, Joanna Scott, Lydia Davis, and Steven Millhauser, arguing that in the work of these writers, most of it little known to the public at large and written virtually without compensation, American fiction "might be free enough to muster one more golden age" (89) to rival those of Irving, Hawthorne, Poe, and James in the nineteenth century, Hemingway, Fitzgerald, Faulkner, and O'Connor in the twentieth. The aesthetic diversity of this new work may be gleaned from the fact that while Passaro praises the short story writers of the 1990s for being "formally innovative" and "successfully experimental," for writing in opposition to an "unexperimental," traditional "idea of what a literary story ought to be," a tradition exemplified in the tight, "commercial fiction of Hemingway and Fitzgerald" (81), Robert Stone has praised many of these same writers for reviving realism and for their willingness to "accept traditional forms without self-consciousness."[6]

Contemporary writers have also raised the bar on the story *collection* as a unified work of art. Books like Butler's *Good Scent from a Strange Mountain,* Erdrich's *Love Medicine,* Denis Johnson's *Jesus' Son,* or William T. Vollmann's *The Atlas* attempt far more than most collections of previously published material. They advance a single theme or a unified set of themes, create a particular place, or even deal with the lives of a common cast of characters— a family, say, or the people in a single town. The individual stories, often brilliant on their own, gain a kind of cumulative power when placed alongside each other in a particular order, a unity of purpose and design we more normally associate with the novel. Of course, one might argue that there is nothing particularly new in this. Books like Sherwood Anderson's *Winesburg, Ohio,* Hemingway's *In Our Time,* or Faulkner's *Go Down, Moses* did the same thing. But not since the time of these writers has the novelistic tendency in story collections been so fully realized or so well done.

A further example of the formal achievements of the contemporary American story comes in the revival of the novella form. Two writers in particular, Stanley Elkin and Jim Harrison, have raised the novella or long story to heights unseen in our literature since the tales of Henry James. Elkin's *Van Gogh's Room at Arles* (1993), a book comprising three novellas, was a finalist for the 1994 PEN/Faulkner Award, a remarkable accomplishment for a collection of novellas; Harrison's novellas, especially *Revenge* and *Legends of the Fall,* are masterpieces of summary exposition, an element of narrative craft that many complain has all but disappeared in the years since Hemingway brought action and dialogue to the fore.

And let us not forget what contemporary writers have begun to accomplish in the novel form. Books like Proulx's *The Shipping News,* McCarthy's *All the Pretty Horses,* or Allison's *Bastard Out of Carolina,* and, more recently, Don DeLillo's *Underworld* (1997), are in their way as structurally sophisticated as any work of literary postmodernism, even as they remain realistic with regard to setting and character. *The Shipping News*'s successive chapters take their names from the different seaman's knots in Clifford W. Ashley's *Ashley Book of Knots* (1944)—the Love Knot, the Strangle Knot, the Cast Away, the Rolling Hitch, and so on—with each knot representing either an important plot development, such as the ties binding particular characters, or a further illustration of the manifold ways in which the book itself is tied together. *All the Pretty Horses* finds its form in an archetypal journey motif with roots in both the Garden of Eden and Exodus. *Bastard Out of Carolina,* on its surface a fairly traditional *Bildungsroman,* becomes by its end a work that explores the structure and efficacy of traditional religious testimony.

The dominant formal device at work in Jane Smiley's novel *A Thousand Acres,* which won both the 1992 Pulitzer Prize and the National Book Critics Circle Award for that year, is akin to what T.S. Eliot, referring to Joyce's use of Homer in *Ulysses,* called the "mythic method." Using Shakespeare's *King Lear* as a model, Smiley tells the story of the decline of a family farm in Iowa, uncovering along the way the hidden weaknesses and hatreds of all the family's members, from its patriarch, Larry Cook, who decides on a whim to divide his one thousand acres among his three daughters, to each of these daughters, their husbands, and their neighbors.

The idea for *A Thousand Acres* grew out of Smiley's experience as a reader of Shakespeare's *King Lear*—she had long been fascinated by the unstated reasons for the rage of Lear's daughters—as well as her own observation of modern agricultural practices in Iowa and the probable environmental consequences of these practices. Below the surface in both *Lear* and life on the contemporary American farm, Smiley thought, "were an arrogance toward and a need to dominate nature, and by extension, women."[7]

What is initially so impressive about the book, however, is the way Shakespeare's play is subtly evoked and explored without ever coming to dominate or intrude on Smiley's own work. Without being told beforehand, even those readers most familiar with *Lear* would not recognize it as the novel's analogue or inspiration until the scene in which Larry Cook divides his farm, perhaps not even then. This is because the novel's mastery of local detail, its documentary realism with regard to every aspect of modern agriculture, is so thoroughly researched and convincing. For example, the book's first few chapters contrast Larry Cook's conservative, modern agricultural practices with his neighbor Cal Ericson's "sloppy," old-time methods, simultaneously introducing readers to the high-tech farming practices Smiley will later critique and paving the way for future plot developments, such as when the Ericsons lose their mortgaged land to the Cooks. "Acreage and financing were facts as basic as name and gender in Zebulon County," Ginny, the novel's narrator, observes:

Harold Clark and my father used to argue at our kitchen table about who should get the Ericson land when they finally lost their mortgage. I was aware of this whenever I played with Ruthie Ericson, whenever my mother, my sister Rose, and I went over to help can garden produce, whenever Mrs. Ericson brought over some pies or doughnuts, whenever my father loaned Mr. Ericson a tool, whenever we ate Sunday dinner in the Ericsons' kitchen. I recognized the justice of Harold Clark's opinion that the Ericson land was on his side of the road, but even so, I thought it should be us. For one thing, Dinah Ericson's bedroom had a window seat in the closet that I coveted. For another, I thought it appropriate and desirable that the great circle of flat earth spreading out from the T intersection of County Road 686 and Cabot Street Road be ours. A thousand acres. It was that simple.[8]

The narrator is eight years old when she sees "the farm and the future in this way" (4). It is the natural outcome of the system of beliefs she has been raised to observe, the "catechism," as she calls it, that she has learned from her father and other farmers:

> What is a farmer?
> A farmer is a man who feeds the world.
> What is a farmer's first duty?
> To grow more food.
> What is a farmer's second duty?
> To buy more land.
> What are the signs of a good farm?
> Clean fields, neatly painted buildings, breakfast at six, no debts, no standing water.
> How will you know a good farmer when you meet him?
> He will not ask you for any favors. (45)

Details such as these, which convince readers of their authenticity and lend the novel as a whole a powerful authority, are the groundwork upon which the novel's conclusions will later be built.

Although *A Thousand Acres* takes its form from *King Lear,* the reasons behind the tragedy it unfolds come not from Shakespeare but from the novel's own content: the Cooks' relationship with the land they farm, which, as Smiley sees it, is skewed in favor of production. It is this relationship, land lust coupled with the abuse of agricultural chemicals, that eventually leads to Larry Cook's madness, Ginny's several miscarriages, and her sister Rose's breast cancer: the farm's groundwater has been poisoned. Even the revelation of incest is somehow related. Larry Cook's attitudes toward his daughters is essentially the same as his attitude toward the land: ownership at all costs.

By so unselfconsciously appropriating the form of Shakespearean tragedy in *A Thousand Acres,* Smiley displays what is a common attitude in contemporary American fiction. Not only may the forms of previous literature be used, but they may be used *without irony.* In the end, the formal triumph Smiley achieves here stands out precisely because it does not overshadow the novel's content.

In his essay "Tradition and the Individual Talent," T.S. Eliot argued that "[n]o poet, no artist of any art, has his complete meaning alone." The artist's "significance, his appreciation is the appreciation of his relation to the dead poets and artists." Not only "the best," but "the most individual parts" of any artist's work were often "those in which the dead poets, his ancestors, assert their immortality most vigorously." Yet in attending to his relation to past works of art, the contemporary artist was not performing a mere act of homage. If successful, his work changed the existing canon as greatly as it was influenced by it. "The existing monuments form an ideal order among themselves," Eliot wrote, "which is modified by the introduction of the new (the really new) work of art among them."[9]

Eliot's ideas in this essay, which apply most immediately to modernism's relationship to the classics of Western literature, also describe the relationship between the best contemporary American fiction and the classics of our tradition, the sophisticated manner in which contemporary fiction petitions the existing canon. One of the most compelling aspects of the work I have been considering, aside from its topicality, is the ways in which it continues an American tradition that was largely ignored by the literary postmodernists of the sixties and seventies, who, like Eliot, looked to Europe for tradition and example. Writers like Erdrich, Morrison, and McCarthy, by contrast, have been most powerfully influenced not by European models but by an American tradition that includes Hawthorne, Melville, Twain, and William Faulkner. Faulkner, in particular, has left his mark on the structure of Erdrich's novels (which typically feature a gallery of first-person narrators), on the moral topography of Morrison's novels (which often deal with the same themes as Faulkner's best work), and on, if nothing else, the prose style of McCarthy's novels (which pays direct homage to the earlier writer's idiosyncracies of diction and punctuation).

Morrison, who has been hailed since her Nobel Prize as "the last classic American writer, squarely in the tradition of Poe, Melville, Twain and Faulkner," provides a powerful example of Eliot's contention that great contemporary writers change the very canon of which they become a part.[10]

Arguing that Morrison will be "a strange addition to the Kiwanis Club of American literature," by which she means "Irving, Cooper, Hawthorne, Poe, Melville, James, Twain, Faulkner, Fitzgerald, and Hemingway," another critic nevertheless insists that Morrison's "inclusion in this group is now axiomatic, not arbitrary, and to a great extent a challenge" to "the superstructure" of the American canon.[11] We have already seen, in the previous chapter, the powerful ways in which Cormac McCarthy both petitions and changes the canon of classic American literature

Taken together, these attributes of contemporary American fiction—its originality in terms of setting and character, its accomplishments on a formal level, and its complex, two-way relationship to the canon of existing works— mark the period from 1980 to 2000 as a rich one in American literary history. Returning to their roots, American writers of this period have nevertheless created something altogether new.

It seems fitting to conclude this book, written at the end of one century and published at the beginning of the next, with a brief consideration of what I take to be one of the masterpieces of late-twentieth-century American fiction, a work that not only consciously takes up many of the millennial themes I have been tracking—particularly the theme of "connections," or the lack thereof, in American life—but does so with an authority over detail borrowed from the broad tradition of realism, and an uncommon artistry born, at least in part, of the formal innovations of literary postmodernism.

Underworld (1997) is Don DeLillo's eleventh novel and a work of enormous scale and ambition, bearing immediate comparison with several other mega-novels of recent years, including David Foster Wallace's *Infinite Jest*, William T. Vollmann's *Fathers and Crows*, William H. Gass's *The Tunnel*, Thomas Pynchon's *Mason & Dixon*, and Leslie Marmon Silko's *Almanac of the Dead*. To give some idea of the scale of these works: consider that the whole of Cormac McCarthy's Border Trilogy totals only 1,020 pages, while *Infinite Jest* weighs in at 1,079 pages, *Fathers and Crows* at nearly 1,000. In the above company, *Underworld* appears relatively slim at 827 pages; more important, it actually justifies its length and, of all these works, is the most accomplished formally.[12]

Despite its length and complexity, however, DeLillo does not consider *Underworld* a work of literary postmodernism. "When people say *White Noise* is postmodern, I don't really complain," he observed in a January 1998 interview. "But I don't see *Underworld* as postmodern. Maybe it's the last modernist gasp."[13] The novel is "about memory," DeLillo continues, "and the way in which the past is constantly with us." It was this theme, more than anything else, that DeLillo aimed for in working out the novel's intricate structure, which shifts back and forth between the 1950s and the 1990s, the beginning and end of the cold war. "Maybe I felt, in a novel so long, that I needed a more overt structure, more connections, than I would normally have ventured toward."

The novel covers roughly five decades of American life, beginning on 3 October 1951—a date that is important for a couple of different reasons, as we shall see—and continuing right up to the advent and expansion of the Internet in the mid- to late 1990s. Along the way, DeLillo introduces a huge cast of characters, including some actual historical figures such as J. Edgar Hoover and Lennie Bruce (shades of E.L. Doctorow), and moves freely back and forth through time, early 1950s to early 1990s, examining within this span what might be called the psychic history of the cold war from the American point of view, a theme that is explored by way of a number of recurring topics or motifs, the most important of which are baseball, the bomb, and garbage.

The book's overall strategy is to seek out and highlight connections between these seemingly disparate themes, and this task is carried out on any number of levels, but especially by the tracking of an single object, a baseball, across time and through the hands of owners and would-be owners, everyone from a poor black kid to a rich white lawyer to a memorabilia collector and conspiracy theorist to the novel's protagonist and primary consciousness, Nick Shay, waste disposal expert and one-time child of the 1950s Bronx. This is not just any baseball, it turns out, but the "Shot Heard Round the World" home-run ball—the ball that Bobby Thomson hit into the left-field stands at the Polo Grounds on 3 October 1951 in the final game of that year's National League pennant race between the Brooklyn Dodgers and New York Giants. Nor is 3 October 1951 just any day, but a day on which the Soviet Union conducted a secret test of their new atomic bomb. It is out of this unexpected, seemingly meaningless connection that DeLillo will build all of the book's manifold connections.

J. Edgar Hoover, for example, appears in the novel because he provides the most immediate connection between the Soviet test bomb, which he almost certainly knew about, and this specific baseball game, which it turns out he attended in the unlikely company of Frank Sinatra, Jackie Gleason, and Toots Shor. Lenny Bruce shows up periodically, delivering a string of coast-to-coast comedy routines during the week of the Cuban missile crisis, the recurrent punch line of which is, *We're all gonna die!* There are all manner of connections between the novel's various characters, too—connections of love, longing, infidelity, and so on. The baseball's various owners cross paths from time to time, or at least their paths cross, as when the plane flown by one of the ball's early owners is painted by a former lover of the ball's final owner. Thematic connections are explored, as in that between weapons and waste, and out of these connections arise a series of conspiracy theories, an "everything's connected" view of the world that is shared by a number of the novel's characters (including both Hoover and Lenny Bruce). As one of these characters, a defense worker, wonders in the middle of a drug-induced paranoid episode, "And how can you tell the difference between orange juice and agent orange if the same massive system connects them at levels outside your comprehension?" (465).

On a structural level, the novel operates according to what DeLillo has called "two time structures," the first a "huge mass sweeping backwards from the 1990s to the 1950s," the second "these little quantum pieces" of a single day, the so-called Manx Martin chapters, which move forward like an "underground stream" and are set apart from the rest of the text by black pages, so that they stand out as "demarked fragments." At the end of the third of these fragments, "these two time-lines connect, so that there is a dovetailing of these two otherwise completely different schemes."[14] The end result is a time structure that closely resembles the action of memory and at the same time replicates the "unexpected connection" that was, for DeLillo, the novel's singular moment of inspiration.

Underworld begins with a twenty-five-thousand-word tour de force prologue that is one of the great set pieces of recent American fiction, bearing comparison with the opening sequence of McCarthy's *Crossing* and the middle novella of William T. Vollmann's *The Atlas*. Originally published in *Harper's*, the prologue had its origins in a newspaper article DeLillo read late in 1991 about the fortieth anniversary of Thomson's home run. DeLillo felt an immediate connection to the material, and a few weeks later he found himself at the library, researching the game. Reeling microfilm through the library's viewer, DeLillo came upon the appropriate page and, as he has recalled in his essay on *Underworld*, "an unexpected connection, a symmetry that seemed to be waiting for someone to discover it." That "unexpected connection" took the form of "a pair of mated headlines," each the same typeface, the same font size, each three columns wide and three lines deep:

GIANTS
CAPTURE
PENNANT

SOVIETS
EXPLODE
ATOMIC BOMB

What he was looking at, DeLillo decided, was "the power of history": "The home run that won the game soon to be known, vaingloriously, as 'The Shot Heard Round the World' had found its vast and awful counterpoint. A Russian mushroom cloud."

DeLillo's allusion to the Hardy poem "The Convergence of the Twain," which juxtaposes the building of the *Titanic* with the growth of the iceberg that will later sink her, raises the question of whether the convergence of Thomson's homer and the Soviet test is mere coincidence or a matter of some larger cosmic significance. The most obvious allusion occurs in DeLillo's use of the word "vainglorious," which Hardy, in his darkly comic way, puts in the mouths of fishes viewing the *Titanic* on the ocean floor: "What does this vaingloriousness down here?" But there is also a rhythmic allusion. Compare DeLillo's line "'The Shot Heard Round the World' had found its vast and awful counterpoint. A Russian mushroom cloud" with Hardy's eighth stanza: "And as the smart ship grew / In stature, grace, and hue, / In shadowy silent distance grew the Iceberg too."[15] In the Hardy poem, striving, overconfident Industrial Man receives his comeuppance when Nature, guided by what Hardy calls the "Immanent Will," slides an iceberg into his path, creating an "august event," a "consummation" that "jars two hemispheres." In DeLillo's formulation, this ultimate consummation—in the form of nuclear annihilation—remains conjectural, a looming possibility rather than an accomplished fact. Nevertheless, it is under this looming threat that what I have called the psychic history of the cold war will unfold.

No character in the prologue understands this better than J. Edgar Hoover, who looks about himself in the innings before Thomson's homer and thinks, "All these people formed by language and climate and popular song and breakfast foods and the jokes they tell and the cars they drive have never had anything in common so much as this, that they are sitting in the furrow of destruction"[16] Only Hoover, whose "sequestered heart holds every festering secret in the Western world," is able to see so early how the bomb, symbol of the cold war, provides "the connection between Us and Them," USA and

USSR, how it is "not enough to hate your enemy. You have to understand how the two of you bring each other to deep completion" (28). Like everyone else in the crowd that day, Hoover longs for a sense of "belonging" or connection, but he's beyond that now. He knows too much—as we, too, will soon know too much.

Russ Hodges, who announces the game over the radio, wants to believe that a thing like Thomson's homer, a shared bit of sports magic, is big enough to keep us "safe in some undetermined way" (60), but that belief is every bit as vainglorious as the notion of building an unsinkable ship; by morning, when DeLillo's "pair of mated headlines" hits the news stands, this belief will be little more than a memory. Thus the lasting importance of the Shot Heard Round the World; for the people who remember the event, it was maybe "the last time people spontaneously went out of their houses for something. Some wonder, some amazement. Like a footnote to the end of the war" (94).

So far, I have described *Underworld* as a mega-novel of vast range and cultural reference. But it is also, as Joseph Conte has observed, the first of DeLillo's novels "thoroughly devoted to an examination of the place of ethnicity—specifically that of Italian Americans—in the panorama of American life."[17] The book is, in other words, a kind of return for DeLillo. "When I first started writing," he remembers, "I wrote short stories about the Italian Bronx. But I wasn't very good at it. Then, with *Americana,* I made an enormous leap, and I think this is what made me a writer. But it took me all those years, all those decades, to gain sufficient perspective to go back . . . into areas I'd avoided—religion, ethnic identity, all of that."[18]

DeLillo's previous books, among them the 1985 National Book Award–winning *White Noise* and the 1988 PEN/Faulkner Award–winning *Libra,* brilliantly tracked the obsessions of postwar America but were thought to be a little cold—"beautifully tender anxiety dreams" defined by their "cool formal artistry," as Martin Amis has said of *White Noise* and *Mao II.*[19] *Underworld* made different demands on the author's talents, and the result is a different kind of achievement. "I wouldn't say it was working class fiction," he has said of part 6 of the novel, set entirely in the Bronx of the 1950s, "but certainly the characters and the physical labors they perform—the garbagemen, the butchers, the seamstress and so on—did have an effect on the prose itself."[20]

Writing of this process in a January 1998 essay on *Underworld,* DeLillo lets loose a kind of rhapsody on what he calls "the word-related pleasures of memory": "The smatter of language of old street games and the rhythms of a thousand street-corner conversations, adolescent and raw. The quirky language of baseball and the glossy adspeak of Madison Avenue. And what rich rude tang in the Italian-American vulgate, all those unspellable dialect words and derivations of the lost Bronx, and what stealthy pleasure to work out the spellings, and how surely this range of small personal recollection served to quicken and enlarge the language that ensued."[21] It was to all this, and more, that Don DeLillo returned in writing *Underworld*. For the first time in his published career, DeLillo becomes every bit as much of an "ethnic" writer as Anaya or Erdrich or Amy Tan, yet in doing so he surrenders none of the artistry of his previous novels.

Seven hundred pages after the prologue's close, in a superb epilogue, the waste disposal expert Nick Shay, grown up and out of the Italian Bronx, who has succeeded in buying the Thomson home-run ball for $34,500, travels into the heart of the New Russia, post–cold war, where everything is for sale and where nuclear waste is destroyed by way of nuclear explosions. In this brave new world, America is connected to its former foe not by terror or assured mutual destruction, but by the flow of capital and instant information. In this world, the bomb no longer reigns supreme, and the "real miracle is the web, the net, where everybody is everywhere at once" (808), where "there are only connections. Everything is connected. All human knowledge is gathered and linked, hyperlinked, this site leading to that, this fact referenced to that, a keystroke, a mouse-click, a password—world without end, amen" (825).

Between the prologue and epilogue, in the heart of this powerful book, lies the great American desert, a landscape of terrifying emptiness, the same landscape Billy Parham traversed at the end of McCarthy's *Crossing*, where once test bombs threw up a terrific and unnatural light, and where, in the present of DeLillo's novel, a conceptual artist named Klara Sax, sometime lover of Nick Shay, has received permission from the United States government to paint row upon row of retired B-52 bomber aircraft. It is a landscape of victory but also of uncertainty and loss, inspiring, in Klara and Nick and many of the novel's other characters an ironic nostalgia for what is described elsewhere as the honesty and dependability of the cold war. As Klara Sax observes, "Now that power is in shatters or tatters and now that those Soviet borders don't even exist in the same way, I think we understand, we look back, we see ourselves more clearly, and them as well. Power meant something thirty, forty years ago. It was stable, it was focused, it was a tangible thing. It was greatness, danger, terror, all those things. And it held us together, the Soviets and us. Maybe it held the world together" (76).

In the aftermath of the cold war, "[t]hings have no limits" (76). Money and violence have no limits; they are "undone, unstuck," "uprooted," and "out of control" (76). For those who grew to adulthood in Hoover's "furrow of destruction," nothing, it seems, makes sense anymore. Hence, the relentless hunt across time for a specific baseball is only the outward expression of an inner nostalgia and longing for the past, just as the salvaging and preservation of bomber aircraft in the desert is an attempt to freeze time in a moment of perceived stability and focus.

In forming such a thought, and building his novel around its manifold associations, Don DeLillo has staked his best claim to our memory on an interpretation of our past that doubles as a prophecy of our uncertain future. *Underworld* may well be the last great work of twentieth-century American literature.

Notes

Notes

Notes

Notes

1. After Postmodernism

1. Robert Scholes, *Fabulation and Metafiction* (Urbana: University of Illinois Press), 212.

2. Charles Newman, *The Post-Modern Aura: The Act of Fiction in an Age of Inflation* (Evanston, Ill.: Northwestern University Press, 1985), 92; hereafter cited in text.

3. Frederick Karl, *American Fictions, 1940–1980: A Comprehensive History and Critical Evaluation* (New York: Harper & Row, 1983), xiii; hereafter cited in text.

4. Philip Roth, *Reading Myself and Others* (New York: Farrar, Straus and Giroux, 1975), 120.

5. John Barth, *The Friday Book: Essays and Other Nonfiction* (New York: Perigee, 1984), 67; hereafter cited in text. By the phrase "those who succeeded Joyce and Kafka" Barth meant Samuel Beckett and Jorge Luis Borges, who, along with Vladimir Nabokov, represented for Barth "just about the only contemporaries of my reading acquaintance mentionable with the 'old masters' of twentieth-century fiction" (67).

6. Susan Sontag, *Against Interpretation* (New York: Deli, 1966), 5.

7. Larry McCaffery, *The Metafictional Muse: The Works of Robert Coover, Donald Barthelme, and William H. Gass* (Pittsburgh: University of Pittsburgh Press, 1982), 261–62.

8. Paula Geyh, Fred G. Leebron, and Andrew Levy, eds., introduction to *Postmodern American Fiction: A Norton Anthology* (New York: W.W. Norton, 1998), xi; hereafter cited in text.

9. "Archaeology of the postmodern" is a phrase from Steven Best and Douglas Kellner's *Postmodern Theory: Critical Interrogations* (New York: Guilford Press, 1991), 5; this is a useful introduction to the wider debate surrounding postmodernism that has included, at one time or another, statements by such figures as Foucault, Deleuze and Guattari, Baudrillard, Lyotard, and others. As should be clear, I am most

interested in the term as it has been applied to American literature, especially contemporary American fiction.

10. Jerome Klinkowitz, *Literary Disruptions: The Making of a Post-Contemporary American Fiction* (Urbana: University of Illinois Press, 1975), ix–x.

11. Larry McCaffery, ed., introduction to *After Yesterday's Crash: The Avant-Pop Anthology* (New York: Penguin, 1995), xvii–xviii; hereafter cited in text.

12. Leslie A. Fiedler, *The Collected Essays of Leslie Fiedler* (New York: Stein and Day, 1971), 2:461.

13. In *Horizons of Assent* (Baltimore: Johns Hopkins University Press, 1981), Wilde attempts a categorization of modernism, what he terms "late modernism," and postmodernism on the grounds of the distinctive form of irony (absolute, mediate, or suspensive) each employs. This is an interesting idea, but again, the problem comes when Wilde begins to assign authors to each of his categories. The modern and late modern periods are illustrated through the works of British writers such as E.M. Forster and Virginia Woolf (modernism) and Christopher Isherwood and Ivy Compton-Burnett (late modernism), while the postmodern appears to be dominated entirely by Americans such as Ronald Sukenick and Raymond Federman whose connections to the earlier writers seem tenuous at best.

In Brian McHale's *Postmodernist Fiction* (New York: Methuen, 1987), the project of categorization is carried out by use of the following thesis, that "postmodernist fiction differs from modernist fiction just as a poetics dominated by ontological issues differs from one dominated by epistomological issues" (xii). Like Klinkowitz and Wilde, McHale tends to view postmodernism in a positive light. Indeed, his final chapter is entitled "How I learned to stop worrying and love postmodernism."

Such enthusiasm is not necessarily to be associated with the work of Ihab Hassan, the critic perhaps most associated with this debate. In "Postface 1982: Toward a Concept of Postmodernism," perhaps his most definitive statement on this subject, Hassan argues that postmodernism is "an artistic, philosophical, and social phenomenon," one that moves simultaneously in two opposite directions, the one tending toward "a discourse of ironies and fragments, a 'white ideology' of absences and fractures, a desire of diffractions, an invocation of complex, articulate silences," the other toward more "pervasive procedures, ubiquitous interactions, immanent codes, media, languages." Hassan's term for the cumulative effect of these two "central, constitutive tendencies" within postmodernism is "indetermance," a neologism designed to capture and combine the separate meanings of "indeterminancy" and "immanence." "Thus," Hassan concludes, striking the apocalyptic note for which much of his writing of this period is known, "our earth seems caught in the process of planetization, transhumanization, even as it breaks into sects, tribes, factions of every kind," all of which leaves Hassan wondering if the world circa 1982 is not on the verge of "some decisive historical mutation." My source for Hassan's essay is Stanley Trachtenberg, ed., *Critical Essays on American Postmodernism* (New York: G.K. Hall, 1995), 81–92.

While the central metaphor behind Newman's *Post-Modern Aura*—inflation— may seem more appropriate to the era in which it was written than to our era, the distinction he draws between modernism and postmodernism still holds up: "[W]hereas the Modern and the Post-Modern share an unbroken (and largely unexamined) aesthetic tradition, their differences in idiom are due essentially to the differences of the institutions against which they are reacting. Post-Modernism is defined by the confusion which comes from bringing forth the dogmatic aesthetic techniques of Modernism against an entirely unprecedented form of production, transmission and administration of knowledge, a system no less binding because it is unstructured" (10). Thus, for Newman, "[m]odernism in its heroic phase is a retrospective revolt against a retrograde mechanical industrialism. Post-Modernism is an ahistorical rebellion without heroes against a blindly innovative information society" (10). Unlike some of these other writers, Newman never equates postmodernity with postmodernism, but understands them to be parallel, distinct phenomena.

14. Irving Howe, *A World More Attractive: A View of Modern Literature and Politics* (New York: Horizon Press, 1963), 93.

15. Harry Levin, *Refractions: Essays in Comparative Literature* (New York: Oxford University Press, 1966), 277, 282.

16. Fiedler, "Cross the Border—Close the Gap," in Fiedler, *Collected Essays,* 2:468.

17. Barth, *Friday Book,* 63–64.

18. C. Barry Chabot, "The Problem of the Postmodern," in *Critical Essays on American Postmodernism,* ed. Stanley Trachtenberg (New York: G.K. Hall, 1995), 109.

19. Gerald Graff, *Literature Against Itself: Literary Ideas in Modern Society* (Chicago: University of Chicago Press, 1979), 32.

20. Tom Wolfe, "Stalking the Billion-Footed Beast: A Literary Manifesto for the New Social Novel," *Harper's,* November 1989, 50–51.

21. Robert Stone, introduction to *The Best American Short Stories 1992,* ed. Katrina Kenison (New York: Houghton Mifflin, 1992), xviii.

22. McHale, *Postmodernist Fiction,* 220.

23. Graff, *Literature Against Itself,* 9. For his efforts Graff has been branded, by McHale and others, a defender of staid tradition and an apologist for an "uncomplicated" realism—essentially a return to the nineteenth century. Yet it is Graff, not the postmodernists, who declares unequivocally that "the representation of objective reality cannot be restricted to a single literary method" (12). Propagandists for realism in the late nineteenth and early twentieth centuries "did their cause a disservice," according to Graff, by arguing for "a limited stock of conventions" such as the "illusionistic presentation" of local detail and a "linear narrative concentrating on everyday events" (11). So too, we might add, do propagandists for literary postmodernism do their cause a disservice by insisting on their own limited stock of conventions, such as formal experimentation and self-consciousness in narration.

Meanwhile, Charles Newman has rightly ridiculed Barth's stance in both "The Literature of Exhaustion" and "The Literature of Replenishment" as what he calls "Can't go backness." "Just what is it about the 20th century experience," Newman asks, "which makes us so unable to utilize the past? The Modernists, for all their obsessive up-to-dateness, certainly had no reluctance to going back to make it new. If Barth himself can 'go back' to Smollett and Defoe and Fielding, then why not to Tolstoy and Dickens?" (*Post-Modern Aura*, 38).

24. Keith Opdahl, "The Nine Lives of Literary Realism," in *Contemporary American Fiction*, ed. Malcolm Bradbury and Sigmund Ro (London: Edward Arnold, 1987), 1–3.

25. Vladimir Nabokov, afterword to *Lolita* (New York: Berkeley Books, 1985), 286. It is interesting, in this regard, to note that Bobbie Ann Mason, a so-called "K-Mart realist," to this day considers Nabokov the single greatest influence on her work, and among Mason's publication credits is a work of criticism called *Nabokov's Garden*.

26. Quentin Curtis, "Object Lessons in the American Dream: The Dirty Realists and the Brat Pack are Dead," *Independent*, 12 May 1991.

2. Minimalism and Its Discontents

1. Sam Halpert, *Raymond Carver: An Oral Biography* (Iowa City: University of Iowa Press, 1995), 104.

2. Richard Ford, "The Good Raymond," *New Yorker*, 5 October 1998, 70; hereafter cited in text. Ford's reminiscence, which appeared only a few months after the flak surrounding D.T. Max's exposé of the role Gordon Lish played in creating Carver's early minimal style ("The Carver Chronicles," *New York Times Magazine*, 9 August 1998), is both a defense of Carver on the grounds of friendship and a meditation on the whole idea of influence, which has dogged Ford's career as surely as it has Carver's.

3. In his essay "Writing in the Cold," which appeared in the Spring 1985 issue of *Granta*, former *New American Review* editor Ted Solotaroff writes, "I don't think one can understand the literary situation today without dealing with the one genuine revolutionary development in American letters during the second half of the century: the rise of the creative writing programs" (266).

If you think Solotaroff is indulging in hyperbole, consider this: by 1986, when the institution of creative writing was celebrating its fiftieth anniversary at the University of Iowa, there were already more than 150 graduate writing programs in the United States, at least 100 of them born in the previous ten years (see Maureen Howard, "Can Writing Be Taught at Iowa?" *New York Times*, 25 May 1986). A decade and a half later, at the close of the twentieth century, the Associated Writing Programs' *Official Guide to Writing Programs* listed 320 member programs in the United States, Canada, and Great Britain.

No enterprise can get this big this fast without experiencing the kinds of growing pains that generate criticism from both without and within. There are those who would argue, for example, that the insularity and safety of academe have corrupted creative writers in precisely the ways they so often corrupt scholarly talent. "Because of the peculiar institution of tenure," Ted Solotaroff writes, "the younger writer tends to publish too quickly and the older one too little. It's no wonder that steady academic employment has done strange things to a number of literary careers and, to my mind, has devitalized the relationship between literature, particularly fiction, and society" (266).

There are even those, like the critic John W. Aldridge, who would say that writers *need* to feel isolated, marginalized, hated by their culture and outcasts in it. To support them with fellowships and cushy teaching jobs only kills their outsider status and renders their fiction impotent (see Aldridge's *Talents and Technicians* [New York: Charles Scribner's Sons, 1992]).

No doubt there is some truth to such arguments, although it would also seem that poverty and exile have ruined as many writing careers as they have spawned. On the positive side, steady academic employment has produced the most stable and widespread form of literary patronage the world has ever known. It has also effectively moved the center of American literary culture out of New York City and into a network of cities and towns, including not only New York and Boston and San Francisco, but also New Orleans, Iowa City, and even far-flung places such as Missoula, Montana, and Hattiesburg, Mississippi.

4. For a complete chronology of Carver's career, see Adam Meyer's *Raymond Carver* (New York: Twayne, 1995) or Ewing Campbell's *Raymond Carver: A Study of the Short Fiction* (New York: Twayne, 1992).

5. Raymond Carver, *Fires: Essays, Poems, Stories* (New York: Vintage Contemporaries, 1989). Carver writes, "Gardner was just starting his magazine, MSS, and was about to publish 'The Pederson Kid' in the first issue. I began reading the story in manuscript, but I didn't understand it and . . . I complained to Gardner. This time he didn't tell me I should try it again, he simply took the story away from me" (45).

6. My source is Carver, *Fires*, 23–24; hereafter cited in text.

7. Marshall Gentry and William L. Stull, *Conversations with Raymond Carver* (Jackson: University of Mississippi Press, 1990), 183–84.

8. In the essay "Fires," Carver famously claimed that the most important illumination of his life occurred in an Iowa City laundromat, when he realized, "amid the feelings of helpless frustration that had me close to tears, that nothing . . . that ever happened to me on this earth could come anywhere close, could possibly be as important to me, could make as much difference, as the fact that I had two children" (*Fires*, 33). The chaotic nature of Carver's life, the constant moving, the need to make a buck, and so on, had created a situation where he could only work on short stories and poems. "I had to sit down and write something I could finish now, tonight, or at least tomorrow night, no later, after I got in from work and before I lost interest" (*Fires*,

34). The image Carver gives of this state, borrowed from Henry Miller, is that of the chair he is sitting on being under constant threat of removal, even as he tries to write. The great question for Carver's eventual biographers will be how much the above situation contributed to his drinking—or whether, on the other hand, it was his drinking above all else that created that situation.

9. See D.T. Max, "The Carver Chronicles," *New York Times Magazine,* 9 August 1998. Although this article has been received as an exposé, and in part is, plenty of people knew about Lish's role in Carver's work before this article came out. Adam Meyer mentions Lish's role in his 1995 book on Carver, and Max tells the story of how Carver's widow, the poet Tess Gallagher, blocked an earlier attempt to publish an article on the subject by Brian Evenson, a literary scholar at Oklahoma State.

10. Gentry and Stull, *Conversations with Raymond Carver,* 181–82.

11. Janet Burroway, *Writing Fiction,* 4th ed. (New York: HarperCollins, 1996), 339. See also Burroway, *Writing Fiction,* 5th ed. (New York: Longman, 2000), 343.

12. My source for this story is the collection *Where I'm Calling From: New and Selected Stories* (New York: Random House, 1989); hereafter cited in text.

13. My source for this quote is Sam Hunter and John Jacobus, *Modern Art: Painting/Sculpture/Architecture* (New York: Harry N. Abrams, 1985), 321.

14. Alexander Neubauer, *Conversations on Writing Fiction: Interviews with 13 Distinguished Teachers of Fiction Writing in America* (New York: HarperPerennial, 1994), 195.

15. John Barth, "A Few Words About Minimalism," *New York Times,* 28 December 1986.

16. Madison Bell, "Less Is Less: The Dwindling of the American Short Story," *Harper's,* April 1986, 65; hereafter cited in text.

17. Frederick Barthelme, "On Being Wrong: Convicted Minimalist Spills Beans," *New York Times,* 3 April 1988.

18. Amy Hempel, *Reasons to Live* (New York: Alfred A. Knopf, 1985), 7; hereafter cited in text.

19. Frederick Barthelme, *Moon Deluxe: Stories* (New York: Simon and Schuster, 1983). I have not included page references since these are the first lines of the cited stories.

3. Dirty Realism

1. Bill Buford, introduction to *Granta 8: Dirty Realism* (1983), 4; hereafter cited in text. Both *Granta* and Buford himself would continue this trend of selecting a group of young writers to introduce to the public at large. See, for example, *Granta 54: The Best of Young American Novelists* (Summer 1996) and the *New Yorker's* Future of American Fiction issue (21 and 28 June 1999).

2. Madison Smartt Bell, "*Jesus' Son:* Gospel of Grace Amid Addiction," *USA Today,* 2 March 1992; Gail Caldwell, "A Walk on the Foul Side," *Boston Globe,* 27

December 1992; Simon Prosser, "Laureate of American Low-Life," *Telegraph*, 4 July 1993; anonymous review of *The Pugilist at Rest* in the *Scotsman*, 7 May 1994.

3. See Levin's *Power of Blackness: Hawthorne, Poe, Melville* (New York: Knopf, 1958).

4. Herman Melville, "Hawthorne and His Mosses," in *The Piazza Tales and Other Prose Pieces*, ed. Harrison Hayford *et al.* (Chicago: Northwestern University Press, 1987), 243.

5. Philip D. Beidler, *Re-Writing America: Vietnam Authors in Their Generation* (Athens: University of Georgia Press, 1991), 2.

6. Thom Jones, *The Pugilist at Rest: Stories* (Boston: Little, Brown, 1993); hereafter cited in text.

7. Thom Jones, contributor's note to *Best American Short Stories 1992*, 369.

8. Tim O'Brien, *The Things They Carried* (Boston: Houghton Mifflin/Seymour Lawrence, 1990), 63.

9. Jay McInerney, "Raymond Carver: A Still, Small Voice," *New York Times*, 6 August 1989.

10. Jack Miles, "Jesus' Son," review of *Jesus' Son: Stories*, by Denis Johnson, *Atlantic Monthly*, June 1993, 121; hereafter cited in text.

11. David Streitfeld, "The Ghost in the Addict," review of *Jesus' Son: Stories*, by Denis Johnson, *Washington Post*, 3 February 1993.

12. Denis Johnson, *Jesus' Son: Stories* (New York: Farrar, Straus and Giroux, 1992), 51; hereafter cited in text.

13. See Annie Dillard, *The Writing Life* (New York: Harper & Row, 1989).

14. Bruce Allen, "Epic *Fathers and Crows*; Cryptic, Touching *Gloria*," *USA Today*, 13 August 1992; Steven Moore, "William Vollmann: An Artist in the American Grain," *Washington Post*, 2 August 1992; Charles Monoghan, "The Shock of the Newcomer," *Washington Post*, 13 February 1994.

15. Andy Beckett, "A Nerd in Action," *Independent*, 26 June 1994. I am indebted to this long profile for all of the details of Vollmann's biography not otherwise noted.

16. Madison Smartt Bell, "William T. Vollmann," *New York Times*, 6 February 1994.

17. William T. Vollmann, *The Atlas* (New York: Viking Penguin, 1996), xvi; hereafter cited in text.

18. Larry McCaffery, "An Interview with William T. Vollmann," *Review of Contemporary Fiction* 13, no. 2 (Summer 1993): 9.

19. Tom LeClair, "His Sister's Ghost in Bosnia," *Nation*, 6 May 1996, 75; hereafter cited in text.

20. Madison Smartt Bell, "Where an Author Might Be Standing," *Review of Contemporary Fiction* 13, no. 2 (Summer 1993): 40; hereafter cited in text.

21. William T. Vollmann, *An Afghanistan Picture Show; or, How I Saved the World* (New York: Farrar, Straus and Giroux, 1992), 155.

4. Hick Chic, or, the "White Trash Aesthetic"

1. Duncan Webster, *Looka Yonder!: The Imaginary America of Populist Culture* (New York: Routledge, 1988), 3–4; hereafter cited in text.

2. Nick Hornby, *Contemporary American Fiction* (New York: St. Martin's Press, 1992), 54.

3. Jonathan Yardley, "Hick Chic," *Washington Post,* 25 March 1985. The essay has been reprinted in Yardley, *Out of Step: Notes from a Purple Decade* (New York: Villard, 1991), 123.

4. Ann Hulbert, "Rural Chic," *New Republic,* 2 September 1985, 25; hereafter cited in text.

5. Diane Johnson, "Southern Comfort," review of *In Country,* by Bobbie Ann Mason, and *The Accidental Tourist,* by Anne Tyler, *New York Times,* 7 November 1985.

6. Jack Killey, "Metaphysical Hicks," *Nation,* 3 May 1986, 622.

7. Fred Hobson, *The Southern Writer in the Postmodern World* (Athens: University of Georgia Press, 1991), 15; hereafter cited in text.

8. Larry Brown, *Father and Son* (Chapel Hill, N.C.: Algonquin Books, 1996), 324.

9. Tad Friend and Anya Sacharow, "White Hot Trash!" *New York Magazine,* 22 August 1994, 22; hereafter cited in text.

10. George Garrett, "No Wonder People Got Crazy as They Grew Up," review of *Bastard Out of Carolina,* by Dorothy Allison, *New York Times,* 5 July 1992.

11. Dorothy Allison, *Bastard Out of Carolina* (New York: Plume, 1993), 22–23; hereafter cited in text.

12. Chris Offutt, *Kentucky Straight* (New York: Vintage Contemporaries, 1992), 8; hereafter cited in text.

13. Dale Peck, *Now It's Time to Say Goodbye* (New York: Farrar, Straus, and Giroux, 1998).

14. Wolfe, "Stalking the Billion-Footed Beast," 49.

15. Sara Rimer, "At Home with E. Annie Proulx," *New York Times,* 23 June 1994.

16. Charles Frazier, *Cold Mountain* (New York: Atlantic Monthly Press, 1997), 104.

17. Suzanne L. MacLauchlan, "The Life of an Author in Demand," *Christian Science Monitor,* 22 July 1994, 14.

5. Return of the Native

1. Nathaniel Hawthorne, *The Scarlet Letter* (New York: Penguin, 1983), 40; hereafter cited in text.

2. Flannery O'Connor, "The Catholic Novelist in the Protestant South," in *A*

Modern Southern Reader, ed. Ben Forkner and Patrick Samway, S.J. (Atlanta: Peachtree Publishers, 1986), 503; hereafter cited in text.

3. Eudora Welty, "Place in Fiction," in Forkner and Samway, *A Modern Southern Reader,* 544. According to Welty, "Place in fiction is the named, identified, concrete, exact and exacting, and therefore credible, gathering spot of all that has been felt, is about to be experienced, in the novel's progress" (541).

4. Leonard Lutwack, *The Role of Place in Literature* (Syracuse, N.Y.: Syracuse University Press, 1984), 2.

5. Gerald Vizenor, introduction to *Native American Literature: A Brief Introduction and Anthology* (New York: HarperCollins, 1995), 6; Delia Poey and Virgil Suarez, introduction to *Iguana Dreams: New Latino Fiction* (New York: Harper Perennial, 1992), xvii.

6. Joel Yanofsky, "Happy Endings," *Calgary Herald,* 18 April 1994.

7. Geraldine Baum, "A Mind Filled with Stories," *Los Angeles Times,* 15 November 1993.

8. Ibid.

9. John Skow, "True (as in Proulx) Grit Wins," *Time,* 29 November 1993, 83.

10. Richard Ford, *A Piece of My Heart* (New York: Random House, 1976), 44; hereafter cited in text.

11. Madison Smartt Bell, *Soldier's Joy* (New York: Ticknor & Fields, 1989), 10–11; hereafter cited in text.

12. Frazier, *Cold Mountain,* 124; hereafter cited in text.

13. Michelle Green, "Transient Writer Richard Ford Lets His Muse Roam Free," review of *Wildlife,* by Richard Ford, *People,* 9 July 1990, 63.

14. Michael Neill, "La Pasionaria," review of *Animal Dreams,* by Barbara Kingsolver, *Time,* 11 October 1993, 109.

15. Richard Ford, *Rock Springs* (New York: Vintage, 1988), 149; hereafter cited in text.

16. Russell Martin, "Writers of the Purple Sage," *New York Times,* 25 December 1981.

17. Jane Smiley, "In One Small Town, the Weight of the World," *New York Times,* 2 September 1990.

18. Ursula LeGuin, "The Fabric of Grace," *Washington Post,* 2 September 1990.

19. Barbara Kingsolver, *Animal Dreams* (New York: HarperPerennial, 1991), 198; hereafter cited in text.

20. Thomas McGuane, "Roping, from A to B," in *An Outside Chance* (New York: Farrar, Straus and Giroux, 1980), 208; hereafter cited in text.

21. Dexter Westrum, *Thomas McGuane* (Boston: Twayne, 1991), 17.

22. Curt Suplee, "Tom McGuane, Safe in the Sagebrush," *Washington Post,* 2 October 1986.

23. Richard Ford, "A Stubborn Sense of Place," *Harper's,* August 1986, 42.

24. J. Fritz Lanham, "Coming Apart in Montana," *Houston Chronicle,* 6 December 1992.

25. Guy D. Garcia, "He's Left No Stone Unturned," review of *Keep the Change,* by Thomas McGuane, *Time,* 25 December 1989, 70.

26. Westrum, *Thomas McGuane,* 78.

27. Thomas McGuane, *Nobody's Angel* (New York: Vintage Contemporaries, 1986); hereafter cited in text.

28. Paul Gray, "Call of the Eco-Feminists," *Time,* 24 September 1990, 87.

29. Michiko Kakutani, "Books of the Times: Haunted Characters," review of *To Skin a Cat,* by Thomas McGuane, *New York Times,* 11 October 1986.

30. Mary Hellman, "Kingsolver Creates Sense of Community in the Wide-Open West," *San Diego Union-Tribune,* 6 July 1993.

31. Garcia, "He's Left No Stone Unturned," 70.

32. Thomas Wolfe, *You Can't Go Home Again* (New York: Harper & Brothers, 1940), 706.

6. New West, or, the Borderlands

1. William Kittredge, introduction to *The Best of the West: New Stories from the Wide Side of the Missouri,* vol. 5, ed. James Thomas and Denise Thomas (New York: W.W. Norton, 1992), 12; hereafter cited in text.

2. Martin, "Writers of the Purple Sage."

3. Leslie Fiedler, *The Return of the Vanishing American* (New York: Stein and Day, 1968). Fiedler writes, "The heart of the Western is not the confrontation with the alien landscape (by itself this produces only the Northern), but the encounter with the Indian, that utter stranger for whom our New World is an Old Home" (21). I have expanded Fiedler's ideas here to include novels such a James Welch's *Fools Crow* that tell the story of the confrontation with the "other" from the point of view of Indians. I am indebted particularly to Fiedler's definitions of not only the western and the southern but also what he calls the northern and the eastern.

4. John R. Milton, *The Novel of the American West* (Lincoln: University of Nebraska Press, 1980), 10.

5. Ivan Doig, *This House of Sky: Landscapes of a Western Mind* (New York: Harcourt Brace Jovanovich, 1978); Gretel Ehrlich, *The Solace of Open Spaces* (New York: Viking, 1985); William Least Heat-Moon, *PrairyErth* (Boston: Houghton Mifflin, 1991). I have not bothered with page references since these are the books' openings.

6. Wallace Stegner, *Where the Bluebird Sings to the Lemonade Springs: Living and Writing in the West* (New York: Penguin, 1993), 55.

7. Quoted in Sharman Apt Russell, *Kill the Cowboy: A Battle of Mythology in the New West* (New York: Addison-Wesley Publishing, 1993), 1.

8. For a history of the development of the western film, and multiple reasons for its demise, see "The Western: A Short History," in *The BFI Companion to the Western,* ed. Edward Buscombe (New York: Antheum, 1988), 24.

9. Ibid.

10. Walter Van Tilburg Clark, introduction to *The Big Sky,* by A.B. Guthrie Jr. (New York: Time-Life Books, 1964), xiii.

11. Stegner, *Where the Bluebird Sings,* 103.

12. William Savage Jr., *The Cowboy Hero: His Image in American History and Culture* (Norman: University of Oklahoma Press, 1979), 109.

13. Russell, *Kill the Cowboy,* 3.

14. "And Our Critics Commend," *Los Angeles Times,* 23 June 1985. For the observation that reviews of McMurtry's *Lonesome Dove* and McCarthy's *Blood Meridian* appeared on the same page, I am indebted to Edwin T. Arnold and Diane C. Luce's introduction to the revised edition of *Perspectives on Cormac McCarthy,* ed. Arnold and Luce (Jackson: University Press of Mississippi, 1999), 8.

15. Gail Caldwell, "Cormac McCarthy's High Frontier," *Boston Globe,* 3 May 1992; Madison Smartt Bell, "The Man Who Understood Horses," *New York Times,* 17 May 1992.

16. For a concise listing of some of McMurtry's historical sources in *Lonesome Dove,* see Don Graham, "*Lonesome Dove:* Butch and Sundance Go on a Cattle Drive," in *Taking Stock: A Larry McMurtry Casebook,* ed. Clay Reynolds (Dallas: Southern Methodist University Press, 1989). For a detailed analysis of McCarthy's historical borrowing, see John Emil Sepich, "'What kind of indians was them': Some Historical Sources in Cormac McCarthy's *Blood Meridian,*" in Arnold and Luce, *Perspectives on Cormac McCarthy,* 123–43.

17. Nicholas Lemann, "Tall in the Saddle," in Reynolds, *Taking Stock,* 327.

18. Jonathan Yardley, "In All Its Gore," *Washington Post,* 13 March 1985.

19. Richard Woodward, "Cormac McCarthy's Venomous Fiction," *New York Times,* 19 April 1992.

20. Cormac McCarthy, *Blood Meridian, or the Evening Redness in the West* (New York: Random House, 1985); hereafter cited in text.

21. Vereen M. Bell, *The Achievement of Cormac McCarthy* (Baton Rouge: Louisiana University Press, 1988), 119.

22. Larry McMurtry, *In a Narrow Grave: Essays on Texas* (New York: Touchstone, 1989), xiii.

23. Janis P. Stout, "Journeying as a Metaphor for Cultural Loss in the Novels of Larry McMurtry," in Reynolds, *Taking Stock,* 57.

24. Larry McMurtry, *Horseman, Pass By* (New York: Penguin, 1979), 87–88; hereafter cited in text.

25. Cormac McCarthy, *Suttree* (New York: Vintage International, 1992), 471.

26. Terence Moran, "Blood Meridian, or the Evening Redness in the West," *New Republic,* 6 May 1985, 37–38.

27. Milton, *Novel of the American West*, 195.

28. Russell Martin and Marc Barasch, introduction to *Riders of the Purple Sage: An Anthology of Recent Western Writing* (New York: Viking, 1989), x.

29. Gail Moore Morrison, "John Grady Cole's Expulsion from Paradise," in Arnold and Luce, *Perspectives on Cormac McCarthy*, 175–94. Morrison's divisions for the novel are slightly different than mine. "The novel's four chapters divide the book into distinctive but interrelated sections," Morrison writes:

(1) the long *andante* movement of the journey south, through an increasingly sterile and incomprehensible wasteland, a false purgatory that foreshadows the false redemption that follows; (2) an *allegro* pastoral interlude in an edenic paradise, rife with fertility of landscape and horse and the promise of Eve, the site of temptation for body as well as spirit; (3) the *staccato* expulsion into purgatory of the newly fallen naïf whose education in the dissonances of life's injustices, chaos and confusion has only just begun; and, finally, (4) the rendering of judgment, the component parts of which include the failed quest to regain paradise, retribution and a reintegrative odyssey home. (181–82)

30. Cormac McCarthy, *All the Pretty Horses* (New York: Alfred A. Knopf, 1992), 5; hereafter cited in text.

31. Cormac McCarthy, *The Crossing* (New York: Alfred A. Knopf, 1994), 46; hereafter cited in text. Few people would call Cormac McCarthy an activist for the environment, but with the first section of *The Crossing*, McCarthy has written a fictional account of what many environmentalists believe about wolves—that they are mystical, that they are necessary, that they should be reintroduced in their native ranges, which for the Mexican wolf includes much of the American Southwest. "What is happening to wolves," says one wolf activist, "is symbolic of what is happening to our environment" (Russell, *Kill the Cowboy*, 105). There are now plans in the works to reintroduce wolves in the White Sands Missile Range in New Mexico, Big Bend National Park in Texas, and most significant, the 8.5 million acres of Yellowstone National Park in Wyoming (ibid., 74–123).

32. Morrison, "John Grady Cole's Expulsion from Paradise," in Arnold and Luce, *Perspectives on Cormac McCarthy*, 193.

33. See McCarthy's veiled description of this event in the novel's final three paragraphs. Several critics have pointed out the connection to Trinity. In his essay on the Border Trilogy, Don Graham mentions an article by the critic Alex Hunt in the journal *Southwestern American Literature* ("Outlaw Heart: Cormac McCarthy's Border Trilogy," *Texas Observer*, August 1998), while Diane C. Luce, in her chapter on *The Crossing*, credits a privately distributed paper by James Campbell (Arnold and Luce, *Perspectives on Cormac McCarthy*, 217).

34. See especially Michiko Kakutani, "Moving Along the Border Between Past and Future," *New York Times*, 22 May 1998.

35. Sara Mosle, "Don't Let Your Babies Grow Up to Be Cowboys," *New York Times*, 17 May 1998.

36. Cormac McCarthy, *Cities of the Plain* (New York: Alfred A. Knopf, 1998), 162; hereafter cited in text.

37. Edwin T. Arnold, "The Last of the Trilogy: First Thoughts on *Cities of the Plain*," in Arnold and Luce, *Perspectives on Cormac McCarthy,* 222.

Arnold has been to the Cormac McCarthy Collection at Southwest Texas State University and has read the screenplay upon which *Cities* is based—a screenplay that was already ten years old when *Pretty Horses* was published in 1992 and that Arnold figures as "the story which began the trilogy" and "the ending towards which all else has been aimed" (225–26).

In following this thesis, Arnold offers a full summary of the screenplay, then totes up the differences between it and the novel, the most important of which appears to be the expanded role of Billy Parham in the novel. Arnold writes, " 'Billy' in the screenplay is primarily an older companion to John Grady. He plays much the same role Lacy Rawlins enacts in *All the Pretty Horses,* a voice of common sense, of caution, of reserve. Billy is something of a comic misanthrope in the screenplay who warns John Grady away from love and marriage. . . . Anyone reading the screenplay after knowing Billy from *The Crossing* would be justified in wondering if these two ' Billys' should indeed be considered the same character, for the young, melancholy Billy Parham of *The Crossing* initially seems worlds away from the garrulous, folksy cowboy we find here" (227).

However, as *Cities of the Plain* continues, Arnold argues, "McCarthy reveals to us that earlier Billy, and one might argue that the novel becomes, in fact, more Billy Parham's story than John Grady Cole's, that in creating the background histories to these two characters, McCarthy found himself pulled closer to the older, wounded man than to the young, impulsive boy" (227–28).

Arnold concludes, "[P]erhaps this explains why John Grady's story is so little changed from the screenplay to the novel, while the additions to Billy's are ultimately more profound and provide the novel its soul" (227–28).

38. According to Michael Dirda, this is the military base at Alamagordo, New Mexico. See "The Last Roundup," *Washington Post,* 24 May 1998.

39. Although there has been little agreement among contemporary reviewers about whether McCarthy is being profound in this epilogue or merely portentous, there can be little doubt this is McCarthy's major statement so far on the nature of fiction writing, and for this reason alone the epilogue is sure to be pored over by scholars for years to come. So far, the most full reading is in Edwin T. Arnold's essay "First Thoughts on *Cities of the Plain.*"

For my part, I wish only to add the following brief list of what I take to be the main points about fictional process made in the epilogue: (1) an author has only limited control over his characters, once they have been set in motion; (2) an author must not rob his characters of at least a semblance of autonomy or they will "vanish," or cease to be believable; (3) to be believable, a character must have a "history" (it continues to be interesting that the trilogy itself began—in the screenplay—with two characters for whom McCarthy then had to supply or discover histories, hence volumes 1 and 2); (4) no author has complete free will as regards characters, because, as with life, each new event or action is "revealed only at the surrender of every alternate course" (274); (5) the meaning of a life, for better or worse, is come upon in an hour and place where the whole life converges, and this cannot be predicted or known until it has happened; hence, again, our lives have meaning only in retrospect, and while each man may indeed be said to be "the bard of his own existence" (283), the events he works with are given, or even "forced" upon him.

7. Tribes and Breeds, Coyotes and *Curanderas*

1. James Welch, introduction to *Ploughshares* 20, no. 1 (Spring 1994): 5; hereafter cited in text.

2. Vizenor, introduction, 4–5.

3. Quoted in David Seals, "The Indian Lawyer," review of *The Indian Lawyer*, by James Welch, *Nation,* 26 November 1990, 648.

4. Ibid.

5. Robert F. Gish, "Old and New Wests," *Chicago Tribune,* 23 September 1990.

6. James Welch, *The Indian Lawyer* (New York: Penguin, 1991), 38; hereafter cited in text.

7. Stegner, *Where the Bluebird Sings,* 61, 73.

8. For help with the complex genealogy of characters in the North Dakota series of novels, see Peter G. Beidler and Gay Barton, *A Reader's Guide to the Novels of Louise Erdrich* (University of Missouri Press, 1999).

9. Louise Erdrich, "Where I Ought to Be: A Writer's Sense of Place," *New York Times,* 28 July 1985.

10. Mary McCay, "Playing to Lose," *Times-Picayune,* 30 January 1994.

11. Louise Erdrich, *The Bingo Palace* (New York: HarperCollins, 1994), 16; hereafter cited in text.

12. Josh Getlin, "A Voice No Longer Ignored," *Los Angeles Times,* 13 December 1993.

13. Nicolas Kanellos, introduction to *Hispanic American Literature: A Brief Introduction and Anthology* (New York: HarperCollins, 1995), 1; hereafter cited in text.

14. Earl Shorris, "In Search of the Latino Writer," *New York Times,* 15 July 1990.

15. Ibid.

16. Cristina Garcia, *Dreaming in Cuban* (New York: Ballantine, 1993), 43.

17. Ana Castillo, *So Far from God* (New York: Plume, 1994), 55; hereafter cited in text.

18. Rudolfo Anaya, introduction to *The Last of the Menu Girls,* by Denise Chavez (Houston: Arte Publico Press, 1986), 7.

19. Chavez, *Last of the Menu Girls,* 190.

20. Mary Hellman, "They Call Him El Jefe," *San Diego Union-Tribune,* 3 May 1994.

21. Rudolfo Anaya, *Alburquerque* (New York: Warner Books, 1994), 119; hereafter cited in text.

8. The White Prison Novel as *Bildungsroman*

1. Seth Morgan, *Homeboy* (New York: Random House, 1990), 151; hereafter cited in text.

2. Jack Henry Abbott expresses this idea in his book *In the Belly of the Beast* (New York: Random House, 1981): "I feel that if I ever did adjust to prison, I could by that alone never adjust to society. I would be back in prison within months" (14). Abbott, of course, is back in prison after his highly publicized murder of a Greenwich Village waiter.

3. For a scholarly look at the birth of the prison, see Michael Ignatieff, *A Just Measure of Pain: The Penitentiary in the Industrial Revolution, 1750–1850* (London: Penguin, 1978). For a more speculative look, see Michel Foucault, *Discipline & Punish: The Birth of the Prison* (New York: Vintage, 1979).

4. Malcolm Braly, *On the Yard* (Boston: Little, Brown, 1967).

5. Dennis Massey, *Doing Time in American Prisons* (New York: Greenwood Press, 1989).

6. H. Bruce Franklin, *The Victim as Criminal and Artist* (New York: Oxford University Press, 1978), 245; hereafter cited in text.

7. Edward Bunker, "War Behind Walls," *Harper's,* February 1972, 39–47.

8. Quoted in Massey, *Doing Time in American Prisons,* 186.

9. Deborah Mason, "Hell's Angels in Purgatory," *New York Times,* 6 May 1990.

10. Art Harris, "The Last Ride of a Rebel Writer," *Washington Post,* 12 February 1991.

11. For more on the phenomenon of the "state-raised" convict, the prisoner who grows from boyhood to manhood in penal institutions, see Abbott's chapter in *In the Belly of the Beast.*

12. Edward Bunker, *The Animal Factory* (New York: Viking Press, 1977), 108; hereafter cited in text.

Conclusion

1. Marcus Klein, *After Alienation* (Cleveland: World Publishing, 1964), 197. It's entirely possible, of course, that Morris's work will one day be rediscovered in the manner that Melville's work was by scholars of the 1920s. However, this rarely happens except in those cases in which one book can be hailed as the masterwork (in Melville's case, *Moby-Dick*).

2. Madison Smartt Bell, "At a Cultural Crossroads," *Chicago Tribune*, 23 February 1992.

3. Vince Passaro, "Voices and Dreams of Vietnamese Exiles," *Newsday*, 12 March 1992.

4. Robert Olen Butler, *A Good Scent from a Strange Mountain* (New York: Penguin, 1993); hereafter cited in text.

5. Vince Passaro, "Unlikely Stories: The Quiet Renaissance of American Short Fiction," *Harper's*, August 1999, 81; hereafter cited in text.

6. Stone, introduction, xviii.

7. Christine Bertelson, "Heartfelt: Family Is the Center of Jane Smiley's Work and Life," *St. Louis Post Dispatch*, 19 July 1992.

8. Jane Smiley, *A Thousand Acres* (New York: Ballantine, 1992), 4; hereafter cited in text.

9. T.S. Eliot, "Tradition and the Individual Talent," in *Selected Prose of T.S. Eliot*, ed. Frank Kermode (New York: Harcourt Brace Jovanovich, 1975), 38.

10. David Gates, "Toni Morrison's Latest," *Newsweek*, 27 April 1992.

11. Denise Heinze, *The Dilemma of "Double Consciousness": Toni Morrison's Novels* (Athens: University of Georgia Press, 1993), 2–3.

12. DeLillo has suggested in an interview that there may be "a small undercurrent of protest" behind the composition of all these monster novels. "At some level," he asks, "don't some writers write long, challenging novels as a way of refusing to become part of the process of consumption, of rampant consumption and instant waste?" (David L. Ulin, "Merging Myth and History," *Los Angeles Times*, 8 October 1997).

13. Richard Williams, "Everything Under the Bomb," *Guardian*, 10 January 1998.

14. Ibid.

15. Thomas Hardy, *Selected Shorter Poems of Thomas Hardy*, ed. John Wain (London: Macmillan, 1975), 45–46.

16. Don DeLillo, *Underworld* (New York: Scribner, 1997), 51; hereafter cited in text.

17. Joseph Conte, "A Masterful Half-Century Mosaic of America's Hybrid Culture," *Buffalo News*, 9 October 1997.

18. Williams, "Everything Under the Bomb."

19. Martin Amis, "Survivors of the Cold War," *New York Times*, 5 October 1997.

20. Williams, "Everything Under the Bomb."

21. Don DeLillo, "The Moment the Cold War Began," *Observer*, 4 January 1998.

Index

Wister, Owen, 114, 122
Wolfe, Tom, 17–18, 80
Wolff, Tobias, 22
Wolheim, Richard, 33
wolves, 191n. 31
Woman Hollering Creek (Cisneros), 146
"Work" (Johnson), 49–51
writing: Barbara Kingsolver on, 104;
    Cormac McCarthy on, 192–93n. 39;
    Thomas McGuane on, 104–5;
    postmodernist notions of, 3, 4

"Writing American Fiction" (Roth), 4
Writing Fiction (Burroway), 28
"Writing in the Cold" (Solotaroff), 183–
    84n. 3
Wynema (Callahan), 136

Yardley, Jonathan, 67, 116
...y no se lo tragó la tierra (Rivera), 145
You Bright and Risen Angels (Vollmann),
    54

1   7/06